Strengthening FDI and SME Linkages in Portugal

OECD
BETTER POLICIES FOR BETTER LIVES

Please cite this publication as:
OECD (2022), *Strengthening FDI and SME Linkages in Portugal*, OECD Publishing, Paris, *https://doi.org/10.1787/d718823d-en*.

ISBN 978-92-64-92675-2 (print)
ISBN 978-92-64-56193-9 (pdf)

Photo credits: Cover © Pajomend iStock/Getty images

Corrigenda to publications may be found on line at: *www.oecd.org/about/publishing/corrigenda.htm*.

Preface

Like many other countries, Portugal has been strongly affected by the global economic slowdown related to the COVID-19 pandemic, reflecting in large part a significant population of micro-firms with limited capacity to adapt to stringent containment measures, especially in the tourism sector, as well as relatively high exposure to disruptions in global value chains.

Although the recovery is now in process, with GDP expected to return to pre-crisis levels by mid-2022, there is considerable scope to strengthen the recovery, and reduce vulnerabilities to future shocks by revitalising progress Portugal has made in recent years in developing a dynamic entrepreneurial ecosystem. Significant potential exists to leverage on its population of small and medium-sized enterprises (SMEs), responsible for 68% of value added and 60% of gross exports. SMEs in Portugal are on average relatively more innovative and digitised than those in many other OECD economies. Portugal has also seen significant growth in foreign direct investment (FDI) in export-oriented manufacturing over the past decade, motivated by relatively low labour costs and a skilled workforce, a strong SME sector with research and development capacities, and good infrastructure. This has supported the creation of value chain networks involving multinational enterprises (MNEs) and domestic SMEs, raising the opportunities for knowledge and technology spillovers in the domestic economy.

Not all firms and locations, however, have the same potential to successfully integrate into these networks and in turn boost competitiveness, productivity and inclusiveness. Public policy interventions can enhance the positive spillovers of FDI for SMEs and the broader economy, but such interventions require concerted action. To ensure that SMEs can absorb the benefits of FDI, policymakers need to understand the drivers and factors that can foster stronger SME-MNE value chains and how public policies at national and subnational levels can promote them.

Action is needed, particularly now, as Portugal considers policy options to ensure a strong and resilient post-COVID recovery. It should build on its 'Portugal 2020' national programme, which provides a comprehensive framework for implementing EU Structural and Investment Funds, to strengthen policy coherence and coordination. This includes supporting SMEs, entrepreneurship, and the linkages between FDI and SMEs. Efforts are underway to further attract FDI and boost FDI-SME linkages, particularly in the fields of skills, innovation and digitalisation and licensing, which can benefit from public and private investments, including those financed by the European Recovery and Resilience Facility.

This report aims to support these efforts. It assesses the linkages between inward FDI and SME productivity and recommends how Portugal can increase the potential of foreign investment for local SMEs, and, in turn, support the broader economic recovery. This includes exploring the characteristics of FDI that enhance the ability of SMEs and the local economy to absorb positive spillovers.

The Government of Portugal and the OECD are very pleased to have joined forces in producing this study, which pioneers the development of a multi-year project supported by the European Commission to boost productivity and innovation in EU countries and regions through stronger FDI-SME linkages and ecosystems. We thank all agencies in Portugal and the OECD Secretariat who have contributed to this assessment and the European Commission for the financial support and strategic cooperation.

We hope this assessment will help lay the foundations of a more resilient and inclusive recovery.

Pedro Siza Vieira
Minister of State for the Economy, Portugal

Yoshiki Takeuchi
Deputy Secretary-General, OECD

Foreword

The COVID-19 pandemic hit countries and regions hard in the OECD and European Union (EU) area and beyond. The impact has been very uneven across places, reflecting differences in health and economic resources, and differences in disruptions of business activities and global value chains (GVCs). As economic prospects brighten but high uncertainty remains, national and subnational governments aim to build back better and lay the foundations for more resilient, sustainable and inclusive growth, across all regions.

This will require higher productivity and more innovation, as well as greater knowledge, technological and skills diffusion across heterogeneous places and firms. Two levers of productivity and innovation will need to be strengthened: small and medium-sized enterprises (SMEs) that constitute the industrial fabric of many regions and countries, and foreign direct investment (FDI) that contributes to the knowledge base and capital stock of host countries and regions. Linkages between these two levers also need to be strengthened. FDI can help SMEs increase productivity and innovation, provided diffusion channels and supportive conditions enable spillovers. In turn, SMEs and their innovation capacities are an important determinant for FDI location decisions. Together these can create a virtual circle of spillovers that foster higher SME productivity (and cost effectiveness) and in turn, through upstream integration into the supply chains of MNEs, higher competitiveness of MNEs.

This report provides an assessment of FDI-SME linkages and spillovers in Portugal, and proposes a number of policy options to improve these spillovers. It provides a diagnostic of enabling conditions for FDI diffusion to domestic SMEs and identifies the extent to which different FDI-SME diffusion channels are at play in Portugal. Building on this assessment, the report looks at the institutional and governance framework and policy mix in place for enhancing FDI-SME diffusion in the country. The final chapter of the report looks at FDI-SME spillovers and related policy approaches through a regional lens, focusing on the regions of Alentejo and Norte.

The report contributed to the development of a multi-year project supported by the European Commission to boost productivity and innovation in EU countries and regions through stronger FDI-SME linkages and ecosystems. The report is jointly developed by the OECD Investment Committee and the OECD Committee on SMEs and Entrepreneurship and contributes to their respective FDI Qualities Initiative and work on “Global value chains: Seizing the opportunities for SMEs”.

Acknowledgements

The assessment of FDI-SME linkages and spillovers in Portugal is a joint report produced by the OECD Centre for Entrepreneurship, SMEs, Regions and Cities (CFE), led by Lamia Kamal-Chaoui, and the OECD Directorate for Financial and Enterprise Affairs (DAF), led by Mathilde Mesnard. The report was prepared under the aegis of the OECD Committee on SMEs and Entrepreneurship (CSMEE) and the OECD Investment Committee.

Portugal's assessment was prepared in close collaboration with the Direção-Geral das Atividades Económicas of Portugal, in consultation with an inter-ministerial taskforce created for the purpose of this work. The assessment also benefited from consultations with the European Commission, and the OECD Regional Development Policy Committee. This assessment is part of and contributes to a joint European Commission (EC)-OECD project aiming to help governments harness FDI spillovers on SME productivity and innovation in the EU countries and regions.

Sandrine Kergroach, Head of SME and Entrepreneurship Performance, Policy and Mainstreaming Unit (CFE), and Martin Wermelinger, Head of Investment Qualities and Incentives (DAF), coordinated the overall project and the assessment of Portugal. Celine Kauffmann and Lucia Cusmano, respectively Head and Deputy Head of Entrepreneurship, SME and Tourism Division (CFE), and Ana Novik and Stephen Thomsen, respectively Head and Deputy Head of Investment Division (DAF) provided guidance.

Chapter 1 is a summary of the concept paper developed for the project.

Chapters 2 and 3 on the potential for FDI spillovers, SME absorptive capacities and enabling conditions were prepared by Martin Wermelinger (DAF) with input from Sandrine Kergroach and Thanh Tran (CFE).

Chapters 4 and 5 on the institutional, regulatory and policy framework were prepared by Stratos Kamenis (CFE/DAF), with input from Sandrine Kergroach (CFE) and Martin Wermelinger (DAF).

Chapter 6 on the regional perspective was prepared by Jenny Vyas and Enrique Garcilazo (CFE).

Stratos Kamenis (CFE/DAF) coordinated consultations with the Portuguese taskforce and relevant institutions, as well as the national and regional policy surveys.

Robert Akam (DAF), Pamela Duffin (DAF), Shayne Maclachlan (CFE) and Pilar Philip (CFE) helped prepare the report for publication. Angèle N'Zinga (DAF) and Heather Mortimer-Charroy (CFE) provided project and administrative assistance. Secretariat comments were also received from Fares Al Hussami, and Takashi Yukizawa (DAF).

Table of contents

FIGURES

TABLES

Acronyms and abbreviations

AD&C	Development and Cohesion Agency
AICEP	Portugal Global - Trade and Investment Agency
ANI	National Innovation Agency
ARI	Residence Permit for Investment (ARI) scheme
B2B	Business-to-business
BPF	National Promotional Bank
CO_2	Carbon-dioxide
CCDR	Regional Coordination and Development Commission
CEIE	Strategic Council for the Internationalisation of the Economy
CIC	Inter-ministerial Coordination Commission for Portugal 2020
CIMs/IMCs	Inter-Municipal Councils
CITs	Technological Interface Centres
CNEI	National Council on Entrepreneurship and Innovation
CoLabs	Collaborative Laboratories
COMPETE 2020	Operational Programme for Competitiveness and Internationalisation
CPAI	Permanent Commission for Investor Support
DESI	EU Digital Economy and Society Index
EAFRD	European agricultural fund for rural development
EC	European Commission
EDRF	European Regional Development Fund
EMCE	Task Force for the Capitalisation of Companies
ESF	European Social Fund
ESPON	European Spatial Planning Observation Network
EU	European Union
FATS	Foreign Affiliates Statistics
FDI	Foreign direct investment
FUA	Functional Urban Area
GDP	Gross domestic product
GPEARI	Office for Economic Policy and International Affairs of the Ministry of Finance

GVCs	Global value chains
GVA	Gross value added
IAPMEI	Competitiveness and Innovation Agency
ICT	Information & Communication Technology
INE	National Statistics Institution
INPI	National Industrial Property Institute
IPA	Investment Promotion Agency
IPVC	Polytechnic Institute of Viana do Castelo
KIS	Knowledge-intensive services
M&E	Monitoring and evaluation
MNE	Multinational Enterprise
NEET	People not in education, employment or training
NUTS	Nomenclature of Territorial Units for Statistics
OECD	Organisation for Economic Cooperation and Development
OLI	Ownership-Location-Internationalisation
OMF	Output Monitoring Framework
PCT	Patent cooperation treaty
PDR	Rural Development Programme
PGA	Portugal Global Evaluation Plan
PNAID	National Diaspora Investment Support Programme
PNPOT	National Spatial Planning Policy Programme
QUAR	Evaluation and Accountability Framework
R&D	Research and development
R&D&I	Research and development and innovation
RFAI	Tax regime for investment support
S2B	Science-to-business
SDEA	Azores Business Development Society
SIFIDE	System of Fiscal Incentives for Business Research and Innovation
SI I&DT	Portugal 2020 Incentives System for Research and Technological Development
SMEs	Small and medium sized enterprises
SNG	Subnational governments
TL2/TL3	Territorial Level 2/3
TRNC	Turkish Republic of Northern Cyprus (TRNC
USD	United States Dollars
VET	Vocational education and training
WIPO	World Intellectual Property Organisation

Executive summary

Portugal has been strongly hit by the COVID-19 crisis with a larger fall in GDP than the OECD average, reflecting in large part a significant population of micro-firms with limited capacity to adapt to stringent containment measures, especially in the tourism sector, as well as relatively high exposure to disruptions in global value chains (GVCs). Although the recovery is now in process, with GDP expected to return to pre-crisis levels by mid-2022, there is considerable scope to strengthen the recovery, and reduce vulnerabilities to future shocks by revitalising progress Portugal has made in recent years in developing a dynamic entrepreneurial ecosystem.

This will require higher productivity and more innovation. This will require leveraging the potential of small and medium-sized enterprises (SMEs) that constitute the industrial fabric of many regions and countries, and foreign direct investment (FDI) that contributes to the knowledge base and capital stock of host places.

Portugal has seen significant growth in FDI in export-oriented manufacturing industries (e.g. mineral and metal products, chemicals, machinery, agri-food, transport material) over the past decade, motivated by low labour costs, a skilled workforce, a strong SME sector with research and development (R&D) capacities and good infrastructure (e.g. digital, financial). Despite this strong growth, key indicators – such as value added and export shares in high-tech manufacturing and services, and FDI stocks relative to GDP – remain below those of peer countries (e.g. Czech Republic and Slovak Republic). Further developing these high-tech sectors could strengthen the potential for FDI-SME spillovers, especially because the capacities of SMEs in these activities to absorb knowledge and technologies from foreign affiliates are already well-developed (particularly in the Lisboa Metropolitan Area). Portuguese SMEs contribute significantly to value added and exports and are relatively more innovative and digitised than those in many other OECD economies. However, Portugal has a large population of relatively low productivity micro firms with low absorptive capacity, compared to the OECD average, and FDI is concentrated in the Lisboa Metropolitan Area and the Norte region, which lowers the spillover potential for those micro firms, particularly in other regions.

Value chain linkages between foreign and domestic firms in Portugal are stronger than in some peer countries (e.g. Belgium and Hungary). Foreign affiliates source more intensively from local suppliers (often SMEs), particularly in high-tech manufacturing and lower technology services, increasing the scope for spillovers in these sectors. Additionally, domestic firms benefit more from (quality) inputs produced locally by foreign affiliates than in peer countries. SMEs in Portugal are less well integrated in innovation networks than in other European economies, although partnerships between foreign firms and SMEs are widespread in terms of technology licensing.

Labour mobility from domestic to foreign firms in skill-intensive activities is enabled by wage differentials. The higher wages offered by foreign firms attract skilled workers which (without enabling policies) may have negative impacts on SMEs, especially in less developed regions. Increased skills demand due to increasing FDI in Portugal also incentivises SMEs and workers outside FDI firms to invest in skills and thus further increases supply in the medium term. In the short-run, however, skills are scarce and therefore FDI entry may crowd out skilled workers from domestic firms. This negative productivity spillover is more likely in less developed Portuguese regions – where many low productivity SMEs and micro firms operate.

Many public institutions are involved in the design and implementation of policies that enable FDI spillovers on Portuguese SMEs. The main implementing agencies report to different line ministries and operate within specific policy domains, making inter-institutional coordination imperative for the effective implementation of policies that span several policy areas. Inter-ministerial collaboration is promoted through three high-level advisory councils that focus on the areas of entrepreneurship and innovation, regional development, and the internationalisation of the economy. However, the councils often lack a clear mandate and resources to facilitate policy coordination across the FDI-SME diffusion policy areas. Institutional silos are less pronounced in the management of the EU Structural and Investment Funds, which require a higher degree of collaboration among ministries, implementing agencies, and national and subnational operational bodies. Furthermore, the use of comprehensive monitoring and evaluation frameworks is limited to government institutions involved in the implementation of policies supported by the EU funds. With the exception of the Agency for Development and Cohesion (AD&C), none of the other implementing agencies, whose role is crucial in enabling FDI-SME diffusion, have a dedicated unit or internal capacity to systematically evaluate the impact of their policy initiatives.

One of the major factors influencing Portugal's policy mix is the desire and necessity to accelerate its transition to a knowledge-based economy. Another factor lies in the availability of the EU Structural and Investment Funds, which have been used to fund the government's policy priorities in the areas of investment, SME and entrepreneurship, innovation and regional development through the Portugal 2020 Partnership Agreement. Portugal's policy mix also presents a relatively high degree of selectivity, which is driven by its national and regional smart specialisation strategies; many policies target specific types of firms – in particular SMEs – priority sectors and value chain activities, as well as specific geographic areas. Strengthening SME absorptive capacities and promoting FDI-SME partnerships appear to be the main objectives pursued by the current policy mix. A large number of policies also target the attraction of knowledge-intensive FDI and the establishment of value chain linkages between foreign and domestic firms. The labour mobility and competition/imitation channels receive little attention from policymakers, however.

Financial incentives for R&D and innovation, technology acquisition and digital transformation have been the major instruments used to strengthen FDI-SME spillovers. Many initiatives include additional financial support for the development of products and services through business-to-business and industry--science collaboration, reflecting the importance given to networks in creating, accessing and sharing new knowledge. The type of instrument used to promote FDI-SME spillovers depends, however, on the pursued policy objectives. Whereas most policies supporting SME absorptive capacities make use of financial instruments, the attraction of knowledge-intensive FDI is pursued mainly through regulatory measures such as special investment regimes for different types of FDI and residence-by-investment schemes. Similarly, technical assistance, information and facilitation services are usually offered to promote value chain linkages and strategic partnerships, reflecting the crucial role that matchmaking services, networking events and supplier development programmes play in bringing together foreign investors with local suppliers, business networks, universities and other actors of the Portuguese innovation ecosystem.

The two regions of Portugal analysed, Norte and Alentejo, are distinctively different from each other and also exhibit substantial heterogeneity within themselves: The highly technologically driven Alentejo Litoral is decoupled from the rest of Alentejo's economy; in Norte the important engines of Porto and Braga differ vastly from the inner hinterland regions. This distinction shows the value of place-based policy responses that can complement nationwide policies. There is room to better connect the EU's Smart Specialisation Strategies to policies relating to FDI attraction; for example showcasing Norte's expertise in high technology manufacturing or the strategic location of the port of Sines in Alentejo – avoiding the use of other measures (e.g. financial incentives) that can be counterproductive and lead to a race to the bottom. This can improve the likelihood of FDI-SME linkages occurring. These links can be crucial for regional development but at the same time regional development policies can improve the strength of FDI-SME linkages. Further efforts should be made to improve the interconnectedness, including funding, of these policy objectives. Policies should be designed and implemented at the appropriate scale with input and coordination from all levels of government. And in order to tackle future challenges, resources should be dedicated to developing and circulating regional statistics relating to the monitoring of policy implementation.

1 Scope of FDI spillovers on SMEs: Conceptual framework

This introductory chapter describes the conceptual framework used in this report to assess factors influencing FDI spillovers on domestic SMEs and to identify opportunities for policies and institutional arrangements enhancing such spillovers. The chapter concludes by outlining how this conceptual framework is applied to the case of Portugal.

Context and motivation

Foreign direct investment (FDI) dropped by 32% in 2020.[1] FDI is an important source of finance for developed and developing countries and can play an important role in supporting a resilient and sustainable recovery from the COVID-19 crisis. Harnessing FDI for sustainable development, and particularly productivity and innovation, requires strong linkages with small and medium-sized enterprises (SMEs) in host countries. Foreign multinational enterprises (MNEs) do not just choose countries but locations in specific sub-national regions, and hence, FDI-SME linkages need to be considered and strengthened through place-based approaches.

SMEs contribute significantly to economic growth and social inclusion, and they can also play a key role in building resilience and more sustainable growth during the post COVID-19 recovery. In the OECD area, SMEs account for almost all enterprises, about two-thirds of total employment and 50-60% of value added (OECD, 2021[1]). To achieve their full potential, SMEs need to increase productivity and scale up innovation capacity. They are often less productive and innovative than larger firms where size is often identified as a major barrier to higher performance. Yet, some SMEs can be more productive and innovative than large firms, signalling that size is no fatality. In digital-intensive sectors, for example, smaller firms can show higher productivity levels (OECD, 2019[2]). SMEs play a key role in shifting innovation models by adapting supply to different contexts or user needs and responding to new or niche demand (OECD, 2018[3]).

Changes in the global trading and investment environment offer new opportunities for SME upgrading. Participation in global value chains (GVCs) enables SMEs to enhance productivity by absorbing technology and knowledge spillovers, upgrading workforce and managerial skills and raising innovation capacity (OECD, 2018[3]). This can be achieved by linking their business activities with foreign affiliates of MNEs (and domestic owned companies) and/or by directly integrating in GVCs as exporters, i.e. by supplying companies located abroad.

In this context, beyond the contribution to capital investment and employment generation, FDI can play an important role for knowledge and technology spillovers in host economies, resulting in increased productivity of local firms, especially SMEs. While productivity and innovation capacity of SMEs are influenced by a variety of market, policy and other factors (OECD, 2019[2]; OECD, 2021[1]), this report focuses on the specific role of FDI and related policies in Portugal. This introductory chapter introduces the conceptual framework to assess FDI spillovers on domestic SMEs and outlines how this framework is implemented for the case of Portugal (OECD, 2020[4]).[2]

Conceptual framework to assess FDI spillovers on domestic SMEs

Spillovers from FDI on domestic SMEs depend on a set of main enabling factors:

- **Potential for FDI spillovers:** FDI spillovers are possible as foreign firms are often more productive than domestic ones. Foreign MNEs are often larger than domestic firms, where size is found to be associated with higher productivity and a key determinant to overcome fixed costs for investment abroad (Helpman, Melitz and Yeaple, 2004[5]). Affiliates of foreign firms – through their links with parent companies – have typically greater access to technology, better managerial skills and more adequate resources for capital investment than domestic firms (Alfaro and Chen, 2012[6]). These capacity differences between foreign and domestic firms make it possible for SMEs to benefit from knowledge and technology transfers. The potential for FDI spillovers is further influenced by the volume of FDI inflows (i.e. the economy's relative dependence on FDI) and a number of FDI characteristics that illustrate to what extent FDI is effectively embedded in the local economy. These characteristics include (a) the sector in which the investment occurs and the activities that the foreign company undertakes, (b) the main motivations behind the FDI decision (e.g. market-seeking, resource-seeking, asset-seeking, efficiency-seeking), (c) the type of FDI (e.g. greenfield versus mergers and acquisitions), (d) the country of origin of the foreign investor, including the geographical and cultural proximity to the receiving country and the degree of foreign ownership.[3]

- **Absorptive capacities of local SMEs:** Absorptive capacity refers to the ability of a firm to recognise valuable new knowledge and integrate it productively in its processes, i.e. to innovate (OECD, 2021[1]; 2019[2]). The stronger its absorptive and innovative capacity, the higher its chances to benefit from FDI. SME absorptive capacity depends on the firm's prior capital endowment and level of productivity, i.e. its level of financial, human and knowledge-based capital and its efficiency in creating value from it. Beyond existing endowments of these resources, absorptive capacity also depends on SMEs' ability to access strategic assets related to finance, skills and innovation as well as on the broader business environment. Not all SMEs are the same and their heterogeneity greatly contributes to explain their performance. SMEs vary in terms of age, size, business model, market orientation, sector and geographical area of operation. This means that different types of SMEs have different growth trajectories and therefore different chances to enter into knowledge sharing relationships with foreign multinational enterprises (MNEs) and to benefit from FDI spillovers.
- **Economic geography factors:** This refers to geographical and cultural proximity factors, where the latter is defined by factors such as the differences between home and host countries in terms of language, culture, political systems, level of education, and level of industrial development (Johanson and Vahlne, 1977[7]). The localised nature of FDI means that geographical and cultural proximity between foreign and domestic firms affects the likelihood of knowledge spillovers, which often involve tacit knowledge, and whose strength decays with distance. Thus, productivity spillovers from FDI on local firms are often concentrated in the same region of the investment. Agglomeration effects, notably through the presence of local industrial clusters, have also been reported to affect FDI attraction and FDI spillovers. Clusters embed characteristics such as industrial specialisation (through specialised skilled workers and suppliers) and geographical proximity that make knowledge spillovers more likely to happen, including from MNE operations.
- **Other economic and structural characteristics of the host country:** The degree to which FDI-SME spillovers materialise also depends on other economic and structural characteristics of the host country and its sub-national regions. These factors relate to the regional/national endowment as well as the macro-economic context, structure of the economy, sectoral drivers of growth, productivity and innovation as well as to the level of integration in the global economy, beyond FDI. These factors are often necessary conditions for FDI spillover potential, SME absorptive capacity and economic geography factors to turn into actual productivity gains for domestic SMEs.

While adequate enabling conditions are necessary, FDI spillovers only occur if domestic SMEs are exposed to MNE activities. Such exposure may occur through a set of diffusion channels:

- **Value chain linkages** involve knowledge spillover from foreign MNEs to suppliers (upstream) and customers (downstream). Linkages help domestic companies extend their market for selling and raise the quality and competitiveness of their outputs. They can also generate knowledge spillovers when MNEs require better-quality inputs from local suppliers, particularly SMEs, and are therefore willing to share knowledge and technology with domestic companies to encourage their adoption of better practices.
- **Strategic partnerships** involve knowledge and capacity transfer in formal collaborations, for example in the area of R&D or workforce/managerial skills upgrading. These partnerships can take many forms, including joint ventures, licensing agreements, research collaborations, globalised business networks (i.e. membership-based business organisations, trade associations, stakeholder networks), and R&D and technology alliances.
- **Labour mobility** can be an important source of knowledge spillovers in the context of FDI, notably through the move of MNE workers to local SMEs – either through temporary arrangements such as detachments or long-term arrangements such as open-ended contracts – or through the

creation of start-ups (i.e. corporate spin-offs) by (former) MNE workers. Firms established by MNE managers are often more productive than other local firms. Similarly, workers who moved from foreign-owned to domestic firms retain skills and competences, including management skills, acquired in the foreign firms and thus contribute more to the productivity of their firm than workers without foreign firm experience.

- **Competition effects** occur with the entry of foreign firms, which heightens the level of competition on domestic companies and puts pressure on them to become more innovative and productive – not least to retain skilled workers. The new standards set by foreign firms – in terms of product design, quality control or speed of delivery – can stimulate technical change, the introduction of new products, and the adoption of new management practices in local companies, all of which are possible sources of productivity growth. This rising competitive pressure due to foreign firm entry and related productivity spillovers may also be associated with new incentives for workers to improve skills and SMEs to engage in skills upgrading.
- **Imitation effects** occur when foreign firms can also become a source of emulation for local companies, for example by showing better management practices. Imitation, reverse engineering and tacit learning can therefore become a channel to strengthen enterprise productivity at the local level. Foreign firms may also participate in innovation clusters and collaborative innovation activities where cross-fertilisation of ideas can increase productivity, both of domestic and foreign firms.

The scope for productivity and innovation spillovers on domestic SMEs is ultimately determined by the interaction of enabling factors and diffusion channels (Figure 1.1). Public policies aiming to enhance these spillovers address these different aspects and cut across a range of policy domains, including investment policy and promotion, SME development, innovation and regional development.

Figure 1.1. Understanding FDI spillovers on domestic SMEs: Conceptual framework

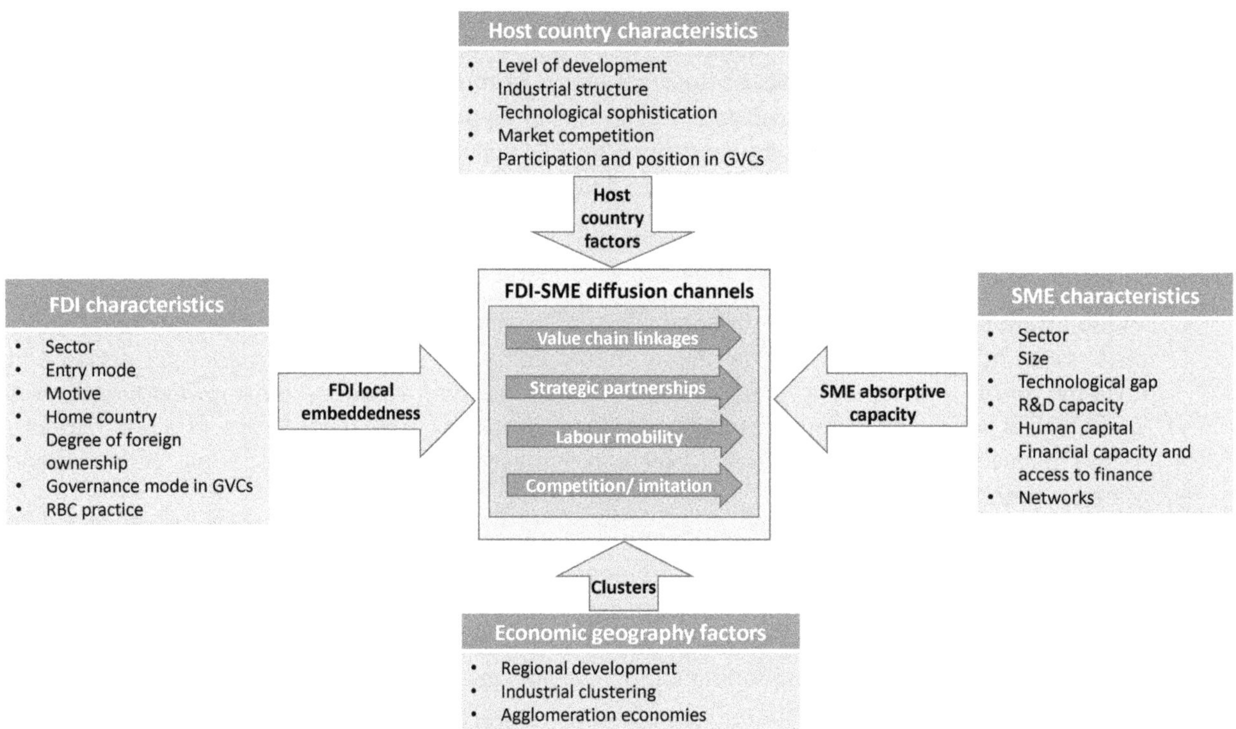

Source: OECD (2022[8]), FDI-SME linkages, productivity and innovation spillovers. Forthcoming.

Implementing the conceptual framework in this report

The next chapter assesses enabling conditions for FDI-SME diffusion in Portugal. It first looks at Portugal's economic context and integration in the global economy and then focuses on the potential for FDI spillovers, SME absorptive capacities and economic geography factors related to FDI and SME development. Whether or not FDI-SME diffusion channels are at play in Portugal is at the centre of discussion in this report and examined in Chapter 3.

Building on the diagnostic assessment of enabling conditions and channels of FDI-SME diffusion, the next two chapters focus on the institutional and governance framework (Chapter 4) and policy mix (Chapter 5) for FDI diffusion on SME productivity and innovation in Portugal. Chapter 4 provides an overview of the institutions that are currently in place to design and implement FDI, SME and entrepreneurship, innovation and regional development policies, and explores the multilevel policy coordination mechanisms to ensure coherence across policy domains, institutions and tiers of government. The chapter also looks at the monitoring and evaluation framework for policies related to FDI-SME diffusion in Portugal, and efforts to enhance stakeholder engagement. Chapter 5 reviews the mix of policies in place for fostering FDI spillovers on the productivity and innovation of Portuguese SMEs. Closely following the conceptual framework, it identifies the FDI-SME diffusion channels and enabling factors that are supported by Portugal's policy framework, and the policy instruments used to promote FDI-SME linkages, noting areas for further policy development or a shift in the policy mix.

The last chapter examines the geographic and regional dimension relevant for FDI investments and its spillovers with the local and regional economy. The chapter also explores the role of subnational policies to complement national FDI and SME policies by examining two Portuguese regions, Alentejo and Norte, as case studies.

References

Alfaro, L. and M. Chen (2012), "Surviving the Global Financial Crisis: Foreign Ownership and Establishment Performance", *American Economic Journal: Economic Policy*, Vol. 4(3): 30-55. [6]

Castro, F. (2000), *Foreign direct investment in the European periphery: The competitiveness of Portugal*, The University of Leeds, https://etheses.whiterose.ac.uk/2612/1/Castro_FB_LUBS_PhD_2000.pdf. [9]

Helpman, E., M. Melitz and S. Yeaple (2004), "Export Versus FDI with Heterogeneous Firms", *American Economic Review*, https://scholar.harvard.edu/files/melitz/files/exportsvsfdi_aer.pdf. [5]

Johanson, J. and J. Vahlne (1977), "The internationalization process of the firm - A model of knowledge development and increasing market commitments", *Journal of International Business Studies*, Vol. Vol. 8, No. 1. [7]

OECD (2022), *FDI-SME linkages, productivity and innovation spillovers*, OECD Publishing, Paris. [8]

OECD (2021), *OECD SME and Enterpreneurship Outlook 2021*, OECD Publishing, Paris. [1]

OECD (2020), *Enabling FDI diffusion channels to boost SME productivity and innovation in EU countries and regions: Towards a Policy Toolkit, Concept Paper for joint EC-OECD project.*. [4]

OECD (2019), *OECD SME and Entrepreneurship Outlook 2019*, OECD Publishing, Paris, https://doi.org/10.1787/d2b72934-en. [2]

OECD (2018), *Promoting innovation in established SMEs, OECD SME Ministerial Conference, Mexico City, Policy Note, 22-23 February 2018*, http://www.oecd.org/cfe/smes/ministerial/documents/2018-SME-Ministerial-Conference-Parallel-Session-4.pdf. [3]

Notes

[1] https://www.oecd.org/investment/FDI-in-Figures-April-2021.pdf.

[2] This conceptual framework has been developed as part of OECD-European Commission's cooperation on supporting EU Member States to harness FDI spillovers on SME productivity and innovation and its long version, including a review of literature, can be consulted at OECD (OECD, 2020[4]). Findings will contribute to OECD Investment Committee's FDI Qualities Initiative and the work on "Global value chains (GVCs): Seizing the opportunities for SMEs" of the OECD Committee on SMEs and Entrepreneurship.

[3] See Chapter 2, Box 2.2, for a discussion of key concepts in the literature; see OECD (2020[4]) and Castro (2000[9]) for a review of the literature.

2 Enabling conditions for FDI spillovers on Portuguese SMEs

This chapter assesses key enabling conditions for FDI spillovers on SMEs in Portugal as described in the conceptual framework in Chapter 1. It first examines Portugal's economic context and structure and then moves to key factors related to the potential for FDI spillovers (FDI trends, local embeddedness and capacity premia of foreign firms), SME absorptive capacities and Portugal's economic geography. The chapter points to Portugal's strengths, challenges and opportunities in these enabling conditions.

2.1. Summary of strengths, challenges and opportunities

The diagnostic assessment of key enabling conditions for FDI spillovers on SMEs in Portugal reveals a number of strengths in current conditions and points to challenges and opportunities to further improve these fundamental conditions for spillovers to take place (Table 2.1). The subsequent chapters (Chapters 4-6) pick up on these challenges and opportunities, identifying policy actions to address them

Table 2.1. Strengths, challenges/opportunities of enabling conditions for FDI spillovers in Portugal

	Strengths	Challenges and opportunities
Economic context and structure	• Strong pre-COVID-19 economic fundamentals and dynamic entrepreneurial ecosystem, which could support recovery • Well-developed export-oriented manufacturing (e.g. mineral and metal products, chemicals, machinery, agri-food, transport material) • Relatively low labour costs of skilled workers; strong R&D skills; good infrastructure (e.g. digital, financial)	• Above average growth decline during pandemic, due to exposure to pandemic affected sectors (tourism, manufacturing) • Rising unemployment; particularly in previously expanding sectors (e.g. sales, tourism, construction, low-tech manufacturing) • Value added and export shares in high-tech manufacturing and services below peers (e.g. Ireland, Czech Republic and Slovak Republic)
Potential for FDI spillovers	• Strong FDI growth in pre-COVID-19 period; relative resilience of FDI, compared to peers in OECD • Capacity gap between foreign/domestic firms low in higher-tech manufacturing, supporting spillover potential • Extensive operations of foreign firms through greenfield investments in higher-tech manufacturing, further supporting strong spillover potential	• Potential for more FDI inflows, given lower stocks compared to peers (e.g. Hungary, Czech Republic) • Limited diversification in terms of FDI origins • Capacity gap between foreign/domestic firms very high in lower-tech manufacturing and services, challenging spillover potential • Opportunity to attract technology-exploiting FDI, given emerging innovation eco-system
Absorptive capacities of SMEs	• SMEs contribute significantly to value added/exports; many SME exporters are foreign-owned • SMEs are relatively more innovative and digitised than those in many other OECD economies • Good entrepreneurial skills; at par with OECD	• More low productivity micro firms, compared to OECD • Access to bank credits and venture capital for SMEs has potential to improve • Weak access to adult learning within SMEs • Rather low computer/electronics and problem solving skills, but training is at par with peers
Economic geography factors	• FDI concentrated in Lisboa and to some extent Norte, making spillover more likely in those regions • Performance gaps of foreign/domestic firms lowest in Lisboa, making spillovers more likely	• Limited FDI diversification across region, limiting spillover potential in many regions • Performance gaps of domestic firms very high in regions other than Lisboa, making spillovers less likely

Note: See Box 2.1 clarifying sectoral groupings (i.e. lower and higher technology manufacturing and lower and higher technology services) used in this table.

2.2. Portugal's economic context and structure

Before assessing strengths, challenges and opportunities of other key enabling conditions for FDI-SME spillovers – namely the potential for FDI spillovers, SME absorptive capacities and Portugal's economic geography – it is important to assess the broad economic context of Portugal. This section assesses (1) recent macroeconomic trends, pre- and post-COVID-19, (2) Portugal's sectoral growth drivers and structure; and (3) its integration in the global economy through trade. FDI is an additional key ingredient for internationalisation, which is assessed in the next section.

Portugal has had robust growth over recent years but has been hit hard by the pandemic

Portugal was heavily affected by the 2008 global financial crisis but economic conditions had improved markedly over the past few years, before the COVID-19 outbreak in 2020 (OECD, 2019[1]). The unemployment rate declined 10 percentage points over 2013-19 to below 7%, one of the largest reductions in any OECD country over the past decade. Like in other small economies, growth in Portugal depends less on domestic consumption, although rising private earnings have led to a solid contribution of consumption to GDP growth over recent years as well.

The pandemic and related travel restrictions and severe supply chain disruptions have led to the most severe economic shock in decades with severe implications on trade, investment, jobs and livelihoods in Portugal. The OECD estimates that real GDP fell by more than 8% in 2020 relative to 2019; a stronger decline than the OECD average decline of 5.5% given the relative exposure of Portugal in pandemic affected industries such as tourism and manufacturing (OECD, 2021[2]). After a strong recovery of employment since 2013, unemployment is expected to increase again in the coming years and put pressure on livelihoods and well-being.

Improving macroeconomic fundamentals during the pre-COVID-19 years indicate that Portugal's recovery from the ongoing economic crisis could be faster than that from the 2009 crisis (OECD, 2019[1]). However, ongoing pandemic-related economic uncertainty in Europe and globally may harm a fast recovery.

Portugal has a dynamic start-up and entrepreneurial ecosystem, which could support the recovery from the pandemic crisis. Unlike most economies (OECD, 2021[3]; OECD, 2019[4]), new firm creations in Portugal have increased steadily over the last decade, notwithstanding the dips around the time of the 2008 financial crisis (Figure 2.1, Panel A). Job destruction due to bankruptcies has accompanied job creation further revealing the dynamic entrepreneurial ecosystem in Portugal (Figure 2.1, Panel B). In recent years, it was net employment change by incumbent firms that has led to a net increase of jobs in Portugal.

Figure 2.1. Enterprise and job creation/destruction over time in Portugal

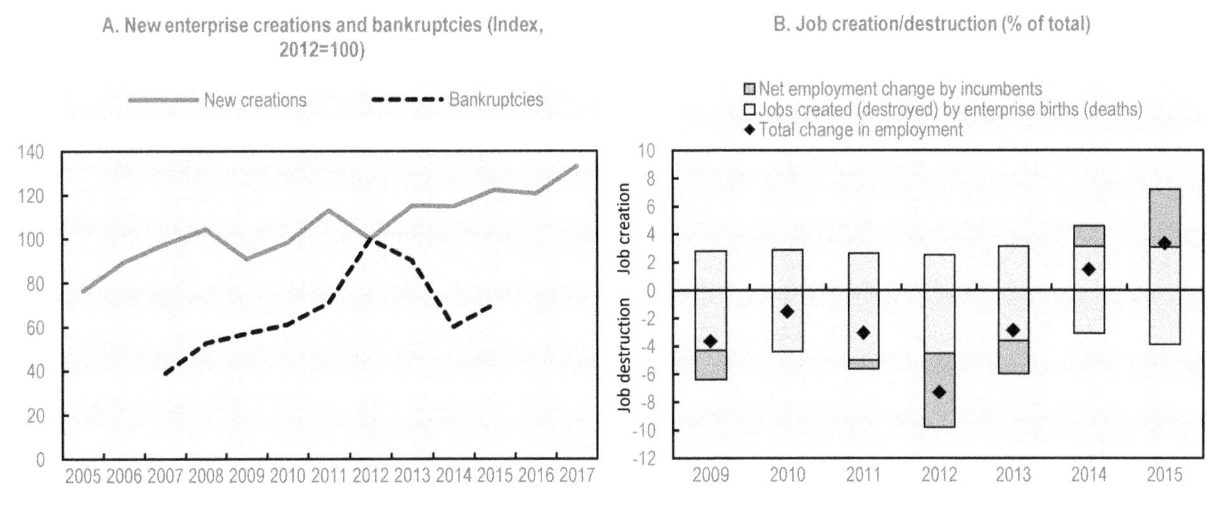

Source: OECD (2019d), OECD SME and Entrepreneurship Outlook 2019

Jobs in sectors that were expanding pre-pandemic are now most at risk. Much of the job creation since the 2008 financial crisis has taken place in low-productivity sectors, e.g. wholesale and retail trade (21% of total jobs created since 2008), accommodation and food services (20%), construction (12%), or in low-tech manufacturing (10%) (OECD, 2019[4]). Job creation in higher productivity and higher wage sectors such as ICT (3%) and professional, scientific and technical activities (8%) was limited. During the ongoing pandemic, it is those jobs in lower productivity sectors that are most at risk (OECD, 2020[5]).

Portugal could further expand high-tech activities to match its European peers

Growth in the pre-pandemic period was driven by the fast expanding tourism sector. It contributed to almost 10% of GDP in recent years and grew twice as fast as the rest of the economy (OECD, 2020[6]). Beyond tourism, Portugal benefited from a boost in a variety of export-oriented manufacturing sectors during the pre-pandemic period (OECD, 2019[1]; Westmore and Adamczyk, 2019[7]). Some of which included lower-tech activities such as mineral and metal products, agri-food, and transport material. Other growth sectors included higher-tech activities such as pharmaceuticals, chemicals and machinery.

Growth in manufacturing was driven by relatively low labour costs, investments in digital infrastructure, access to knowledge-based capital, such as big data analytics, average skills at par with levels seen elsewhere in the OECD, strong R&D skills, a stable financial system and a fairly strong regulatory environment for business and investment (see more details on relative assets of the Portuguese economy in Section 2.4 on absorptive capacities of local SMEs and Chapter 5 on the regulatory environment and policy mix for FDI-SME diffusion) (OECD, 2019[8]).

Understanding technology intensity of economic activity is important to assess the potential FDI and SMEs and their linkages have to drive productivity in Portugal, which is the key endeavour of this report. Higher technology manufacturing and services help to differentiate, customise and upgrade products and often drive aggregate productivity and innovation, particularly in advanced economies like Portugal (OECD, 2020[9]). Box 2.1 clarifies sectoral classifications based on technology intensity used in this report.

Box 2.1. Classification of economic activities by technology-intensity

The conceptual framework described in Chapter 0 explains that FDI's local embeddedness and absorptive capacities of SMEs are key determinants for FDI spillovers on SME productivity and innovation to take place. They depend, among other things, on the economic sectors and activities in which investment takes place and SMEs are operating. Given the focus on productivity and innovation spillovers, the sectoral analysis in this and the following chapters is based on technology- or R&D-intensity. As such, most analysis based on sectors (e.g. regarding economic structure, including of SMEs; GVC integration both through trade and FDI; and FDI-SME diffusion channels) focuses on four main sectoral groupings based on R&D-intensity, which are adapted from Galindo-Rueda and Verger (2016[10]): higher technology manufacturing, lower technology manufacturing, higher technology services and lower technology services. Table 2.2 provides an overview of the industries covered in these groupings. R&D-intensity is measured by the ratio of business R&D expenditure relative to gross value added in each industry covered in a given group. It is important to note that sectoral classifications may vary across data sources covered in this report. Table 2.2 lists industries based on ISIC Rev. 4 two-digit sectors, which is the classification applied for most of the data used (e.g. OECD and Eurostat data). Commercial datasets like Financial Times' fDi Markets and Refinitiv have their own classification of sectors but for the purpose of this report they were also classified according to the four groupings described above.

The classification has the caveat that R&D-intensity is an imperfect measure of innovation and innovation potential across industries. Not all firms that are successful at developing or implementing innovation are necessarily R&D performers. Many of these firms are successful adopters of technology which they have not developed. Measuring R&D intensity or embedded R&D in their purchases may not effectively characterise the innovative performance of firms or industries. Other OECD indicators measure skill intensity, patenting activities and innovation by industries that facilitate a more refined description of the overall knowledge intensity in different economic activities, although these measures are not always widely available across a majority of OECD countries and partner economies (OECD, 2015[11]). Another caveat of this classification is related to the fact that it is not entire sectors that involve either higher or lower technologies but it is specific activities or segments within these sectors that involve different technology intensities. For example, in textiles, most surviving companies in Portugal are no longer low-tech. On the other hand, many of the outsourced segments in the automobile industry, for example, are not exactly high-tech but involve standard processes with no R&D involved. This caveat needs to be considered for any conclusions made in this report.

Table 2.2. Sectoral groupings based on R&D-intensity

Economic grouping	Industries covered based on ISIC Rev. 4
Lower technology manufacturing	Food products, beverages and tobacco; Textiles, wearing apparel, leather and related products; Wood and products of wood and cork; Paper products and printing; Rubber and plastic products; Other non-metallic mineral products; Basic metals; Fabricated metal products
High technology manufacturing	Pharmaceutical products; Computer, electronic and optical products; Electrical equipment; Machinery and equipment; Motor vehicles, trailers and semi-trailers; Other transport equipment; Other manufacturing; repair and installation of machinery and equipment
Lower technology services	Wholesale and retail trade; repair of motor vehicles; Transport and storage; Publishing, audio-visual and broadcasting activities; Financial and insurance activities; Real estate activities
Higher technology services	IT and other information services; other business sector services

Note: A number of industries are not classified into these four groupings as the analysis in this report deliberately avoids focusing on these industries. They include: *Mining and extraction* (Mining and extraction of energy producing products; Coke and refined petroleum products); *Infrastructure* (Electricity, gas, water supply, sewerage, waste and remediation services; Telecommunications); *Other services* (Accommodation and food services; Public admin. and defence; compulsory social security; Education; Human health and social work; Arts, entertainment, recreation and other service activities; Private households with employed persons). These industries are either highly specialised and would require a more focused analysis, or their role/potential for FDI-SME linkages and spillover is limited.

Figure 2.2. Economic structure, by key sectoral groups (% of total value added), 2016

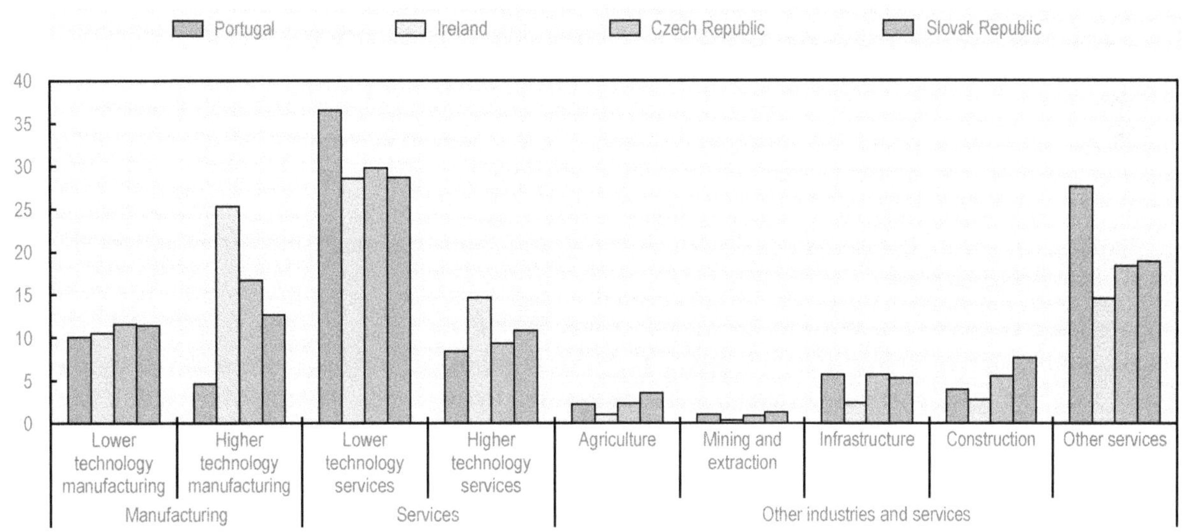

Note: See Box 2.1 clarifying sectoral groupings used in this figure.
Source: OECD based on the OECD Analytical AMNE database, 2019, https://www.oecd.org/sti/ind/analytical-AMNE-database.htm

Despite recent expansion of some advanced manufacturing and high-tech (including digital) services, Portugal still has the potential to further expand in this area. Some comparators such as Ireland, the Czech Republic and the Slovak Republic report larger shares of both higher technology manufacturing and services (Figure 2.2).[1] The services sector is large but dominated in relatively low productivity activities in Portugal. The sector includes a large share of lower technology activities such as wholesale and retail trade, transport and other logistics services (35% of total value added), which are reported as lower productivity activities in Portugal and are dominated by SMEs. The services sector also includes other activities (25% of total value added), driven by tourism. These services and some other industries (agriculture, mining and extraction, infrastructure, construction) are not classified into the four groupings based on technology intensity (Box 2.1). These industries are either highly specialised and would require a more focused analysis, or their role/potential for FDI-SME linkages and spillover is limited. These activities are not in the focus for the remainder of this report.

Portugal is a highly globalised economy and thus the speed of economic recovery also depends on that in its exporting markets

The favourable economic context, pre-COVID-19, led to a boost in foreign investment inflows in manufacturing activities, enabled linkages and diffusion channels between foreign affiliates and domestic SMEs and led to an export boom, including for domestic SMEs (OECD, 2019[1]; OECD, 2019[8]). Section 2.3 emphasises the important role of inward FDI for Portugal's internationalisation process, while Section 2.4 clarifies the important role of SMEs in exporting – which is also an important indicator of absorptive capacity of SMEs.

Strong exports sustained economic activity in the decade prior to COVID-19 and helped expand a variety of manufacturing sectors with rising revealed comparative advantage[2] (e.g. mineral and metal products, chemicals, machinery, agri-food, transport material) (Westmore and Adamczyk, 2019[7]; Fontoura Gouveia, 2018[12]). Rising export competitiveness was driven by improved product quality, weak domestic demand that prompted firms to increase their focus on foreign markets (e.g. through dedicated marketing activities) and decreasing relative export prices. It also coincided with increased integration in global value chains (GVCs), including through growth in inward FDI (see Section 2.3) (Adamczyk and Westmore, 2020[13]).

In line with the value added structure, lower technology activities are responsible for higher shares of exporting in Portugal compared to peers such as Ireland, the Czech Republic and the Slovak Republic (Figure 2.3). Lower technology manufacturing exports include food, textiles and apparel, wood and paper, plastics and metal products and are responsible for about 35% of all exports in Portugal compared to 20% or less in peer countries. On the contrary, the export share of high-tech manufacturing is at about 20% of total exports lower in Portugal compared to other countries reporting shares between 50-60%. Portugal also participates in some lower technology services GVCs, such as wholesale and retail trade and transport logistics. These services amount to almost 20% of total exports in Portugal, at par with the share in Ireland. Exports of knowledge services such as research and development (R&D), design and process management, however, remain relatively small in Portugal and are much more developed in Ireland (almost 30% of total exports).

Portugal's export exposure to lower technology activities, both in manufacturing and services, is a concern for its economic recovery. For example, lower technology manufacturing is more affected by the crisis compared to high-end services related to the digital economy. While Portugal has made strains in expanding more advanced sectors, the bulk of the economy and employment in Portugal depends on the recovery of exports of these lower technology sectors and thus on the recovery of demand in its exporting markets in Europe and beyond.

Figure 2.3. Export structure, by key sectoral groups (% of total exports*), 2016

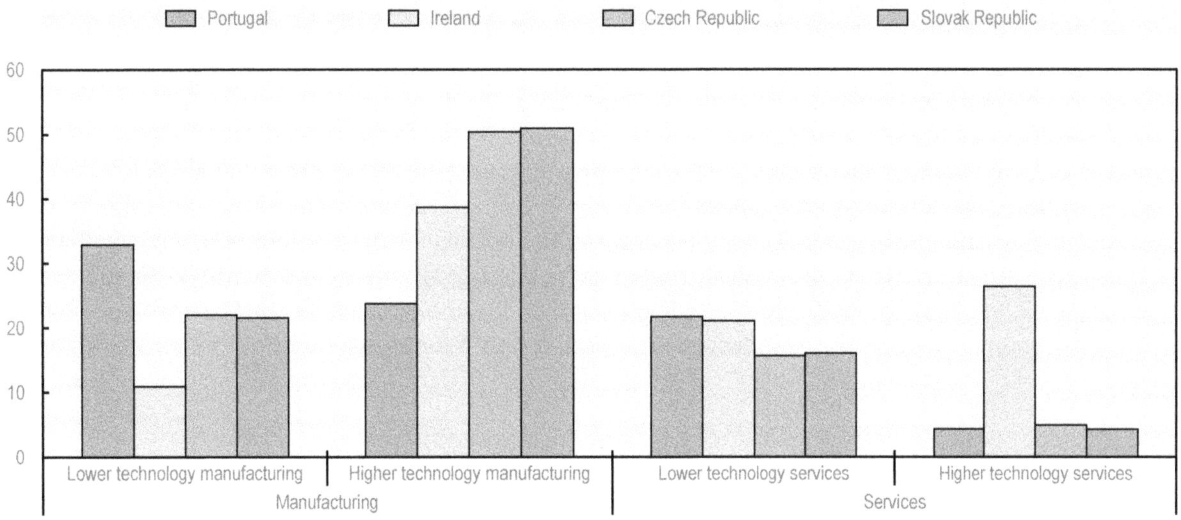

Note: *In this figure, total exports refers to the total of the four industrial groupings. See Box 2.1 clarifying sectoral groupings used in this figure. Covered exports are responsible for approximately 80% of total exports in Portugal.
Source: OECD based on the OECD Analytical AMNE database, 2019, https://www.oecd.org/sti/ind/analytical-AMNE-database.htm

2.3. Potential for FDI spillovers in Portugal

This section clarifies the potential for FDI spillovers in Portugal. Firstly, it illustrates that spillovers are possible due to the capacity or productivity premia of foreign firms compared to domestic ones in Portugal. Secondly, it shows that knowledge and technology transfers from FDI are likely due to significant FDI inflows in recent years and, thirdly, the section explains how FDI is embedded in Portugal, helping to identify strengths, challenges and opportunities for FDI spillover potential.

Foreign firms exhibit important productivity premia over domestic SMEs

Labour productivity, defined as value added per person employed, serves as a good indicator to measure performance differences between foreign and domestic firms. If differences exist, FDI spillovers are possible as foreign firms can transfer their knowledge and technology to domestic firms. Comparing productivity differences doesn't allow to make conclusions on whether or not SME absorptive capacities are sufficient, but identifying differences in capacities allows to infer that the potential for spillovers exists.

There are significant productivity gaps between foreign and domestic firms in Portugal, as in many EU economies. Using Eurostat's Foreign Affiliates Statistics (FATS) shows that affiliates of foreign firms in Portugal are on average 70% more productive than an average firm in Portugal (Figure 2.4, Panel A). This gap is particularly high in Cyprus[3] and Bulgaria and fairly low in economies like Austria and France. While this aggregate indicator provides some insights on potential challenges related to SME capacities to benefit from foreign firms' presence, it is important to dig deeper into sectoral specificities and firm characteristics to better understand domestic capacities in Portugal (see Section 2.4).

Studying labour productivity levels of foreign firms – which are typically larger than average domestic firms (but not always) – and SMEs across value chain functions reveals that foreign firms outperform local ones across all key economic activities in Portugal, in line with countries like Ireland (Figure 2.4, Panel B) (OECD, 2020[14]). This gap is lowest in higher technology manufacturing, where foreign firms are 30% more productive than an average firm in Portugal and 50% more productive than SMEs. Relatively low differences in productivity could illustrate that foreign and domestic firms are operating at par in comparable activities/functions within these industries and thus knowledge exchange is likely. The gap is highest in lower technology manufacturing and services where foreign firms are twice as productive as SMEs. The bulk of fairly low productivity domestic firms (especially SMEs) are operating in these lower value added activities in Portugal (both in terms of value added and employment (see Section 2.4).

The productivity distance between foreign and domestic firms, based on Eurostat's FATS data, has declined only marginally over recent years (Figure 2.4, Panel A) but micro and small firms have seen some progress in closing the gap with medium sized and large domestic firms in some industries. However, using OECD Structural and Demographic Business Statistics to take a closer look at SMEs and specific sectors shows that their productivity levels have increased over the past decade, especially among micro- and small-firms. In this period, labour productivity grew across all SME size classes in the manufacturing sector. It also grew significantly among micro- and small firms in wholesale and retail trade, as well as in professional, scientific and technical activities, closing the gap with large and medium-sized firms (OECD, 2019[8]).

Figure 2.4. Labour productivity differences between foreign and domestic firms

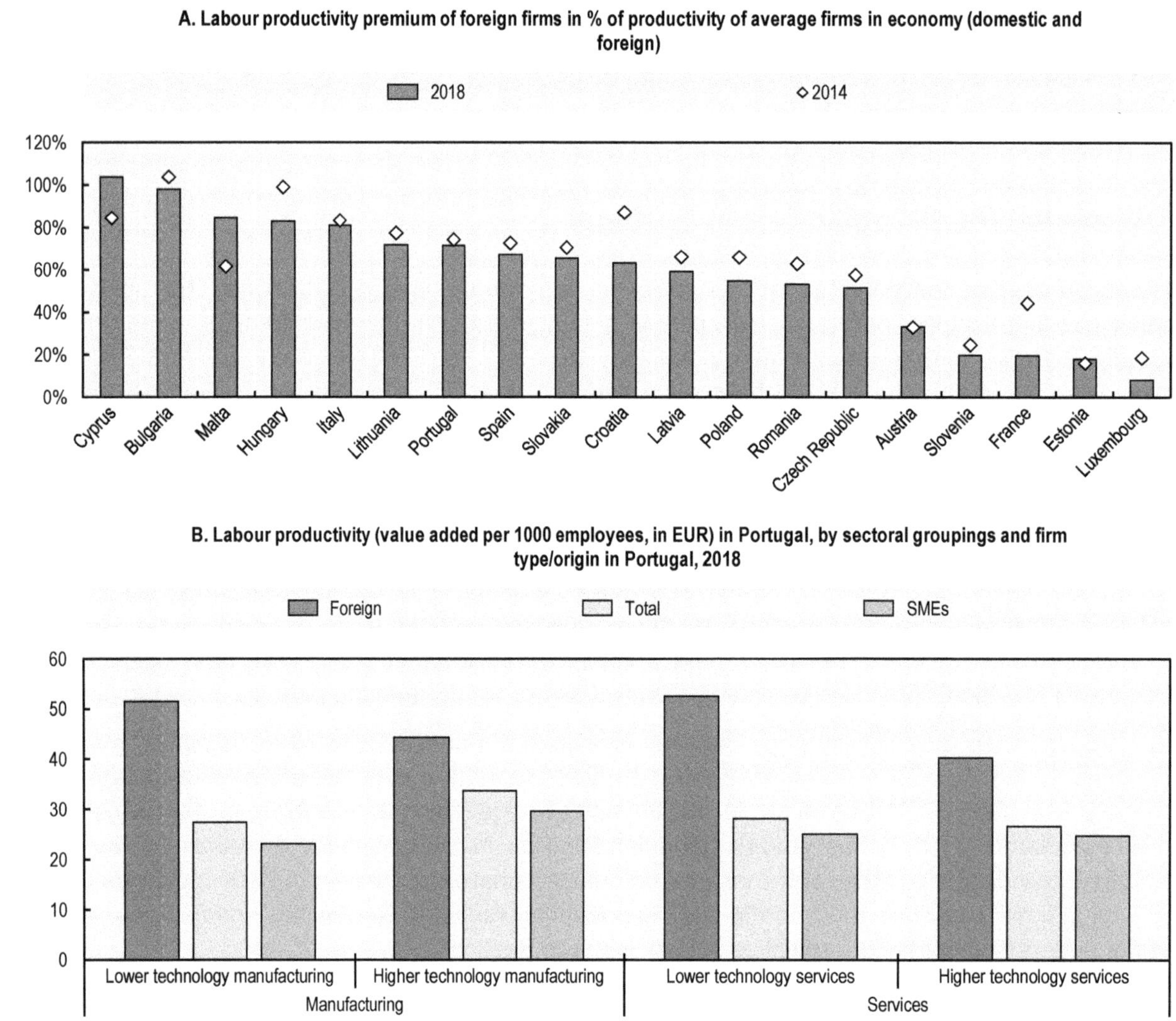

Note: See Box 2.1 clarifying sectoral groupings used in this figure. The information in this document with reference to "Cyprus" relates to the southern part of the Island. There is no single authority representing both Turkish and Greek Cypriot people on the Island. Turkey recognises the Turkish Republic of Northern Cyprus (TRNC). Until a lasting and equitable solution is found within the context of United Nations, Turkey shall preserve its position concerning the "Cyprus" issue.
Source: OECD based on Eurostat's FATS data, 2020.

FDI has been on the rise before the pandemic, with potential for further growth

FDI can have a leverage on SMEs if foreign firms not only have a performance advantage but they also need to have enough economic weight in the host economy. The volume of foreign investment can be illustrated with FDI stocks relative to GDP, foreign firms' share in total value added and employment for example.

Despite rising importance of FDI, there is potential for further FDI growth in Portugal. In Portugal, the share of inward FDI stocks as a percentage of GDP increased from approximately 30% in 2005 to above 60% in 2019, with much of the increase occurring predominately during the post 2008 crisis recovery (Figure 2.5, Panel A). FDI was enabled by increasing efforts to position Portugal as an attractive location for investment and innovation in Europe (see Chapter 5), although it also reflects a general globalisation of investments in Europe and beyond. While its FDI share in GDP is above the EU and OECD average, the stock of FDI remains below that of comparable small European economies such as Hungary, the Czech Republic or Belgium (OECD, 2021[15]). This suggests that there is further potential for FDI growth in Portugal.

Based on available data on immediate origins of investors, FDI diversification in Portugal appears limited with more than 50% of investments coming from the Netherlands, Spain and Luxembourg and almost all investments have their origins within Europe (Figure 2.5, Panel B). However, some FDI in Portugal may originate from immediate investing countries through which investments have been channelled. Investors may channel their investment through different countries globally for strategic reasons related to policy and market conditions in these countries. It is likely that the 20% FDI share of Luxembourg points to this problem, for example. Portugal does not yet publish FDI data in terms of ultimate investing country. Data by ultimate investing country tend to show a more diversified source of FDI and show a greater role for US investors within Europe than would be suggested in the bilateral data. Recent research finds that the more diverse is FDI in terms of country of origin, the higher the positive effect on domestic firm productivity (Zhang and Zhao, 2010[16]).

FDI has been more resilient in Portugal during the COVID-19 crisis compared to the OECD and EU average. The sudden halt of economic activity in important sectors, such as tourism and manufacturing supply chains, along with important demand contractions has led to an almost free fall of inward investment flows in Portugal (OECD, 2021[15]). In 2020, Portugal's FDI inflows fell by almost 50% relative to 2019. This decline was lower relative to the average FDI fall in the OECD and EU where FDI declined by above 50% and 70% relative to 2019 (Figure 2.5, Panel C).

Despite the relative resilience of FDI in Portugal, its sharp drop adds strain to the economic situation and prospects for a fast recovery. Yet, Portugal's existing and significant FDI position can help it during the economic recovery. Evidence from past crises has shown that foreign affiliates, including SME investors, often show greater resilience during crises thanks to their linkages with, and access to the financial resources of, their parent companies (Alfaro and Chen, 2012[17]) (Desai, Foley and Forbes, 2008[18]). Additionally, delayed reinvestments of earnings of foreign firms often materialise after crisis peaks (OECD, 2020[19]).

Figure 2.5. Short- and medium-term inward FDI trends in Portugal

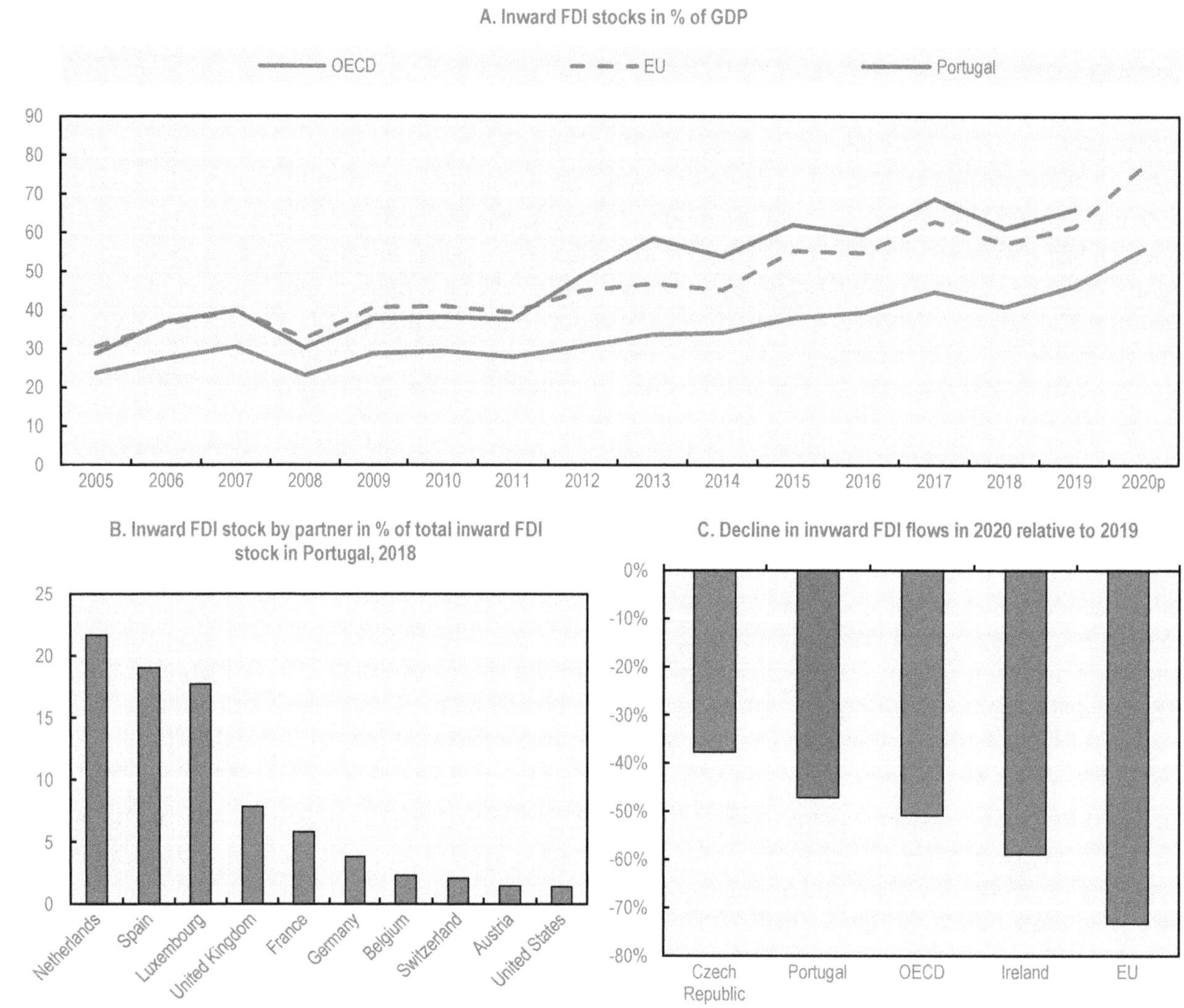

Note: FDI exclude resident special purpose entities (SPEs). Statistics follow OECD Benchmark Definition 4 (BM4).
Source: OECD based on OECD International Direct Investment Statistics and OECD FDI in Figures April 2021, https://www.oecd.org/investment/FDI-in-Figures-April-2021.pdf

Local embeddedness of FDI supports other aspects of spillover potential in Portugal

The potential for FDI spillovers is further influenced by a number of FDI characteristics that illustrate to what extent FDI is effectively embedded in the local economy. These characteristics include (a) the sector in which the investment occurs and the activities that the foreign company undertakes, (b) the type of FDI (e.g. greenfield versus mergers and acquisitions), and (c) the main motives behind the FDI decision (e.g. market-seeking, resource-seeking, asset-seeking, efficiency-seeking) (Box 2.2). They are discussed in this section, while local embeddedness relative to the location of FDI within Portugal is discussed in Section 2.5.

Portugal is revealed to have strong FDI spillover potential in higher technology manufacturing, given extensive operations of foreign firms in these activities. Foreign firms in Portugal are contributing to value added and exports across all sectors. They are responsible for at least 15% of value added and at least 45% of exports within each sectoral grouping based on technology intensity (Figure 2.6). In high technology manufacturing such as electronics and pharmaceuticals, foreign firms are responsible for almost all exports. They account for 80% of total exports, up from around 70% in 2006, and for 50% of total value added, up from 40% in 2006. Existing research shows that FDI spillovers on SME productivity are often observed in higher technology sectors (Nicolini and Resmini, 2010[20]; Keller and Yeaple, 2009[21]), suggesting that Portugal's FDI dominance in these activities further supports the spillover potential of FDI.

Box 2.2. FDI motivations: Key concepts in the literature

The Ownership-Location-Internalisation (OLI) paradigm proposed by Dunning (1977[22]) provides a useful way of thinking about MNEs and what determines their internationalisation decisions. *Ownership advantages* are assets that enable firms to overcome the costs associated with setting up affiliates abroad. *Location advantages* originate from the characteristics of a specific country or region – for instance, natural resources, manpower and skills on the supply side, or a large consumer base on the demand side. *Internationalisation advantages* exist in the presence of high transaction costs, which induce the firm to internalise activities through affiliates, rather than purchasing goods or services through trade. According to this framework, trade and investment are either complementary (vertical FDI) or substitutes (horizontal FDI), and why companies invest abroad is tied to the hold-up problem: the impossibility of writing complete contracts imposes high transaction costs (Grossman and Hart, 1986[23]).

Global production networks have undergone a profound transformation in terms of firms' internationalisation strategies. The OLI paradigm formulated 40 years ago remains a useful tool but shows several limitations when confronted to today's business reality. Horizontal and vertical FDI are not the only strategies behind investment, and trade and investment are not simply substitutes or complements (Alfaro and Charlton, 2009[24]; Herger and McCorriston, 2016[25]). MNEs combine horizontal strategies of FDI in some countries and vertical strategies in others (Buckley and Casson, 1976[26]). In some cases, MNEs might decide to concentrate their value chain abroad (vertical investment) while at the same time serving proximate foreign markets through horizontal investment as in the case of "export-platform FDI" (Ekholm, Forslid and Markusen, 2003[27]).

Another limitation is that a significant share of investment is neither purely vertical nor horizontal (Herger and McCorriston, 2016[25]), which raises the question as to why MNEs establish affiliates that do not provide inputs to the parent company and do not serve foreign markets. A fourth category of 'strategic asset-seeking' FDI was later acknowledged by Dunning (1993[28]) himself, as somehow neglected by the traditional OLI framework. This is because MNEs are understood to have ownership advantages *ex ante* which allow them to overcome the costs associated with setting up an affiliate abroad. The strategic asset seeking motive describes rather the opposite phenomenon: MNEs try to access assets and capabilities which are not inside the firm. This acknowledgment of MNEs seeking new and complementary assets is an important extension of the OLI framework (Castro, 2000[29]).

Figure 2.6. Foreign firms' value added and exports, by sectoral groups (in % of total)

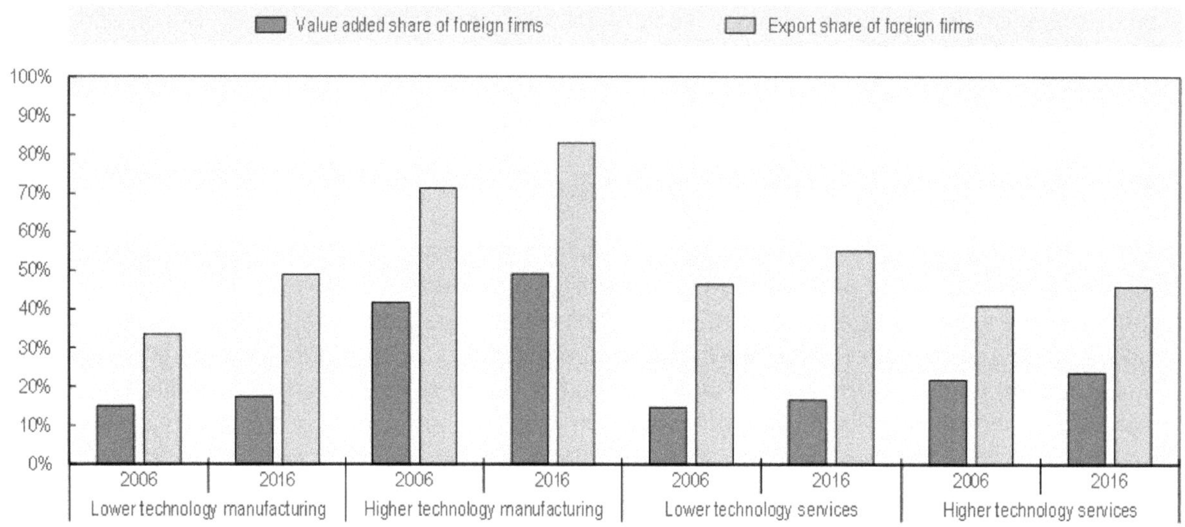

Note: See Box 2.1 clarifying sectoral groupings used in this figure.
Source: OECD based on the OECD Analytical AMNE database, 2019, https://www.oecd.org/sti/ind/analytical-AMNE-database.htm

Greenfield investments are concentrated in higher technology manufacturing and transport and other logistics services; they are more likely to involve transfers of knowledge and technology than acquisitions (particularly in the short-run), further supporting FDI spillover potential. The establishment of subsidiaries of foreign MNEs in Portugal (greenfield investment) is most prevalent in higher technology manufacturing and lower technology services (particularly transport and other logistics services) (Figure 2.7). Taken together, these activities are responsible for more than 80% of all greenfield investments made since 2003. As greenfield investments are likely to involve productivity spillovers, and these spillovers are often larger in higher technology sectors, Portugal's type of FDI and sectoral positioning seems to be well formed to enable diffusion of knowledge.[4]

Acquisitions of domestic firms by foreign investors almost exclusively occur in lower technology services in Portugal, where spillovers may occur in the longer term. Close to 90% of all deals have taken place in lower technology services since 2003; mainly in banking, logistics and consumer services. In the case of acquisitions, the deployment of the foreign investor's technology is likely to be implemented more gradually, making knowledge spillovers to domestic firms less likely in the short-term but they may still occur in the longer term (Crespo, Fontoura and Proenca, 2009[30]; Braconier, Ekholm and Knarvik, 2001[31]; Branstetter, Fisman and Foley, 2006[32]). Foreign entry in these services is also likely to enhance competitive pressure in the market and thus involve more indirect spillover potential (OECD, 2019[33]).

Figure 2.7. Distribution of greenfield FDI and cross-border M&A stocks, 2020

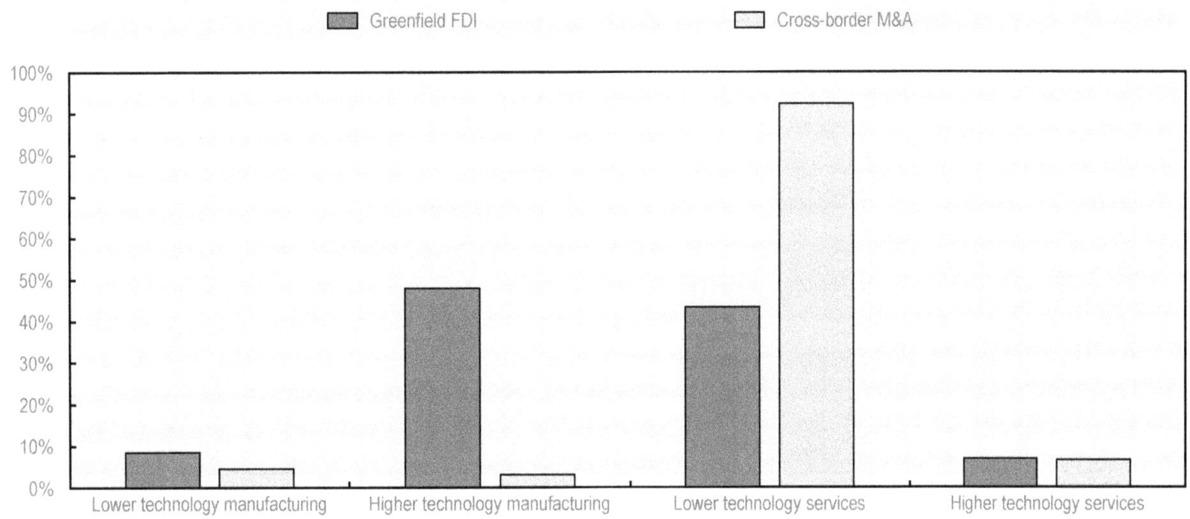

Note: See Box 2.1 clarifying sectoral groupings used in this figure. Detailed sector/activity classifications from Financial Times' fDi Markets and Refinitiv data underlying the analysis in this figure differ marginally from standard classifications based on ISIC rev. 4 used in other figures in this report. Percentages are based on total capital investment (greenfield FDI) and total M&A deal values over 2003-2020.
Source: OECD based on Financial Times fDi Markets database and Refinitiv.

The small Portuguese market and its labour and administrative cost advantage relative to larger markets within Europe (e.g. Germany or France) make it particularly attractive for efficiency-seeking FDI. While less developed countries may attract efficiency-seeking FDI in lower technology manufacturing, Portugal does so at the higher technology end, including services activities. This is also related to Portugal's relatively high level of advanced skills combined with relatively low labour costs (see discussion in Section 2.4). Dominance of efficiency-seeking FDI in knowledge-intensive activities in Portugal is further supported when examining FDI across all sectors in the economy. FDI is concentrated in sectors with higher average labour productivity and higher R&D-intensity levels relative to the rest of the economy (Figure 2.8, Panel A and B), while relative wages in FDI-dominated activities are lower compared to activities in other sectors (Panel C). It is important to recall that the analysis on technology-intensity in this report is based on fairly aggregate sector data. Analysis based on detailed firm activities would allow to further examine the types of FDI in Portugal (see Box 2.1)

Dynamic and innovative clusters in the higher technology manufacturing segment – involving competitive domestic firms – is emerging in Portugal, shifting future FDI motives from efficiency-seeking to technology-exploiting FDI, which is shown to have the highest FDI spillover potential (Driffield and Love, 2007[34]). In general, FDI motives are often interlinked, so that they cannot be fully separated but rather emerge in combination.

Figure 2.8. FDI concentration in terms of sectoral labour productivity, R&D-intensity and wages

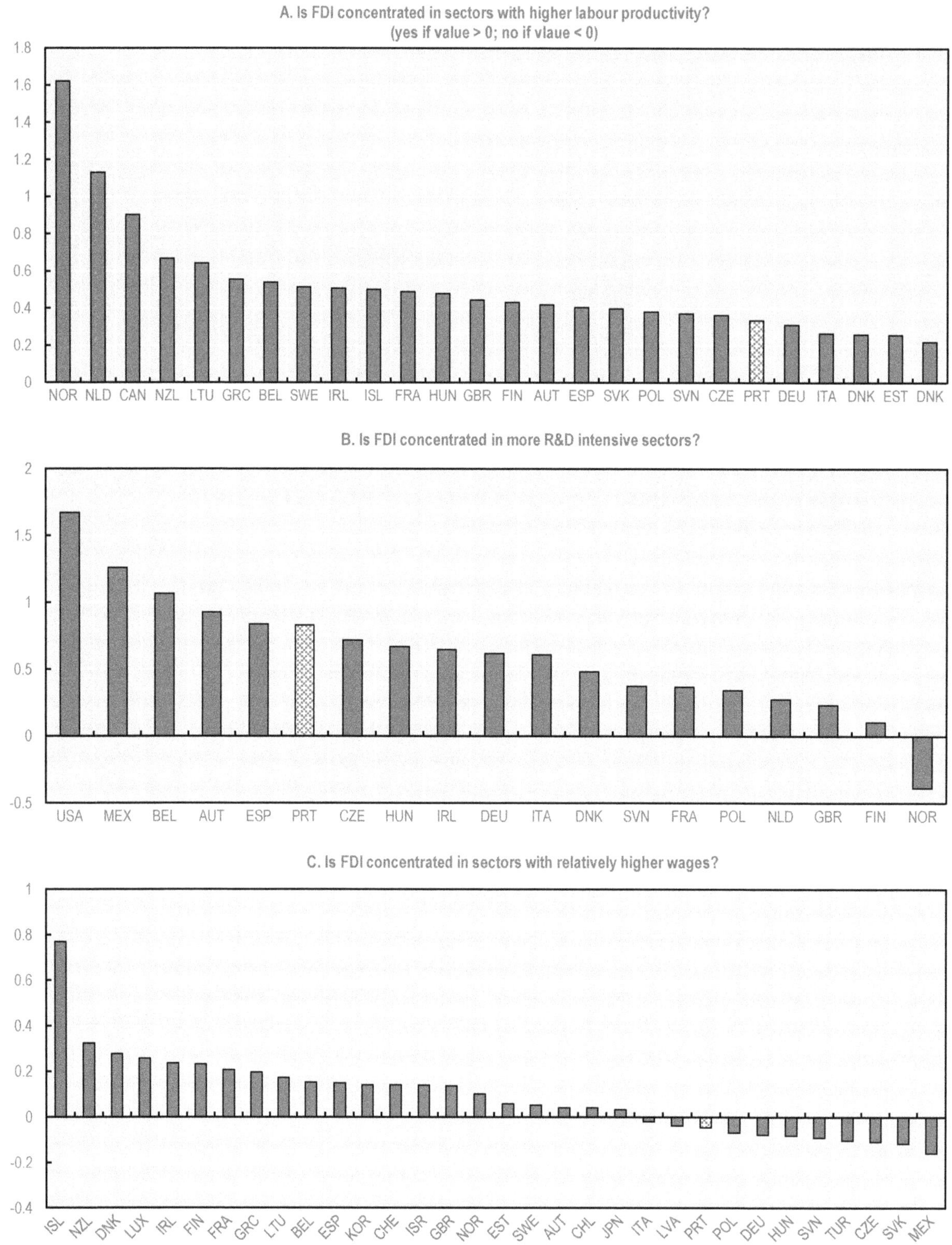

Note: See (OECD, 2019[35]) for a description of the methodology and data. Labour productivity = value added per employee; R&D intensity = R&D expenditures per unity of value added; wages = wage per employee

Source: OECD FDI Qualities Indicators based on Financial Times' fDi Markets database, 2020, OECD National Accounts and OECD MSTI database, 2020

2.4. Absorptive capacities of Portuguese SMEs

Global production networks and the presence of MNEs provide local SMEs with an important opportunity to increase productivity and acquire knowledge. Technology transfers are more effective when firms possess previously accumulated knowledge and innovative capabilities. This set of knowledge and capabilities is generally identified by the literature as absorptive capacity (OECD, 2020[9]). More specifically, absorptive capacity is defined as the ability of the firm to utilise available information or knowledge that comes through the interaction with other firms (Cohen and Levinthal, 1990[36]). It involves the ability to acquire, assimilate and exploit the value of the information and knowledge (Todorova and Durisin, 2007[37]).

Using the conceptual framework of the OECD SME and Entrepreneurship Outlook (OECD, 2019[4]), this section starts with an overview of SMEs contribution to Portugal's economy and trade and then provides an analysis of absorptive capacities, including comparisons with other OECD countries and across economic activities.

Low productivity micro firms make up most of Portugal's business population

Portuguese micro-firms account for a very large share of the total number of enterprises as compared to micro-firms in other OECD and EU economies (OECD, 2021[3]).[5] Portugal also counts relatively more self-employed compared to the rest of the OECD. On the other hand, SMEs (excluding micro firms and self-employed) account for only 4% of the total business population, which is lower than shares seen in many other OECD countries, raising the question of "missing middle" firms in Portugal and their lower capacity to scale up (OECD, 2021[3]). This is further supported by micro firms' large share of employment (above 40%), but relatively small share in total value added (25%) (Figure 2.9, Panel A). Their labour productivity is also below the OECD average, weighing down productivity of the entire economy. Conversely, Portuguese medium-sized firms are comparatively more productive than their OECD counterparts.

In terms of employment, the share of SMEs is generally high in Portugal and in fact higher compared to the OECD average in selected manufacturing industries (e.g. basic metals, chemicals and machinery) (OECD, 2019[4]). In services, employment shares of SMEs are more aligned with services sectors in other OECD economies.

In term of value added, SMEs are less represented in higher technology manufacturing compared to other sectors, which is less the case in some comparator economies like Ireland (OECD, 2020[38]). SMEs in Portugal – in line with other OECD countries – are most present in services but also account for an important share in manufacturing (Figure 2.9, Panel B). SMEs in Portugal are concentrated in domestically-oriented services such as advertising, legal, accounting, management, scientific and technical services but also in larger service sectors such as logistics and transport. In both lower and higher technology services, SMEs' share in value added is above 70%. While this is significant due to the very large lower technology services sector in Portugal, SME dominance in higher technology services takes a smaller weight for the economy as a whole.

Figure 2.9. Employment and value added by firm size and sectoral groups

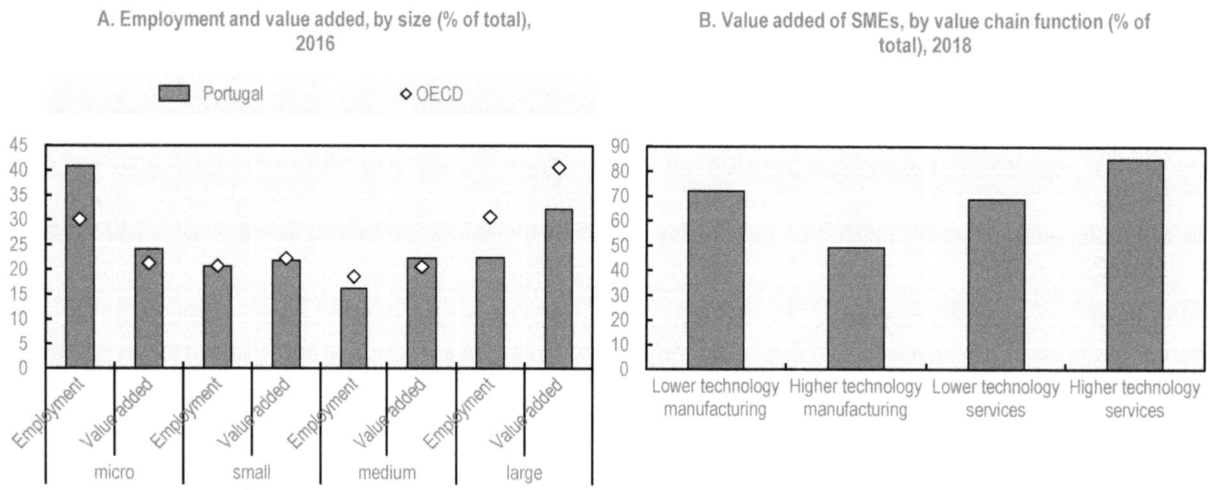

Source: OECD based on OECD Structural and Demographic Business Statistics Database, 2020, https://www.oecd.org/sdd/business-stats/structuralanddemographicbusinessstatisticssdbsoecd.htm

Many SME exporters in services and manufacturing are foreign-owned

Except in higher technology manufacturing, most exporters in Portugal are SMEs (Figure 2.10, Panel B). SMEs in Portugal are responsible for more than 70% of exports in services and 60% of exports in lower technology manufacturing; these export shares are similar to SMEs' contribution to total value added in these value chain functions. In services, almost half of all Portuguese exports are due to foreign firms (see Section), which further illustrates that many SME exporters in services (at least 20%) are actually foreign-owned.[6]

Due to its capital intensity, high technology manufacturing is dominated by large foreign investors in Portugal and SMEs have not been able to fully establish their footprint in this export market, unlike in some other economies such as Ireland, Germany, and Switzerland. SMEs are responsible for approximately 25% of all exports in high technology manufacturing of which some SMEs are foreign-owned. In terms of value added, SMEs in high technology manufacturing are responsible for a larger share (approximately 50%), illustrating the role SMEs may play to supply domestic demand in this sector.

While SMEs play an important role for internationalisation in Portugal, they are currently one of the weakest performers in this area in the EU (EC, 2019[39]). A relatively high percentage of Portuguese businesses are micro-businesses that do not have the capacity to become significant exporters.

Figure 2.10. Value added and exports of SMEs, by value chain function (in % of total of each value chain function), 2018

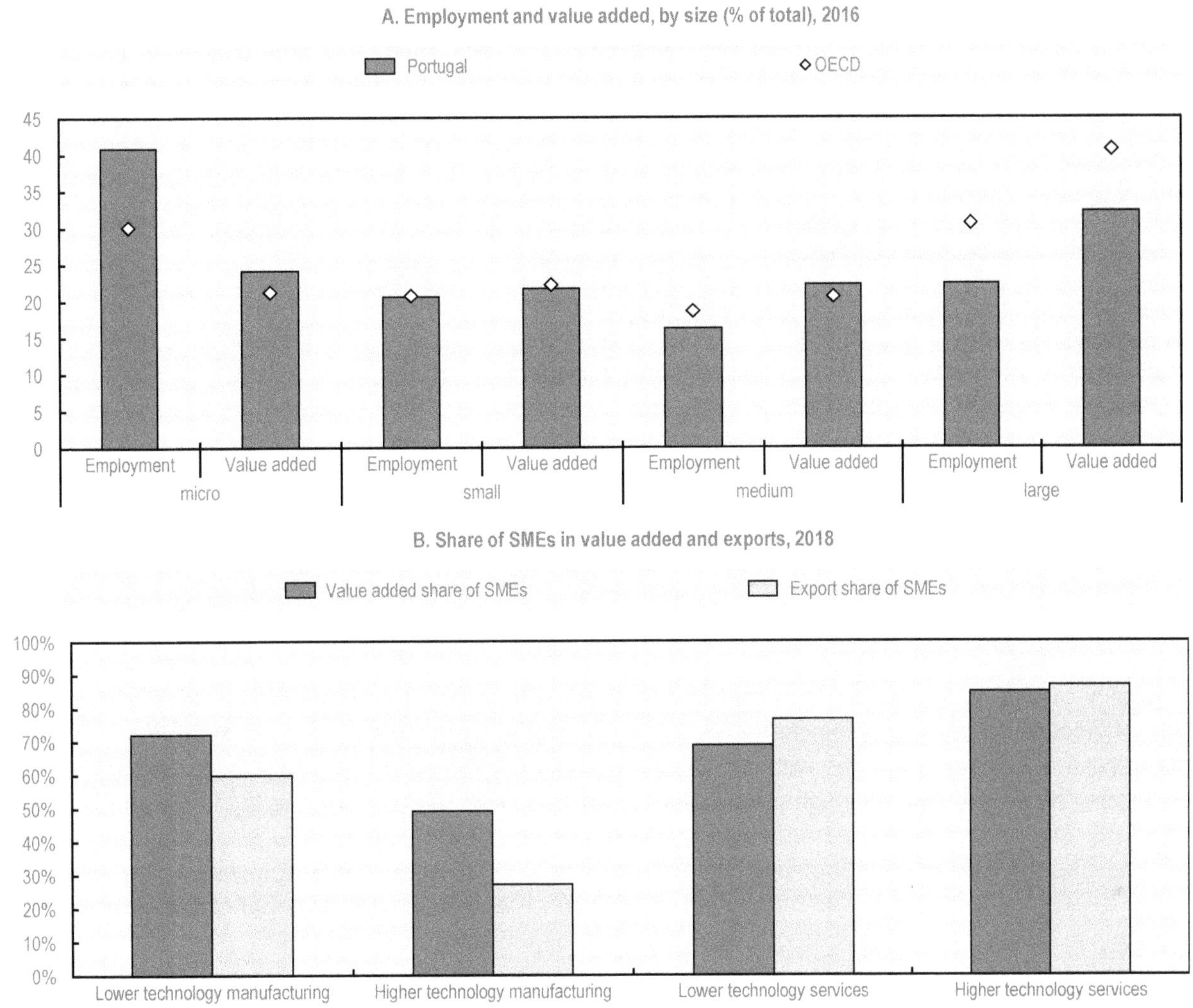

Note: See note in Figure 2.2 for detailed classification of value chain functions.
Source: OECD based on OECD Structural and Demographic Business Statistics Database, 2020, https://www.oecd.org/sdd/business-stats/structuralanddemographicbusinessstatisticssdbsoecd.htm, and OECD Trade by Enterprise Characteristics Database, 2020, https://www.oecd.org/sdd/its/trade-by-enterprise-characteristics.htm.

Portugal has competitive financial, knowledge-based and human capital with potential for improvement

In Portugal, access to bank credits has potential to improve. Accessing appropriate sources of finance across all stages of their life cycle is critical for SMEs to start, innovate and grow. Bank lending as the most common source of external finance for SMEs has largely recovered after the financial crisis, making it easier for SMEs to access credit in the OECD. Despite decreasing interest rate spreads and rejection rates in Portugal, SMEs face tightening lending conditions. SME lending decreased over 2009-18, in line with a drop in total business credits and a sharp decline in short-term SME loans (-62% in 2010-2018) (OECD, 2019[8]; OECD, 2020[40]). However, SMEs in Portugal are facing competitive interest rates (3% in 2018) and are more likely to receive new bank credits compared to SMEs in many other OECD economies (Figure 2.11, Panel A).

Access to venture capital is at the lower end in the OECD. Alternative sources, including asset-based and equity funding, have also become more widespread across the OECD, offering multiple and competing options to different profiles of firms and investors. Yet, SMEs remain undercapitalised and heavily reliant on straight debt. Barriers both on the supply side (i.e. information asymmetries, lack of collateral and higher transaction costs, etc.) and on the demand side (i.e. lack of awareness and financial skills, etc.) persist, and recent evidence suggests that financial institutions have become even more risk-averse, placing an extra burden on high-risk SMEs or on firms without collateral. In Portugal, venture capital recovered in 2017 (+58%) after the fall in 2016 and experienced a boost of four-fold growth in 2018 (OECD, 2020[40]). Yet, challenges remain – access to venture capital for Portuguese SMEs is at the lower end in the OECD (Figure 2.11, Panel A). The government has put high priority on securing SME access to finance, which is discussed in more details in Chapter 5.

Portuguese SMEs are relatively more innovative and digitised than those in many other OECD economies. Portuguese SMEs are proactive in adopting high-speed broadband and new digital technologies, but they remain weakly integrated into innovation networks compared to SMEs in most other OECD economies (Figure 2.11, Panel B). SMEs in Portugal are, however, performing fairly well compared to peers in other economies in terms of R&D and innovation outputs. SMEs have considerably improved their innovation performance relative to EU peers over the last decade both in terms of introducing new processes and products, developing new marketing and organisational approaches and collaborating with other firms to produce innovation outputs (Figure 2.12). SMEs in Portugal do relatively better across these metrics of innovation performance compared to SMEs in other small open economies in Europe, such as the Czech Republic, Ireland, Lithuania and the Slovak Republic. This reflects Portugal's determined efforts in recent years to develop an innovation ecosystem for SMEs (see Chapters 4 and 5).

The quality of entrepreneurial skills in Portugal is at par with those in peer countries, but gaps remain in terms of access to training within firms. In Portugal, student proficiency in core disciplines and adult entrepreneurial abilities are in line with the OECD average (OECD, 2020[41]), but a large gap still exists in the number of adults who are highly educated or who access training (Figure 2.11, Panel C). SMEs, particularly micro businesses, perform weakly compared to SMEs in other EU economies in terms of providing life-long learning opportunities for their workers (EC, 2019[39]). Skills acquired at the work place are key assets for technology and innovation absorption, managing organisational changes or enabling integration in GVCs through exports or linkages with foreign affiliates at home.

In the area of innovation and digitalisation skills, a number of sources point to weaknesses that hamper the potential for innovation and further productivity gains in Portugal: Portugal is a rather low performer in the area of computer and electronics skills and complex problem solving (OECD, 2021[3]). The share of businesses that provide ICT skills training to their employees has been falling since 2014 but remains at par with EU average levels. The share of firms providing digital training across firm size classes is also in line with EU comparators like the Czech Republic, Ireland and Finland, for example (Figure 2.13). Nonetheless, evidence indicates that the resources devoted to continuous training and the percentage of staff trained are relatively low in Portugal, particularly in micro-enterprises (EC, 2019[39]).

Figure 2.11. SMEs' access to strategic resources in Portugal

Note: See methodology in (OECD, 2019b). Index of benchmark (OECD median = 100), from more stringent or less supportive framework conditions or lower country value (low) to less stringent or more supportive framework conditions or higher country value (high). Indicators that reflect potential barriers to SME performance are marked with * and are reversed, so that, when a country ranks high, it effectively performs well as compared to the OECD median.
Source: OECD (2019b), OECD SME and Entrepreneurship Outlook 2019.

Figure 2.12. SME innovation performance (Index, 100= EU average)

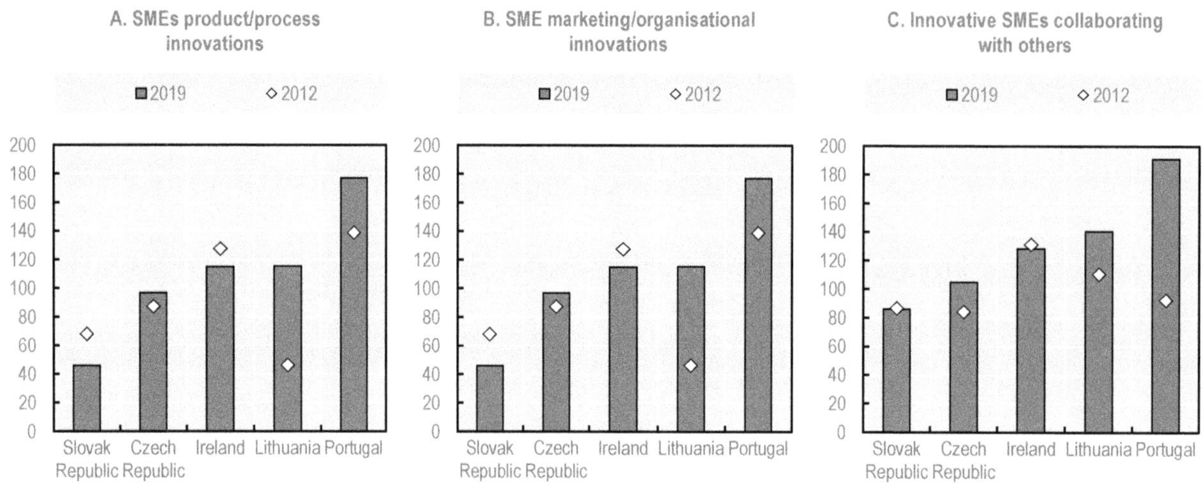

Note: Underlying data relate to share of SMEs who introduced product/process, marketing/organisational innovations or that engage in innovation cooperation activities with other firms (https://ec.europa.eu/docsroom/documents/36282/attachments/1/translations/en/renditions/native).
Source: OECD based on Eurostat, 2020, https://ec.europa.eu/eurostat/de/home

Figure 2.13. Firms providing ICT skills training (% of firms in each size class), 2019

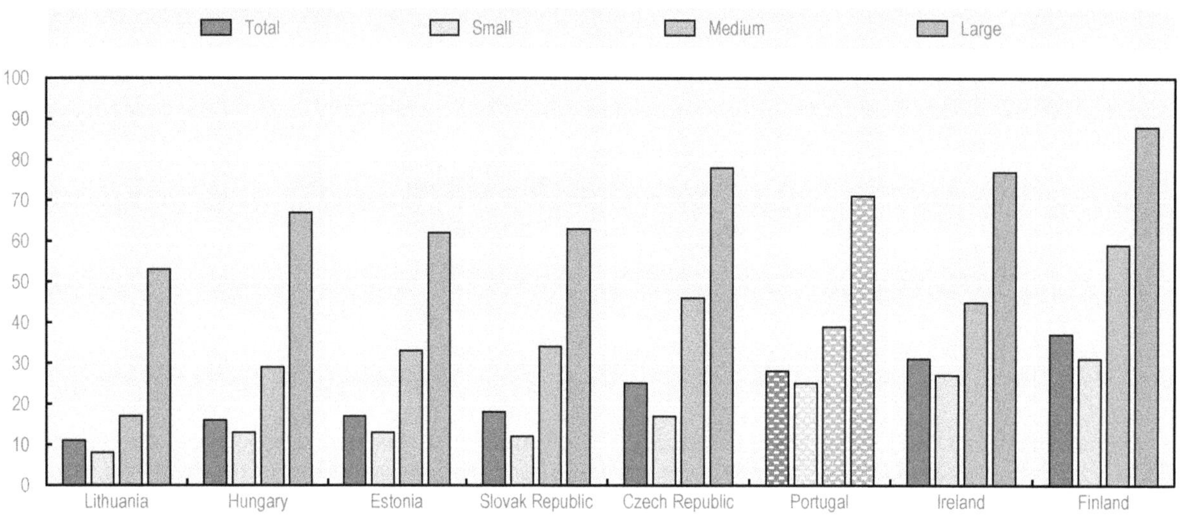

Source: OECD based on Eurostat, 2020, https://ec.europa.eu/eurostat/de/home

2.5. Economic geography factors and FDI-SME spillovers in Portugal

When deciding where to invest, foreign firms are increasingly considering region - rather than just country - specific factors. SME activity is also unevenly distributed within countries. Whilst it was traditionally thought that this is only applicable for specific sectors e.g., the location of natural resources for mining projects, as firms' production processes become more disaggregated, they are progressively placing functions in the most suitable locations. As such, a region's economic, social and structural features are being scrutinised. This is why it is essential for a country to look beyond the national level and understand their regions' relative strengths and weaknesses. Given the importance of locations in the discussion, Chapter 6 is dedicated to FDI-SME diffusion and related policy in Alentejo and Norte.

References

Adamczyk, P. and B. Westmore (2020), “Unpicking Portugal’s export performance: A microdata analysis”, *OECD Economics Department Working Papers* No. 1618, https://dx.doi.org/10.1787/71df6aa3-en. [13]

Alfaro, L. and A. Charlton (2009), “Intra-industry foreign direct investment”, *American Economic Review*, Vol. 99(5), 2096-2119, http://dx.doi.org/10.1257/aer.99.5.2096. [24]

Alfaro, L. and M. Chen (2012), “Surviving the Global Financial Crisis: Foreign Ownership and Establishment Performance”, *American Economic Journal: Economic Policy*, Vol. 4(3): 30-55. [17]

Braconier, H., K. Ekholm and K. Knarvik (2001), “In Search of FDI-Transmitted R&D Spillovers: A Study Based on Swedish Data”, *Weltwirtschaftliches Archiv*, Vol. 137 (4): 644–65. [31]

Branstetter, L., R. Fisman and F. Foley (2006), “Do Stronger Intellectual Property Rights Increase International Technology Transfer? Empirical Evidence from U. S. Firm-Level Panel Data”, *The Quarterly Journal of Economics,*, Vol. Volume 121, Issue 1. [32]

Buckley, P. and M. Casson (1976), *The future of the multinational enterprise*, MacMillan. [26]

Castro, F. (2000), *Foreign direct investment in the European periphery: The competitiveness of Portugal*, The University of Leeds, https://etheses.whiterose.ac.uk/2612/1/Castro_FB_LUBS_PhD_2000.pdf. [29]

Cohen, W. and D. Levinthal (1990), “Absorptive Capacity: A New Perspective on Learning and Innovation”, *Administrative Science Quarterly*, Vol. 35(1), 128-152. [36]

Crespo, N., M. Fontoura and I. Proenca (2009), “FDI spillovers at regional level: Evidence from Portugal”, *Papers in Regional Science*, Vol. 88(3): 591–607. [30]

Desai, M., C. Foley and K. Forbes (2008), “Financial Constraints and Growth: Multinational and Local Firm Responses to Currency Depreciation”, *Review of Financial Studies*, Vol. 21 (6):2857-88. [18]

Driffield, N. and J. Love (2007), “Linking FDI Motivation and Host Economy Productivity Effects: Conceptual and Empirical Analysis”, *Journal of International Business Studies*, Vol. 38(3): 460–7. [34]

Dunning, J. (1993), *Multinational Enterprises and the Global Economy, Addison-Wesley, Harlow*, http://dx.doi.org/10.1057/palgrave.jibs.8400426. [28]

Dunning, J. (1977), *Trade, Location of Economic Activity and the Multinational Enterprise: a search for an eclectic approach*, Macmillan, London, https://doi.org/10.1007/978-1-349-03196-2_38. [22]

EC (2019), *2019 SBA Fact Sheet PORTUGAL*, https://ec.europa.eu/growth/smes/sme-strategy/performance-review_en#sba-fact-sheets. [39]

Ekholm, K., R. Forslid and J. Markusen (2003), “Export-Platform Foreign Direct Investment”, *NBER Working Paper Series*, Vol. No. 9517, http://dx.doi.org/10.3386/w9517. [27]

Fontoura Gouveia, A. (2018), *The Portuguese economy: Short essays on structural changes*, https://www.iseg.ulisboa.pt/aquila/homepage/fleal/investigacao/working-papers/the-portuguese-economy:-short-essays-on-structural-changes. [12]

Galindo-Rueda, F. and F. Verger (2016), *OECD Taxonomy of Economic Activities Based on R&D Intensity*, OECD Publishing, Paris, https://doi.org/10.1787/5jlv73sqqp8r-en. [10]

Grossman, S. and O. Hart (1986), "The Costs and Benefits of Ownership: A Theory of Vertical and Lateral Integration", *Journal of Political Economy*, Vol. 94(4), 691-719, http://dx.doi.org/10.1086/261404. [23]

Herger, N. and S. McCorriston (2016), "Horizontal, Vertical, and Conglomerate Cross-Border Acquisitions", *IMF Economic Review*, Vol. 64(2), 319-353, http://dx.doi.org/10.1057/imfer.2015.42. [25]

Keller, W. and S. Yeaple (2009), "Multinational enterprises, international trade, and productivity growth: firm-level evidence from the United States", *The Review of Economics and Statistics*, Vol. 91(4), 821-831. [21]

Nicolini, M. and L. Resmini (2010), "FDI spillovers in new EU member states", *Economics of Transition*, Vol. 18(3), 487-511, https://doi.org/10.1787/39a88ab1-en. [20]

OECD (2021), *FDI in Figures, April 2021*, https://www.oecd.org/investment/FDI-in-Figures-April-2021.pdf. [15]

OECD (2021), *OECD Economic Outlook, Interim Report March 2021*, OECD Publishing, Paris, https://doi.org/10.1787/34bfd999-en. [2]

OECD (2021), *OECD SME and Enterpreneurship Outlook 2021*, OECD Publishing, Paris. [3]

OECD (2020), *Coronavirus (COVID-19): SME Policy Responses – OECD*, OECD Publishing, Paris, https://read.oecd-ilibrary.org/view/?ref=119_119680-di6h3qgi4x&title=Covid-19_SME_Policy_Responses. [5]

OECD (2020), *Education Policy Outlook in Portugal*, OECD Publishing, Paris, https://doi.org/10.1787/0e254ee5-en. [41]

OECD (2020), *Enabling FDI diffusion channels to boost SME productivity and innovation in EU countries and regions: Towards a Policy Toolkit, Concept Paper for EC-OECD project.* [9]

OECD (2020), *FDI Qualities Assessment of Ireland*, http://www.oecd.org/investment/FDI-Qualities-Assessment-of-Ireland.pdf. [14]

OECD (2020), *Financing SMEs and Entrepreneurs 2020: An OECD Scoreboard, Portugal*, OECD Publishing, Paris, https://doi.org/10.1787/061fe03d-en. [40]

OECD (2020), *Foreign Direct Investment Flows in the time of COVID-19*, http://www.oecd.org/coronavirus/policy-responses/foreign-direct-investment-flows-in-the-time-of-covid-19-a2fa20c4/. [19]

OECD (2020), *OECD Structural Enterprise Statistics*, OECD Publishing, Paris, https://doi.org/10.1787/sdbs-data-en. [38]

OECD (2020), *OECD Tourism Trends and Policies 2020: Portugal*, OECD Publishing, Paris, https://doi.org/10.1787/46decc94-en. [6]

OECD (2019), *FDI Qualities Indicators: Measuring the sustainable development impacts of investment*, https://www.oecd.org/investment/fdi-qualities-indicators.htm. [35]

OECD (2019), *Investment Policy Review of Southeast Asia*, https://www.oecd.org/investment/oecd-investment-policy-review-southeast-asia.htm. [33]

OECD (2019), *OECD Economic Surveys: Portugal 2019*, OECD Publishing, Paris, https://doi.org/10.1787/eco_surveys-prt-2019-en. [1]

OECD (2019), *OECD SME and Entrepreneurship Outlook 2019: Portugal*, OECD Publishing, Paris, https://doi.org/10.1787/d2b72934-en. [4]

OECD (2019), *SME and Entrepreneurship Outlook 2019, Portugal*, OECD Publishing, Paris, https://doi.org/10.1787/d2b72934-en. [8]

OECD (2015), *The Innovation Imperative: Contributing to Productivity, Growth and Well-Being*, OECD Publishing, Paris, http://dx.doi.org/10.1787/9789264239814-en. [11]

Todorova, G. and B. Durisin (2007), "Absorptive Capacity: Valuing a Reconceptualization", *Academy of Management Review*, Vol. Vol. 32, pp. 774-786. [37]

Westmore, B. and P. Adamczyk (2019), *Public policy reforms to further improve Portuguese export performance*, OECD Publishing, Paris, https://doi.org/10.1787/4d416a6b-en. [7]

Zhang, K. and Z. Zhao (2010), "FDI and Industrial Productivity in China: Evidence from Panel Data in 2001–06", *Review of Development Economics*, Vol. 14(3):656-665, https://doi.org/10.1111/j.1467-9361.2010.00580.x. [16]

Notes

[1] These three countries are considered as comparators in this report, together sometimes with Hungary and Lithuania. They were chosen based on their economic size, outward orientation driven by foreign investors and EU membership.

[2] A country has a revealed comparative advantage in international trade when the export share of a product in their export basket is higher than the corresponding share of that product in world exports.

[3] The information in this document with reference to "Cyprus" relates to the southern part of the Island. There is no single authority representing both Turkish and Greek Cypriot people on the Island. Turkey recognises the Turkish Republic of Northern Cyprus (TRNC). Until a lasting and equitable solution is found within the context of United Nations, Turkey shall preserve its position concerning the "Cyprus" issue.

[4] A greenfield investment is likely to involve the introduction of a new technology in the host country and is therefore accompanied by a direct transfer of knowledge and technology from the parent firm to the new affiliate. However, greenfield FDI can pull skilled workers away from domestic firms, which may involve that incumbent firms are lowering their absorptive capacities and therefore this argument needs to be taken with a pinch of salt. See discussion on labour mobility in Chapter 3.

[5] Micro firms have 1-9 employees; small firms have 10-49 employees; and medium sized firms have 50-249 employees; SMEs have 10-249 employees, excluding micro firms. See for details: https://www.oecd.org/sdd/business-stats

[6] Portuguese SME exports are also important in the mining, agriculture and construction. These sectors are not covered in Figure 2.10.

3 FDI diffusion at play for Portuguese SMEs

This chapter studies the extent of FDI-SME diffusion in Portugal based on the conceptual framework introduced in Chapter 1. It examines where Portugal stands in the core channels of FDI-SME diffusion – value chain relationships (buy/supply linkages and strategic partnerships), labour mobility and skills effects, competition and imitation effects – relative to peers in the OECD and European Union and across economic activities.

3.1. Summary of strengths, challenges and opportunities

The diagnostic assessment of key diffusion channels through which FDI spillovers on Portuguese SMEs can take place reveals a number of strengths and points to challenges and opportunities (Table 3.1). The subsequent chapters (Chapters 4-6) pick up on these challenges and opportunities, identifying policy actions to address them.

Table 3.1. Strengths and challenges/opportunities across FDI-SME diffusion channels in Portugal

	Strengths	Challenges and opportunities
Value chain linkages	• More extensive sourcing of foreign affiliates from local suppliers (often SMEs) than in peers (e.g. Ireland and Hungary) • Suppliers in higher technology manufacturing and lower technology services benefit most from demand of foreign affiliates (in USD volume), increasing chances for spillovers • Domestic firms increasingly source inputs from abroad, indicating their upgrading and integration in GVCs • Domestic firms benefit more from (quality) inputs produced locally by foreign affiliates than in peers (e.g. Belgium, Ireland)	• Foreign affiliates not sourcing from each other, contrary to comparators, pointing to limited clustering of foreign firms • Low demand for suppliers in higher technology services (in USD volume), limiting spillover potential
Strategic partnerships	• Widespread partnerships in terms of technology licensing, at par with peers • Partnerships involving Portuguese SME manufactures deliver innovation, learning and access to markets	• Limited integration of SMEs in innovation networks • Lower access to quality certification compared to peers, constraining partnerships
Labour mobility and skills effects	• Labour mobility (from foreign to domestic firms) facilitated by dynamic FDI and SME sectors • Frequent mobility from domestic to foreign firms in skill-intensive activities in Portugal, enabled by wage differential and involving on-the-job skills development of mobile workers • Increased skills demand due to increasing FDI drives investment in skills and thus increased supply in the medium term	• Crowding out of skilled workers from domestic firms due to FDI entry in the short-term, involving negative productivity spillovers, particularly in less developed Portuguese regions
Competition and imitation effects	• Competition/imitation effects benefit relatively more productive and innovative SMEs	• Competition from FDI is challenging vast sector of low-productivity micro firms

Note: See Chapter 2, Table 2.1, clarifying sectoral groupings (i.e. lower and higher technology manufacturing and lower and higher technology services) used in this table. This report primarily uses Ireland, Czech Republic, Slovak Republic, and sometimes Belgium, Hungary and Lithuania, as comparators/peers. They were chosen based on their economic size, outward orientation driven by foreign investors and EU membership.

3.2. Value chain relationships between foreign investors and SMEs

Domestic Portuguese firms may benefit from the presence of affiliates of foreign MNEs through buy and sell linkages. Domestic backward linkages are formed when foreign affiliates source intermediate inputs from locally established companies. Foreign affiliates can also sell intermediates to local companies. These linkages are referred to as domestic forward linkages. This section benchmarks domestic backward and forward linkages of foreign affiliates in Portugal against linkages observed in some of its peers in the OECD.[1]

Foreign affiliates source more extensively from domestic firms in Portugal compared to affiliates in some comparator economies

Domestic backward linkages of foreign affiliates help domestic companies extend their market for selling and raise the quality and competitiveness of their outputs. They can also generate knowledge spillovers when MNEs require better-quality inputs from local suppliers and are therefore willing to share knowledge and technology with domestic companies to encourage their adoption of better practices (OECD, 2020[1]).

Backward linkages of foreign affiliates in Portugal can be analysed using the new OECD Analytical AMNE database. The data allow to compare the sourcing structure of foreign affiliates across OECD economies, including with respect to sourcing/linkages with domestically-owned firms (Box 3.1). In Portugal, purchased intermediates accounted for about 57% of foreign affiliates' output in 2016 (where value added was responsible for the other 43% of total output). Foreign affiliates in Portugal source intermediate goods both from suppliers abroad (via imports) and firms located in Portugal. The share of inputs purchased internationally represented 38% of foreign firms' total sourcing (Figure 3.1). The rest is local sourcing (62%) and can be further split into sourcing from other foreign affiliates established in Portugal (13%), domestically-owned multinational enterprises (domestic MNEs) (7%) and domestic non-MNEs (42%). The data do not allow to distinguish between domestic large firms and SMEs. However, based on existing knowledge on firms' internationalisation, firms with FDI activity (i.e. MNEs) are often larger than those without. While this assumption may not hold for firms operating in the digital economy, it can be used for firms in more traditional sectors.

The share of local sourcing in total sourcing of foreign affiliates in Portugal is comparable with that of Korea, Finland, Switzerland or the Netherlands (Figure 3.1). Foreign affiliates source comparatively more from domestic non-MNEs (often SMEs) than foreign firms in many other OECD economies. Large economies such as France, the United States, the United Kingdom or Canada report a similar foreign firm sourcing pattern from domestic non-MNEs as Portugal. Foreign affiliates in many other small open economies – like Ireland or Hungary – depend relatively more on imported inputs and source less from domestic non-MNEs than foreign firms in Portugal do. This is a general pattern seen in such economies and typically relates to smaller markets for domestic input sourcing in these countries (less variety of intermediates might be available in smaller markets) as shown in a recent study on Ireland for example (OECD, 2020[2]).

Figure 3.1. Sourcing structure of foreign affiliates, by supplier type/origin, 2016

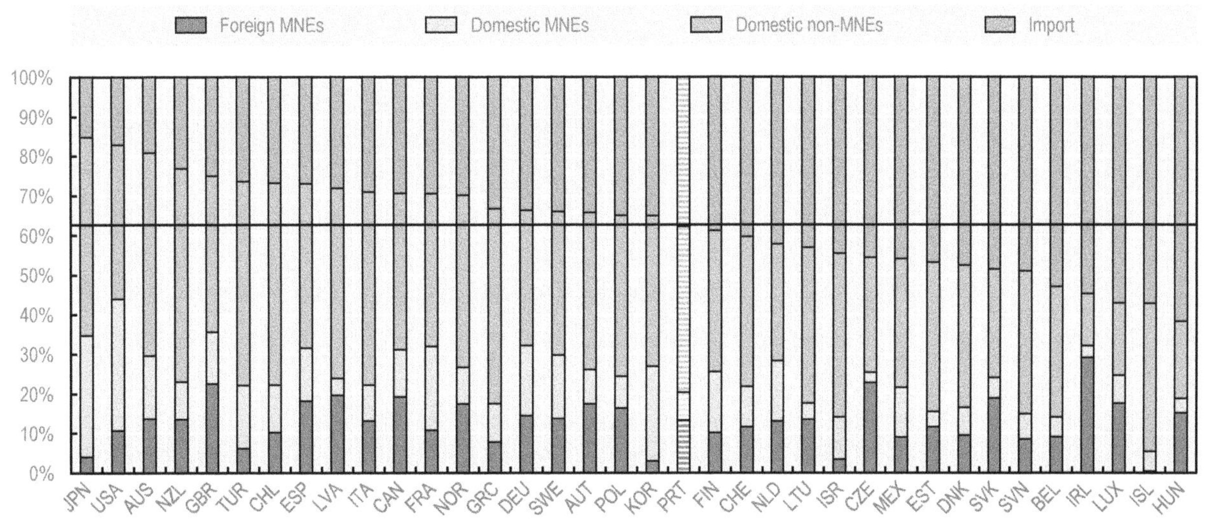

Note: Foreign MNEs = foreign affiliates of multinational enterprises; domestic MNEs = domestically owned firms with foreign affiliates abroad; domestic non-MNEs = domestically owned firms with no operations abroad. **Trend = OECD average** domestic sourcing share of foreign affiliates in total sourcing of foreign affiliates (sum of shares reflecting sourcing from other foreign affiliates, domestic MNEs and domestic non-MNEs).
Source: OECD based on the OECD Analytical AMNE database, 2019, https://www.oecd.org/sti/ind/analytical-AMNE-database.htm

On the other hand, sourcing of foreign affiliates from other foreign affiliates established in Portugal is somewhat less common in Portugal than in Ireland or the Czech Republic for example. The share is however still in the middle range compared to other OECD countries. Relatively low sourcing from other foreign firms indicate that clusters of foreign MNEs that buy from and sell to each are relatively more present in other small EU economies, while foreign firms' motives for establishment could relate to other considerations such as labour and production costs, availability of skills and other assets (as shown in Chapter 2).

Local sourcing of foreign affiliates is more prevalent in services than in manufacturing in Portugal. In higher technology services (such as R&D, technical services and design) and lower technology services (such as logistics and sales), the share of local sourcing is around 80% of total input sourcing.[2] This share has remained stable since the mid-2010s (Figure 3.2, Panel B). In lower technology manufacturing activities about half of all inputs are sourced in Portugal; this share has decreased over the past decade in higher technology manufacturing and stood at 40% in 2016. The patterns of local sourcing in services and manufacturing value chain functions in Portugal are comparable with those in other OECD and developing countries and thus reflect common sourcing practices across value chain functions across countries and not a specificity of Portugal (Cadestin et al., 2019[3]).

In absolute terms, local suppliers in higher technology manufacturing and lower technology services benefit most from demand of foreign affiliates. Firstly, foreign firms in Portugal are sourcing the largest amounts of inputs (both goods and services) in lower technology services; USD 7 billion in 2016 (Panel D). However, foreign manufacturers have sourced even more locally; if lower and higher technology manufacturing is put together, sourcing stood at USD 8.5 billion in 2016. Despite a very high share of local sourcing in higher technology services, their sourcing in absolute values at around USD 2 billion is much lower.

Domestic firms in Portugal source less domestically than their foreign peers. The analysis of the FDI sector in Portugal needs to be compared to the relatively larger sector of domestic firms, measured in terms of value added (Panel C). Across all value chain functions, foreign firms in Portugal are sourcing relatively more locally than domestic firms (Panel A). Domestic firms have reduced local sourcing over the past decade in all value chain functions. In higher technology services the local sourcing share of domestic firms was 70% in 2016, down from 80% in 2006; 60% in lower technology services, down from 70%; 35% in lower technology manufacturing, down from 55%; and 15% in higher technology manufacturing down from 35% over the same ten year period.

Box 3.1. Foreign affiliates' output, value added and sourcing - concepts

To understand foreign firms' (foreign affiliates') buy linkages with domestically established firms, it is important to clarify how firm output, value added and sourcing related to each other. Foreign firms' output can be split into value added and sourcing of intermediate inputs (see figure).

This section focuses on the extent to which foreign firms source intermediates directly from firms established in Portugal as opposed to sourcing of inputs from abroad through imports. In particular, the section looks at the extent of sourcing from domestic firms, i.e. Portuguese domestically-owned firms. The domestic sourcing structure is therefore further split into sourcing from other foreign affiliates established in Portugal, domestic MNEs (i.e. Portuguese firms with establishments abroad, which are often – but not exclusively – larger firms) and domestic non-MNEs (i.e. Portuguese firms with no establishments abroad, which are often SMEs).

The section does not specifically focus on better understanding to what extent value added generated by foreign affiliates stays in Portugal or may be repatriated to home economies, which is also of key interest in the context of direct contributions of foreign firms have to host economy growth and development. Part of foreign affiliates' value added is used to pay salaries of their (mostly local) employees and therefore 'stays' in the domestic economy. The remaining part, including earnings, may or may not leave the host economy. The latter is particularly important in the context of tax policy.

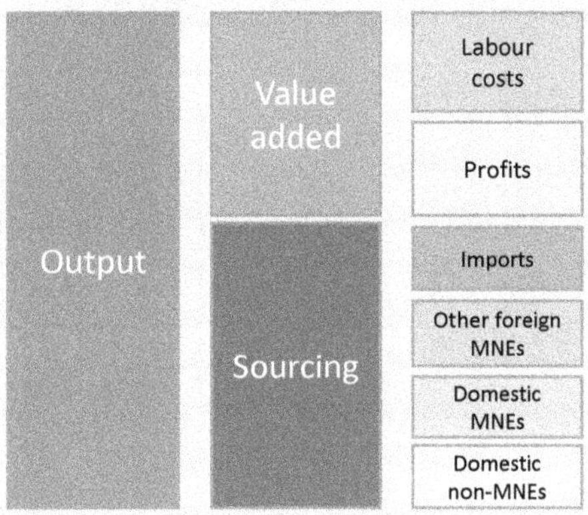

Source: OECD based on (Cadestin et al., 2019[3])

This shift in supply chain practices of domestic firms reflects increased integration in GVCs of domestic firms, which is also observed in many other OECD and EU economies over the past decade, and is often associated with a process of their technology upgrading (Cadestin et al., 2019[3]; OECD, 2020[2]; OECD-UNIDO, 2019[4]). Integration in global value chains, which typically includes importing higher quality and cost-effective goods and services, has enabled domestic firms, particularly SMEs, in OECD and partner economies to move up the value chain, improve productivity and increase their market for exporting (OECD, 2019[5]; OECD-UNIDO, 2019[4]; Farole and Winkler, 2014[6]; López González et al., 2019[7]). This finding can thus be considered as positive for two reasons: On the one hand, domestic firms in Portugal have enhanced their integration in GVCs over recent years and, on the other hand, foreign affiliates established in Portugal take extensive advantage of the local economy by sourcing from domestically owned firms.

Figure 3.2. Sourcing of domestic and foreign firms by sectoral groups in Portugal

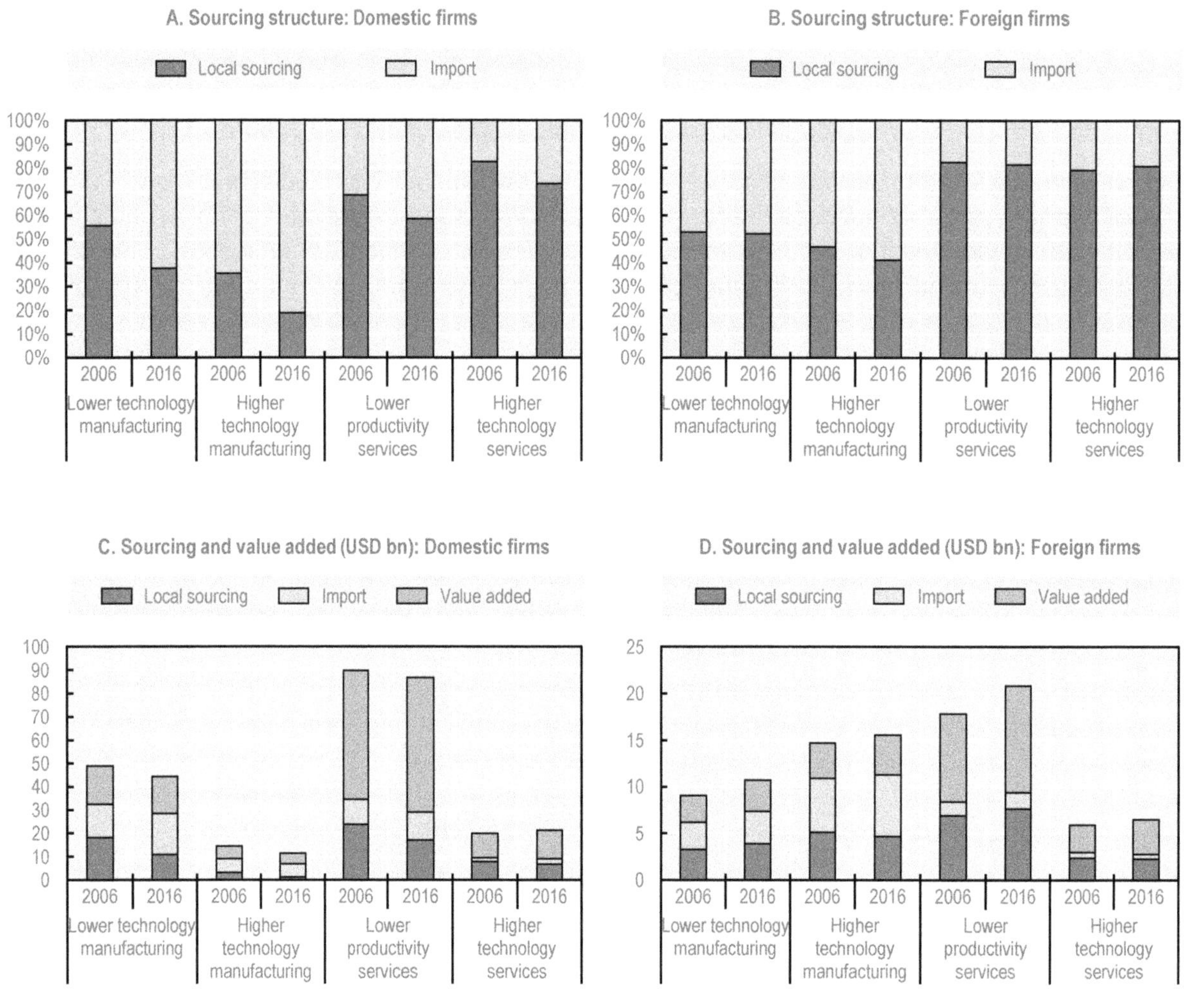

Source: OECD based on the OECD Analytical AMNE database, 2019, https://www.oecd.org/sti/ind/analytical-AMNE-database.htm

Production of foreign affiliates feeds back into domestic value chains and more so than in some of peer countries

Domestic firms in Portugal benefit more from (quality) inputs produced locally by foreign affiliates than in some peers according to the OECD Analytical AMNE database (Figure 3.3). In Portugal, more than 60% of the production of foreign affiliates feeds back into domestic value chains: in 2016, 24% of foreign affiliates' output was used as an input by domestic non-MNEs, 4% by domestic MNEs and 7% by other foreign affiliates in Portugal. Another 24% was sold in the domestic market for final consumption. Hence, foreign affiliates produce relatively more intermediates (35%) than final goods for the domestic market in Portugal. The 35% output share acquired by domestically operating firms as inputs into their production, corresponds to the OECD average (see trend line in the figure). A number of other small economies – like Belgium, Ireland and the Slovak Republic – benefit relatively less from the use of intermediates produced locally by foreign firms. Forward linkages between MNEs and local buyers often have a positive impact on local enterprise productivity mostly through the acquisition of better quality inputs which were not locally available before. In addition, many MNEs, especially in industrial sectors such as machinery, often offer training to their customers on the use of their products and provide information on international quality standards (Jindra, 2006[8]). They may also help set the standards for the industry, which in turn can help better diffuse innovation. Firms adopting those international standards can more easily integrate in markets abroad.

Given the relatively smaller size of the Portuguese economy and the focus of public policies on attracting export-intensive FDI during the post 2008 crisis recovery (see Chapter 5), a relatively higher share of the production of foreign affiliates in Portugal is destined to international markets compared to the OECD overall: 40% in Portugal versus 30% in the OECD (Figure 3.3, OECD average export share not reflected in figure). Some other small open OECD economies show similar export orientation of foreign affiliates (e.g. Poland or Austria), while a number of other small economies have yet higher shares of exports in total output of foreign affiliates, such as Ireland, Belgium, or the Slovak Republic. Due to larger domestic markets in OECD economies like Japan, United States or Germany, market seeking motives of foreign firms appear as relatively more important. In these economies, foreign affiliates export lower shares of output, i.e. around 20-30%.

Figure 3.3. Use of outputs of foreign affiliates, by buyer type/origin, 2016

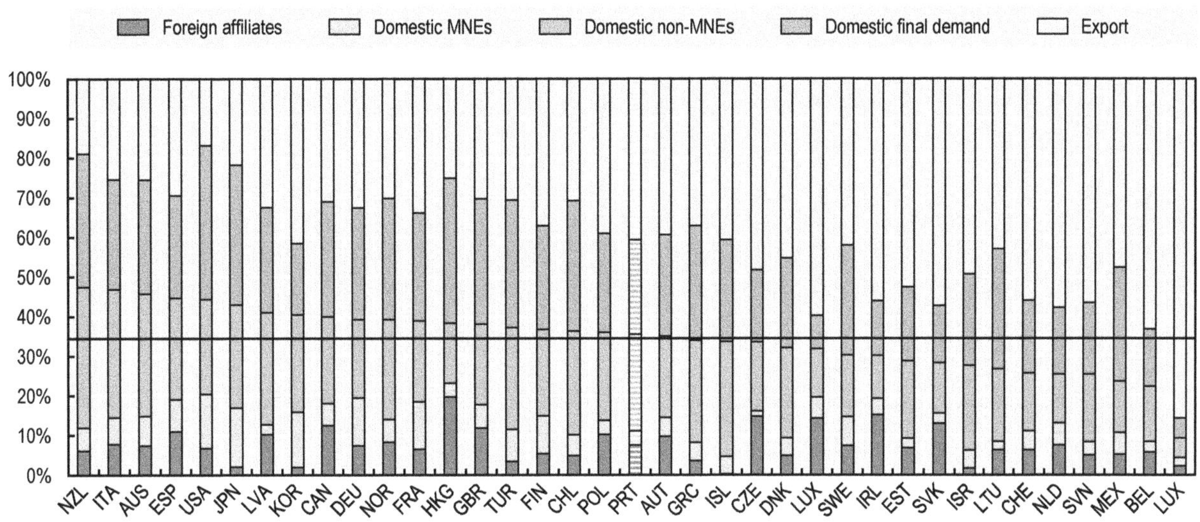

Note: Foreign affiliates = foreign affiliates of MNEs; domestic MNEs = domestically owned firms with foreign affiliates abroad; domestic non-MNEs = domestically owned firms with no operations abroad. **Trend line = OECD average** use of foreign affiliates' intermediates in domestic value chains (sum of shares reflecting acquisitions/use by other foreign affiliates, domestic MNEs and domestic non-MNEs).
Source: OECD based on the OECD Analytical AMNE database, 2019, https://www.oecd.org/sti/ind/analytical-AMNE-database.htm.

3.3. Strategic partnerships between foreign firms and SMEs in Portugal

The emergence of GVCs has brought new types of FDI-SME partnerships, especially in high-technology and knowledge-intensive industries, which are based on the transfer of technology and the development of cross-border R&D projects and thus contribute extensively to spillovers of FDI. These partnerships can take many forms, including joint ventures, licensing agreements, research collaborations, globalised business networks (i.e. membership-based business organisations, trade associations, stakeholder networks), and R&D and technology alliances.3 A study for Portugal produced during the post-2008 crisis recovery showed that SMEs involved in partnerships, cooperation and networking arrangements (with other SMEs, large companies, public institutions, higher education and research and development institutions, social partner organisations and professional organisations) deal better with restructuring and are more innovative than other firms (Pereira and Correia Leitão, 2013[9]). This sections provides some insights on strengths and opportunities related to strategic Partnerships in Portugal.

SMEs could improve integration in innovation networks, while partnerships in terms of technology licensing are widespread

As analysed in Chapter 1, Portuguese SMEs remain weakly integrated into innovation networks on average compared to SMEs in most other OECD economies, despite their relatively good performance with respect to innovation outcomes and digitalisation. Part of this weakness may be due to comparatively fewer firms with internationally recognised quality certificates in Portugal. Across all types, manufacturers in Portugal are less likely to have quality certificates compared to the same types of firms in other OECD economies for which data are available (including Estonia, Hungary, Latvia, Lithuania, Poland, the Slovak Republic and Slovenia) (Figure 3.4, Panel B). As expected, larger and foreign-owned firms are more likely to have certificates compared to smaller domestic firms. It would useful to further examine the costs of certification and monitoring and evaluation of certification processes across sectors and countries, but related data were not available for this study (see Chapter 5 on policy efforts in Portugal to enhance certification).

Figure 3.4. Foreign technology licensing and international certification in the Portuguese manufacturing sector, 2019

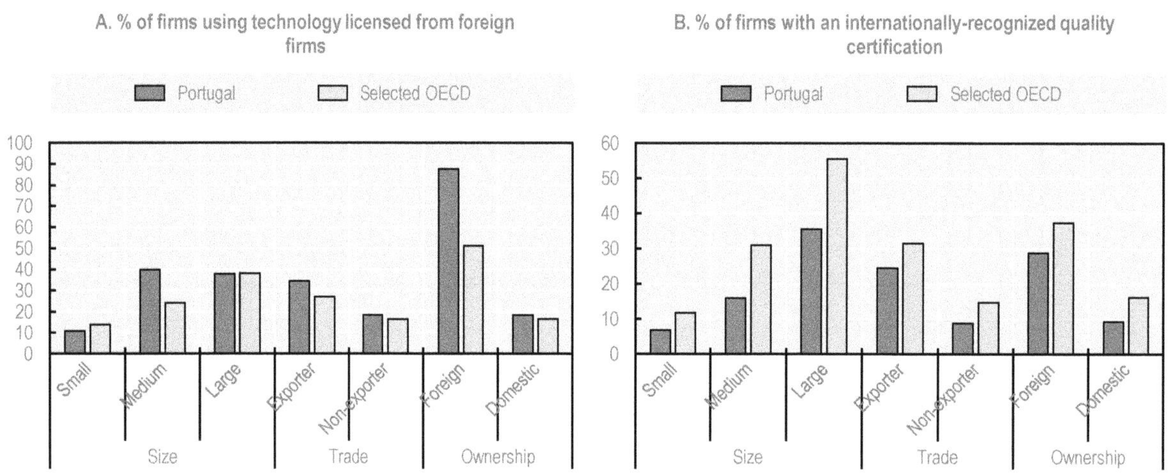

Note: Selected OECD include: Estonia, Hungary, Latvia, Lithuania, Poland, Slovak Republic and Slovenia
Source: OECD based on World Bank Enterprise Surveys.

Focusing on a specific form of partnerships – namely technology licensing – reveals a more encouraging perspective on partnerships in manufacturing sectors of Portugal. Domestic firms – including medium-sized firms – extensively engage in licensing agreements with foreign firms, which as showed in numerous existing studies helps to deepen linkages between SMEs and foreign MNEs and thereby supports performance improvements. Approximately 40% of medium-sized and large manufacturing firms have technology licensing agreements with foreign companies (Figure 3.4, Panel A); this share is lower for small firms and non-exporting firms. Almost all affiliates of foreign manufacturers in Portugal (90%) use technologies licensed from (other) foreign firms; this share is much higher compared to foreign-invested companies in other selected OECD countries for which data are available. This underlines that foreign firms engage in operations in Portugal that require a certain level of technological sophistication, supporting skills improvements and productivity of the local workforce. The gap between foreign and domestic firms in terms of use of foreign licensing is lowest in the Lisbon Metropolitan area (see Chapter 1, Figure 1.16).

Partnerships of SMEs deliver innovation and learning opportunities and market access

A 2020 survey of SME owners/managers in the Portuguese automobile and parts sector (Franco and Haase, 2020[10]), shows that innovation and learning (e.g. consolidation of market position, quality improvement, sharing of resources and competences) is their main motive to engage in business partnerships with other firms (Figure 3.5). Other key motives for inter-firm partnerships relate to exploiting market opportunities (e.g. achieve competitive advantages and gain access to new markets).

The survey further shows that 45 of the 65 SMEs (or 70% of the SMEs) engage in only formal or both formal and informal partnerships with clients and suppliers (Table 3.2). The majority of these arrangements take place with partners within Portugal

Figure 3.5. Motives for inter-firm partnerships of SMEs in the automobile sector in Portugal

Average score, based on 65 responses of SME owners/managers (0=indifferent, 1=important, 2=very important)

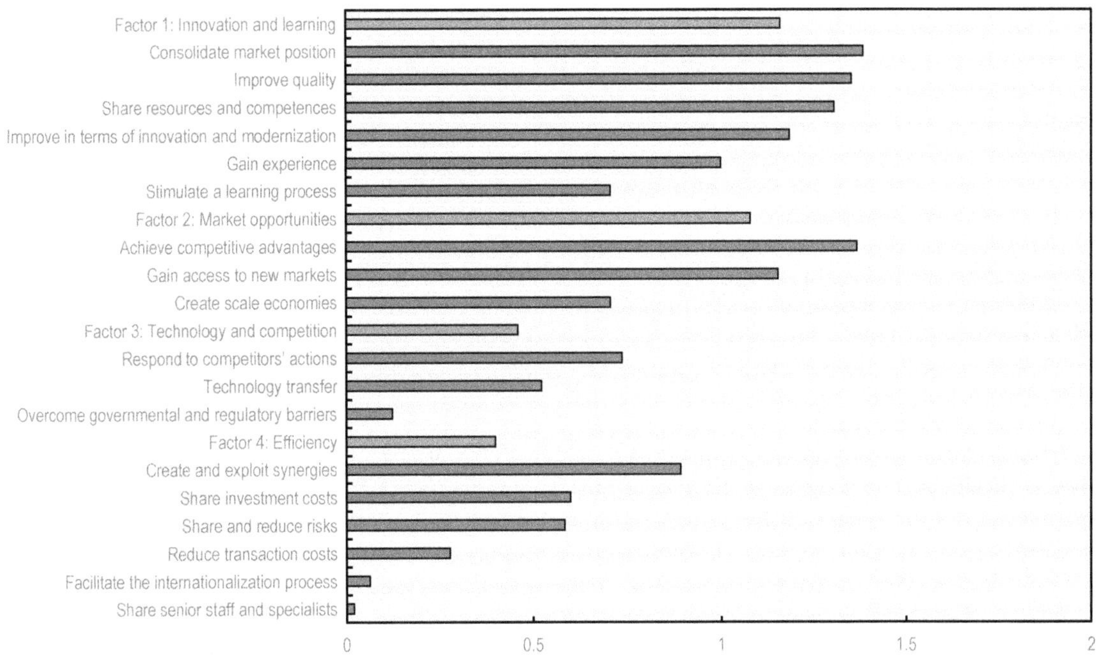

Note: This figure is based on interviews with 65 SME owners/managers in the Portuguese automotive and parts sector.
Source: OECD based on Franco and Haase (2020[10]).

Table 3.2. Characterisation of inter-firm partnerships in the Portuguese automotive sector, 2020

% of SMEs out of a sample of 65 SMEs interviewed

Inter-firm partnerships' characteristics	%
Type of partner Supplier	**23**
Supplier and client	23
Client and complementary firm	15.4
Others	38.6
Formality of the agreement	
Formal	41.6
Informal	30.7
Formal and informal	27.7
Number of partners	
1 firm	20
2 firms	15.4
3 to 6 firms	35.4
7 to 9 firms	7.7
More than 10 firms	21.5
Geographical Area	
Portugal	60
Abroad	15.4
Portugal and abroad	24.6

Note: This table is based on interviews with 65 SME owners/managers in the Portuguese automotive and parts sector.
Source OECD based on Franco and Haase (2020[10]).

3.4. Labour mobility and skills effects related to FDI entry in Portugal

Labour mobility can be an important source of knowledge spillovers in the context of FDI, notably through the move of MNE workers to local SMEs. This can occur through temporary arrangements such as detachments, long-term arrangements such as open-ended contracts, or through the creation of start-ups (i.e. corporate spin-offs) by (former) MNE workers. However, mobility can also occur in the opposite direction, also involving potential for spillovers. This section assesses spillover potential through labour mobility and associated skills effects in Portugal.

Dynamic FDI and SME sectors in Portugal facilitate labour mobility from foreign firms to SMEs

Up-to-date evidence on labour mobility practices and related productivity spillovers on SMEs is currently lacking for Portugal. Detailed evidence from studies in the early 2000s, tracing all spells of inter-firm worker mobility in Portugal (covering both the manufacturing and services sectors) over 1990-2000 provides some insights whose implications may be relevant for today's discussion (Martins, 2011[11]; Martins, 2005[12]).

The studies reveal that labour mobility between foreign affiliates and domestic firms was a rather rare phenomenon in Portugal in the 1990s. Those few workers that moved from foreign to domestic firms experienced a decrease in average wages, which could be interpreted by involuntary mobility during a period of a significant fall of FDI inflows in Portugal related to a slowdown of privatisation, economic recession in Europe and radical geopolitical changes, namely the fall of the Soviet Union (Castro and Buckley, 2001[13]). This low mobility from foreign to domestic firms suggests that worker mobility was most likely not a major source of productivity spillovers from foreign to domestic firms in the 1990s.

Over recent years (pre-COVID-19), however, Portugal experienced an opposite trend with FDI stocks increasing from 30% to 60% of GDP over 2005-2020 and a dynamic and innovative SME and start-up sector has been developing (see Chapter 2). Accordingly, a pattern of increased labour mobility due to a more dynamic economy could have occurred recently, as evidenced by the case of Ireland that has experienced a similar rise of FDI over recent year (OECD, 2020[2]). Evidence in support of this hypothesis is currently not available.

FDI in high technology activities in Portugal is associated with an increase of supply of skills in the medium term

The analysis in Chapter 1 shows that Portugal is competing for FDI in high technology activities, particularly in manufacturing. While this strategy supports Portugal's productivity growth and overall upgrading, it is important to recognise that any new establishment of high technology foreign firms involves new demand for skilled workers in the vicinity of the foreign firms' location (Becker et al., 2020[14]).

As foreign firms are often more productive than their domestic peers, due to their higher capital, technological and managerial endowments, they can typically pay higher wages and attract the most talented workers. In Portugal, workers employed by foreign manufacturers earn 80% higher wages compared to those employed by average domestic firms; similar wage premia of workers in foreign firms are observed in the Czech Republic and Hungary for example (Figure 3.6, Panel A). Recent evidence shows that in Portugal large firms pay 20% higher wages than SMEs (OECD, 2019[15]); accordingly, the premia provided by foreign firms are likely to relate to their large size and higher productivity. Evidence of labour mobility from domestic to foreign firms in Portugal and other EU countries further confirms that such movements translate into considerable pay increases for workers (Becker et al., 2020[14]; Martins, 2011[11]).

Given the relative technological sophistication of foreign firms vis-à-vis domestic (mostly smaller) firms, workers are likely to acquire new knowledge in foreign firms, which then translates into productivity spillovers from this type of labour mobility. Beyond acquiring knowledge from foreign firms on-the-job, formal in-house training may also occur. The training and on-the-job learning opportunities offered by MNEs may also be extended to the workforce of local companies with which they develop linkages. These training opportunities are prevalent in the context of value chain relationships (vertical linkages) by which foreign-owned firms provide staff training to domestic suppliers as a way to ensure efficiency and product quality (OECD, 2019[5]).

Skills are a scarce resource in any OECD and partner economy, including in Portugal, and particularly in remote and less developed regions. The presence of foreign firms in high technology sectors is thus likely to put pressure on the labour market and increase demand for highly skilled workers. Increased demand will not only contribute to increased salaries for workers at foreign firms but will provide any worker with incentives to train themselves and for domestic SMEs to engage in training activities for their workers. This is likely to increase supply of skills in the medium-term. In Portugal (as well as in the Czech Republic for example), domestic firms are relatively more likely to engage in formal training as compared to foreign firms, illustrating domestic firms' appetite to improve skills and remain competitive (Figure 3.6, Panel B). Establishing partnerships and collaboration with domestic vocational schools or higher education institutions (HEIs) (e.g. joint dual education programmes) is another way for foreign MNEs to address skills shortages in the local labour market and lower staff recruitment and requalification costs, with positive effects on skills endowments of the local workforce in the longer term (OECD, 2021[16]).

This is further supported by the OECD scoreboard on skills and global value chains (OECD, 2017[17]): the scoreboard uses selected indicators from the Programme for the International Assessment of Adult Competencies (PIAAC) and the Programme for International Student Assessment (PISA) to identify the extent to which relevant skills for the integration in GVCs have improved (e.g. decreasing shares of unskilled adults, improvements of cognitive skills among adults and secondary school students, or growth in tertiary graduation). Portugal outperformed all other OECD economies in terms of skills improvements relevant for GVC integration over 2000-15. This finding supports the argument that FDI entry, GVC integration through trade, capacities of SMEs and workers are interdependent; improvements or growth in one area may support improvements in another area. Determined policy action for skills development has been key in Portugal in this context and will be discussed further in Chapter 5, also see (OECD, 2018[18]).

Figure 3.6. Foreign firms' premia relative to domestic firms, 2019

Wage and formal training premium of average foreign firms in % of wages and shares of formal training of average domesic firms

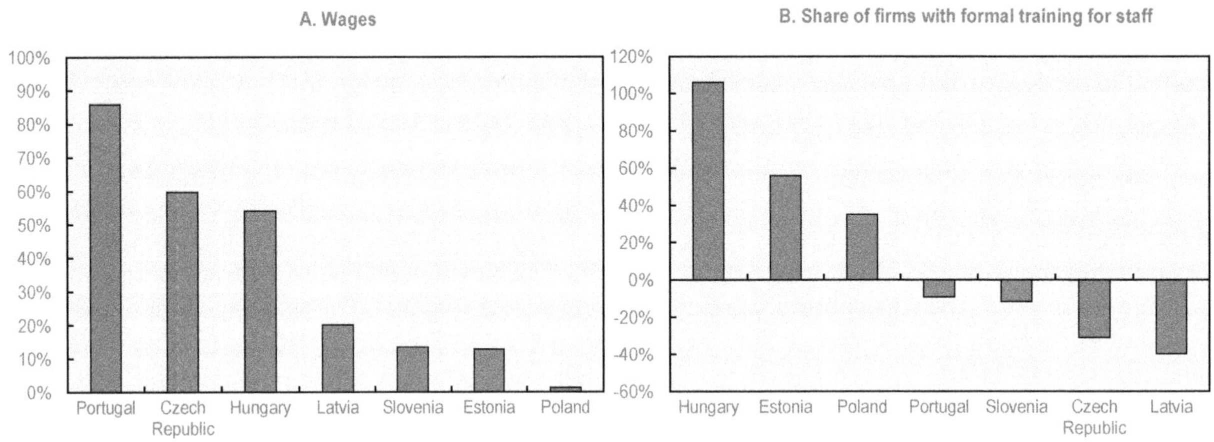

Note: See methodology in OECD (2019[5]).
Source: OECD FDI Qualities Indicators 2019 based on World Bank Enterprise Surveys, 2020

Figure 3.7. Changes in participation in global value chains and skills

OECD countries, 2000-15

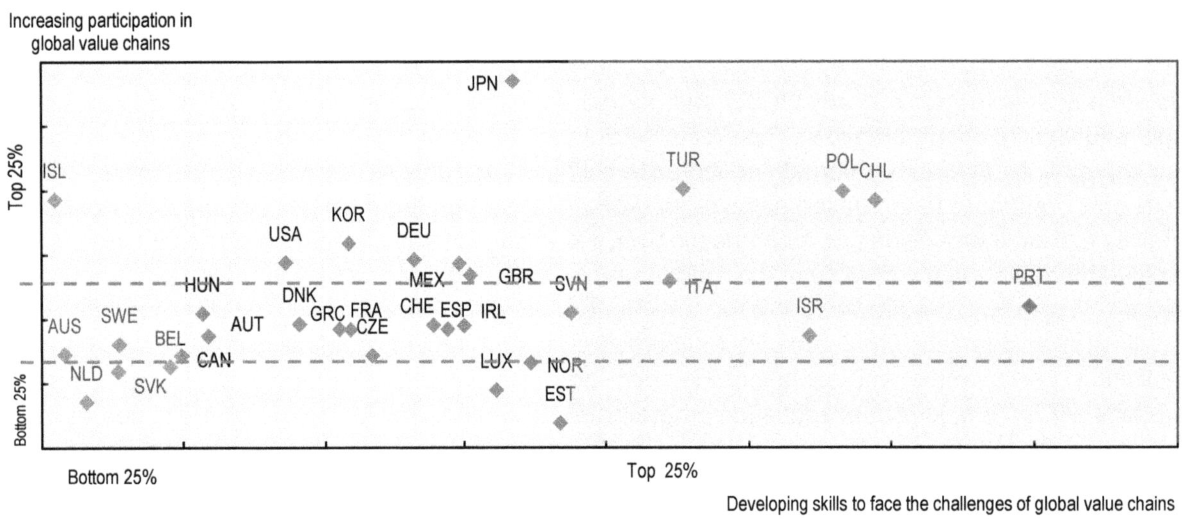

Note: The figure shows the scoreboard indicators capturing the development of participation in GVCs and the evolution of skills relevant for GVC integration (OECD, 2017[17]). Countries in the upper part of the figure are among the top 25% that have increased their participation in GVCs the most while those in the lower part of the figure are among the bottom 25% that have increased their participation in GVCs the least. Countries in the right-hand side of the figure are among the top 25% that have increased their skills the most while those in the left-hand side of the figure are among the bottom 25% that have increased their skills the least. Countries in the middle of the figure are around the average.
Source: (OECD, 2017[17]).

3.5. Competition and imitation effects of FDI

Existing concepts on FDI-SME diffusion also look at competition and imitation effects of FDI on SME productivity and innovation. This section discusses how and to what extent such effects might be at play in the Portuguese FDI and SME sectors, arguing that these effects take place in specific situations of market interactions (including competition for talent and skills), value chain linkages, strategic partnerships and labour mobility The section thus builds extensively on the discussion above and in Chapter 2.

Competition and imitation effects are likely to benefit relatively more productive and innovative SMEs in Portugal

Beyond labour mobility effects, the previous section also argued that the entry of foreign firms heightens the level of competition on domestic companies, putting pressure on them to become more innovative and productive – not least to retain skilled workers (Becker et al., 2020[14]). The new standards set by foreign firms – in terms of product design, quality control or speed of delivery – can stimulate technical change, the introduction of new products, and the adoption of new management practices in local companies, all of which are possible sources of productivity growth (OECD, 2020[1]). This rising competitive pressure due to foreign firm entry and related productivity spillovers may also be associated with new incentives for workers to improve skills and SMEs to engage in skills upgrading in the medium term, as shown for Portugal in the previous section (Figure 3.7).

Foreign firms can also become a source of emulation for local companies, for example by showing better management practices. Imitation, reverse engineering and tacit learning can, therefore, become a channel to strengthen enterprise productivity at the local level. Foreign firms may also participate in innovation clusters and collaborative innovation activities where cross-fertilisation of ideas can increase productivity both of domestic and foreign firms. Section 3.3 showed that, on average, SMEs in Portugal engage relatively less often in collaboration networks, in which peer-to-peer learning including with foreign firms may take place, compared to SMEs in other OECD economies. Yet, the small sub-group of SMEs that is innovating new products or processes in Portugal often does so in contexts of cooperation with other firms. This illustrates that positive imitation/demonstration effects through cooperation with other firms take place in Portugal but could be further strengthened.

FDI involves increased competitive pressure for domestic SMEs

If local companies are not quick or not able to adapt, competition from foreign-owned companies may also result in the exit of some domestically-owned firms. This will of course also depend on other factors such as the market size and growth rate of the market, whether or not foreign firms serve the same market (engage in the same activities) and on the number of producers in the market. Increased competition for talent may also make it more difficult for local companies to recruit skilled workers (Lembcke and Wildnerova, 2020[19]) (see also Section 3.4). These effects are more likely to happen to local companies which operate in the same sector or value chain function of the foreign-owned company, which is the main reason why positive horizontal spillovers from FDI are so rare and, when they happen, they mostly involve larger domestic companies (Gorodnichenko, Svejnar and Terrell, 2014[20]; Farole and Winkler, 2014[6]).

As discussed throughout this report, the capacity of domestic firms to absorb knowledge from foreign firms will determine whether increased competition results in higher or lower productivity (positive or negative spillovers). Comparing performance of European countries in Becker et al. (2020[14]) reveals that limited spillovers in less developed regions, including in Portugal, are related to challenges to absorb foreign knowledge. This is also supported by other evidence for Portugal showing that geographical proximity between the locations of MNEs and domestic firms facilitates the occurrence of FDI spillovers (Crespo, Fontoura and Proenca, 2009[21]). The impact is negative in the case of horizontal externalities, i.e. domestic firms experience a negative productivity impact in proximity of foreign firms in the same sector, which may result from the competition effect at the regional level and limited absorptive capacities. With regard to vertical externalities (value chain linkages), a positive productivity shock is observed, further supporting arguments made in Section 3.2 on the importance of value chain relationships.

Evidence for Portugal further indicates that the presence of foreign firms benefits the small fraction of highly productive domestic firms but not necessarily the bulk of less productive firms (Fernandes, 2013[22]). Inequality in productivity among Portuguese companies has increased over time, evidencing a slowdown in the catching up process of companies during a period of strong FDI inflows (CompNet, 2020[23]). In this context, the productivity of the top performing companies (the most productive in each industry) presents an important contribution in the evolution of aggregate productivity, both through their performance as well as by the way they spread new technologies and business practices in the economy. This further illustrates that the potential for FDI spillovers is higher when firms have a sufficient set of absorptive capacities (Castellani and Pieri, 2010[24]).

References

Becker, B. et al. (2020), "FDI in hot labour markets: The implications of the war for talent", *Journal of International Business Policy*, Vol. 3, 107–133. [14]

Cadestin, C. et al. (2019), *Multinational enterprises in domestic value chains*, OECD Publishing, Paris, https://doi.org/10.1787/9abfa931-en. [3]

Castellani, D. and F. Pieri (2010), *The Effect of Foreign Investments on European*. [24]

Castro, F. and P. Buckley (2001), "Foreign direct investment and the competitiveness of Portugal", https://www.fep.up.pt/docentes/fcastro/CISEP2001.pdf. [13]

CompNet (2020), *Firm Productivity Report*, https://www.comp-net.org/fileadmin/_compnet/user_upload/Documents/Productivity_Report_FINAL-.pdf. [23]

Crespo, N., M. Fontoura and I. Proenca (2009), "FDI spillovers at regional level: Evidence from Portugal",", *Papers in Regional Science*, Vol. 88(3): 591–607. [21]

Farole, T. and D. Winkler (2014), *Making Foreign Direct Investment Work for Sub-Saharan Africa: Local Spillovers and Competitiveness in Global Value Chains*, World Bank, Washington, DC, http://dx.doi.org/10.1596/978-1-4648-0126-6. [6]

Fernandes, N. (2013), *Investimento Directo Estrangeito e Produtividade: uma análise ao Nível da Empresa*, Universidade do Minho, https://repositorium.sdum.uminho.pt/bitstream/1822/26813/1/TESE_Nuno%20Miguel%20Ribeiro%20Fernandes_2013.pdf. [22]

Franco, M. and H. Haase (2020), "Interfirm Partnerships and Organisational Innovation: Study of SMEs in the Automotive Sector", *Journal of Open Innovation Technology Market and Complexity*, Vol. 6(193). [10]

Gorodnichenko, Y., J. Svejnar and K. Terrell (2014), "When does FDI have positive spillovers? Evidence from 17 transition market economies", *Journal of Comparative Economics*, Vol. 42(4), 954-969. [20]

J., S. (ed.) (2006), *The Theoretical Framework: FDI and Technology Transfer*, Palgrave Macmillan, London. [8]

Lembcke, A. and L. Wildnerova (2020), *Does FDI benefit incumbent SMEs? FDI spillovers and competition effects at the local level*, OECD Publishing, Paris, p. No. 2020/02, https://doi.org/10.1787/47763241-en. [19]

López González, J. et al. (2019), *Participation and benefits of SMEs in GVCs in Southeast Asia*, OECD Publishing, Paris, https://doi.org/10.1787/3f5f2618-en. [7]

Martins, P. (2011), "Paying More to Hire the Best? Foreign Firms, Wages, and Worker Mobility", *Economic Inquiry,*, Vol. 49 (2), 349-363, http://ftp.iza.org/dp3607.pdf. [11]

Martins, P. (2005), "Inter-Firm Employee Mobility, Displacement, and Foreign Direct Investment Spillovers", https://www.researchgate.net/publication/228614727_Inter-Firm_Employee_Mobility_Displacement_and_Foreign_Direct_Investment_Spillovers. [12]

OECD (2021), *Geography of Higher Education (GoHE)*, https://www.oecd.org/cfe/smes/geo-higher-education.htm. [16]

OECD (2020), *Enabling FDI diffusion channels to boost SME productivity and innovation in EU countries and regions: Towards a Policy Toolkit, Concept Paper for joint EC-OECD project.*. [1]

OECD (2020), *FDI Qualities Assessment of Ireland*, http://www.oecd.org/investment/FDI-Qualities-Assessment-of-Ireland.pdf. [2]

OECD (2019), *FDI Qualities Indicators: Measuring the sustainable development impacts of investment*, https://www.oecd.org/fr/investissement/fdi-qualities-indicators.htm. [5]

OECD (2019), *SME and Entrepreneurship Outlook 2019, SME and Entrepreneurship Outlook 2019*, OECD Publishing, Paris, https://doi.org/10.1787/d2b72934-en. [15]

OECD (2018), *OECD (2018), Skills Strategy Implementation Guidance for Portugal: Strengthening the Adult-Learning System, OECD Skills Studies*, OECD Publishing, Paris, https://doi.org/10.1787/9789264298705-en. [18]

OECD (2017), *OECD Skills Outlook 2017: Skills and Global Value Chains*, OECD Publishing, Paris, https://doi.org/10.1787/9789264273351-en. [17]

OECD-UNIDO (2019), *Integrating Southeast Asian SMEs in Global Value Chains.Enabling Linkages with Foreign Investors*, http://www.oecd.org/investment/Integrating-Southeast-Asian-SMEs-in-globalvalue-chains.pdf. [4]

Pereira, D. and J. Correia Leitão (2013), *Restructuring in SMEs Portugal*, https://www.researchgate.net/publication/284654674_Restructuring_in_SMEs_Portugal. [9]

Notes

[1] This report primarily uses Ireland, Czech Republic, Slovak Republic, and sometimes Hungary and Lithuania, as comparators. They were chosen based on their economic size, outward orientation driven by foreign investors and EU membership.

[2] See Chapter 2, Box 2.1, for an introduction to the classification of sectors used in this report.

[3] See (OECD, 2020[1]) for a review of the literature.

4 The institutional and governance framework for FDI diffusion on Portuguese SMEs

This chapter focuses on several core issues that underpin the institutional and governance framework for foreign direct investment (FDI) promotion and small and medium-sized enterprises (SMEs) development in Portugal. It provides an overview of the institutions that are currently in place to design and implement FDI, SME, innovation and regional development policies, and explores the multi-level policy coordination mechanisms to ensure coherence across policy domains, institutions and tiers of government. This chapter gives also special attention to the monitoring and evaluation framework of the policy system in Portugal, and efforts to enhance stakeholder engagement.

4.1. Summary of findings and recommendations

Strengthening FDI spillovers on Portuguese SMEs requires public action to be taken in different policy domains related to investment promotion and facilitation, SME internationalisation, innovation and regional development. The institutional framework that governs these policy areas differs from country to country. Different governance structures are feasible as long as appropriate coordination mechanisms are in place to ensure policy alignment across Ministries, implementing agencies and advisory bodies. Effective multi-level governance also plays a crucial role in ensuring consistency between policy interventions taking place at national and local levels. This chapter aims to identify the institutional arrangements and possible governance challenges in Portugal's policy mix for FDI diffusion on domestic SMEs (Table 4.1). It provides an overview of the main Portuguese institutions that operate at the intersection of FDI, SME, innovation and regional development policy and explores their organisational structures as well as the scope and diversity of their mandates. It also sheds light on their internal capabilities for inter-institutional coordination, policy evaluation and stakeholder engagement, which are all important elements of a conducive institutional environment.

Table 4.1. Findings and recommendations on the institutional framework for FDI-SME diffusion

Findings	Recommendations
Creating a conducive institutional environment	
The governance system is represented by many public institutions. The implementation of FD-SME diffusion policies is fragmented along several ministries and government agencies.	Consider the potential benefits of a more centralised governance framework that facilitates cross-cutting policy implementation across the FDI-SME diffusion policy areas. Alternatively, inter-institutional coordination should be strengthened to overcome policy silos.
The Portuguese SME agency (IAPMEI) has a large network of subnational offices and a decentralised governance structure while the investment promotion agency (AICEP) has a limited regional footprint with a small number of local agency representatives in a few cities across Portugal.	Consider local market needs and priorities in the implementation of national business support programmes and strengthen collaboration with subnational actors, in particular municipalities and inter-municipal councils, which have been given enhanced responsibilities in the area of investment attraction following recent decentralisation reforms.
Recent reforms have focused on strengthening the mandate, responsibilities and resources of subnational governments. Regional administrations (CCDRs) play an important role in the implementation of regionally tailored smart specialisation strategies.	Continue efforts to encourage synergies at the local level through the transfer of delegated powers from municipalities to inter-municipal councils (CIMs). Getting the CIMs more involved in investment promotion efforts could be an alternative to subnational IPAs.
Several inter-municipal councils have been established to increase synergies at the local level. However, inter-municipal cooperation on the implementation of investment, SME and innovation policies remains limited.	Leverage the subnational branches of IAPMEI and AICEP to help subnational governments of less developed regions strengthen their capacities in supporting and providing complementary services to local FDI-SME ecosystems.
Ensuring coordination across different institutions, policy areas and tiers of government	
Several high-level government councils are in place bringing together ministries, agencies, and subnational authorities. However, their contribution to cross-ministerial planning and decision-making varies with some councils lacking a clear mandate and resources.	Strengthen the mandate of high-level advisory bodies and ensure they have sufficient financial and human resources to contribute to inter-ministerial coordination and collaboration.
The large number of national strategies increases the risk of policy overlaps and contradictions, potentially leading to ambiguity about the responsibilities of various institutions.	Ensure the alignment of policy objectives across the various national strategies and use robust monitoring tools to minimise potential inconsistencies and contradictions in policy implementation.
Promoting impact evaluations and policy dialogue with stakeholders	
The evaluation of policy impacts is less systematic and does not allow for strategic foresight and planning. The scope of evaluations is often procedural and centred on implementation rather than on impacts.	Establish a comprehensive M&E framework that covers all major policy fields and goes beyond satisfying the monitoring requirements of the EU funds. Focus on measuring results / impacts rather than implementation issues.
The M&E capacities of the main Portuguese implementing agencies are limited, with potential negative consequences on the process of policy learning and adaptation.	Set up dedicated M&E units within each implementing agency and strengthen their analytical and data collection capacities through the provision of specialised training to raise awareness on evaluation methods.
Deliberative processes have improved in recent years with the creation of the CONSULTALEX Portal and the organisation of public consultations for several national strategies.	Expand the use of the CONSULTALEX Portal to also consult on broader policy initiatives in addition to laws and regulations. Consider strengthening the capacity of high-level advisory bodies to convene stakeholders and provide input to policymaking processes.

4.2. Overview of Portugal's governance framework for FDI-SME diffusion

The formulation and implementation of FDI-SME diffusion policies is fragmented along several line ministries and implementing agencies

The governance framework for investment, SME, innovation and regional development policy in Portugal is represented by many public institutions. FDI-SME diffusion policies are designed and implemented through several ministries, task forces, advisory bodies and autonomous government agencies that operate at the intersection of investment promotion, SME development, innovation and regional development policy (Figure 4.1). At the highest level, the Portuguese government (Council of Ministers) has collective responsibility for investment, business and economic policy and for setting strategic directions. It is also responsible for implementing EU Structural and Investment Funds in Portugal within guidelines set by and agreed at EU level.

The primary responsibility for SME and business innovation policy lies with the Ministry of Economy and Digital Transition (*Ministério da Economia e Transição Digital*), which is also in charge of formulating and executing economic growth policies with the aim to foster the competitiveness of the Portuguese economy, promote business innovation, and facilitate the digital transition (Government of Portugal, 2014[1]). The Ministry of Science, Technology and Higher Education (*Ministério de Ciência, Tecnologia e Ensino Superior, MCTES*) is responsible for promoting science, technology and education. As in many countries, support to knowledge and technology transfer to the business sector, including collaborative applied research, is shared between these two ministries (OECD, 2019[2]). The Ministry of Foreign Affairs (*Ministério dos Negócios Estrangeiros, MNE*) coordinates national investment promotion and trade policies in collaboration with other ministries with competences in these policy areas. It is responsible for Portugal's economic diplomacy, supporting the internationalisation of the Portuguese economy and promoting the interests of Portuguese companies abroad on matters related to trade and investment (Government of Portugal, 2011[3]).

Important prerogatives are also in the hands of the Ministry of Planning, which is responsible for the management of the EU Structural and Investment Funds, and the Ministry of Territorial Cohesion, which formulates and implements regional development policies (OECD, 2019[2]). Through its decentralised ministry branches, the Regional Coordination and Development Commissions (CCDRs), the Ministry of Territorial Cohesion plays a significant role in territorial approaches, and is responsible for the formulation and implementation of regional smart specialisation strategies together with the Ministry of Planning, the Ministry of Economy and Digital Transition, the Ministry of Science, Technology and Higher Education.

The implementation of policy initiatives that enable FDI spillovers on Portuguese SMEs is entrusted to four main implementing agencies, which all report to different line Ministries (Table 4.2). **Portugal Global - Trade and Investment Agency** (*Agência para o Investimento e Comércio Externo de Portugal, AICEP*) was created in 2007 as an autonomous agency under the Ministry of Foreign Affairs to promote FDI towards Portugal and support the internationalisation of Portuguese companies in coordination with the Ministry of Economy and Digital Transition. AICEP is the one-stop-shop for facilitation and aftercare services to foreign investors and operates an industrial parks management entity, *AICEP Global Parques*, which manages the Portugal Site Selection platform – a search engine that allows users to find the best locations in Portugal that match their business requirements. A clear distinction is made between the types of companies and investment projects that can be supported by AICEP and the other Portuguese government agencies. AICEP's clients are solely large companies with an annual turnover of EUR 75 million or companies that implement investment projects of over EUR 25 million. As part of its mandate, AICEP is responsible for the screening, administration and management of investment support and incentive schemes for its clients and also supports Portuguese companies regardless of their size and legal form in promoting their brands, products and commercial activities in foreign markets.

Figure 4.1. The institutional environment for FDI-SME diffusion policy areas in Portugal

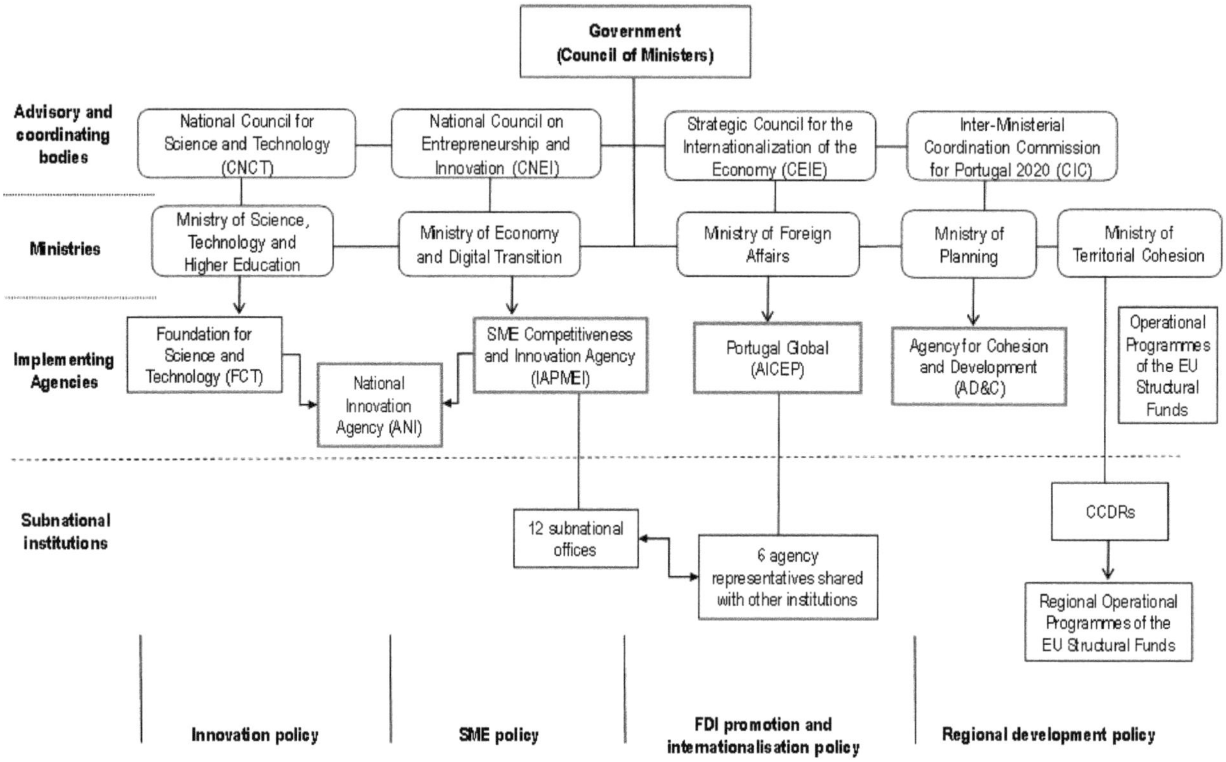

Note: In red frame are the main government agencies implementing policies that strengthen FDI diffusion on Portuguese SMEs.
Source: OECD elaboration.

The **SME Competitiveness and Innovation Agency** (*Agência para a Competitividade e Inovação, IAPMEI*) was established in 1975 as an autonomous agency that supports domestic SMEs and reports to the Ministry of Economy and Digital Transition. The agency targets all sectors except for tourism, which is under the sole responsibility of the National Tourism Authority, *Turismo de Portugal*. In contrast to AICEP, IAPMEI is responsible for supporting Portuguese companies with an annual turnover of less than EUR 75 million and investment projects whose value is less than EUR 25 million. It aims to foster innovation and boost the competitiveness of Portuguese SMEs through financial support schemes, business consulting services and training programmes. IAPMEI places particular emphasis on supporting R&D investment, innovation and technology upgrading as well as the promotion of linkages between companies and entities of the Portuguese scientific, research and innovation ecosystem.

The **National Innovation Agency** (*Agência Nacional de Inovação, ANI*), which was created in 1993 and re-established in 2014, aims to foster technology transfer and knowledge promotion through joint projects between businesses and scientific and research institutions. The agency reports to the Ministry of Economy and Digital Transition and the Ministry of Science, Technology and Higher Education, through a "hybrid" governance structure that is meant to bring together scientific innovation and business development and foster collaboration between the corporate and applied research sectors.[1] The agency coordinates several research infrastructure networks (e.g. Interface Centres, Collaborative Laboratories) and provides funding for collaborative R&D. It is also responsible for administering the tax incentive scheme "System of Fiscal Incentive for Business Research and Innovation" (*Sistema de Incentivos Fiscais à I&D Empresarial, SIFIDE*), which has been the main instrument used by government to support business R&D since its establishment in 1997.

Finally, the **Agency for Development and Cohesion** (*Agência para o Desenvolvimento e Coesão, AD&C*) was established in 2013 to ensure the programming, implementation and evaluation of regional development policies, and the overall coordination of EU funds, including the flagship Portugal 2020 national strategy. AD&C operates as a Department within the Ministry of Planning. In addition, the EU's cohesion policy is administered through seven regional and four thematic operational programmes, which have their own national managing authorities (e.g. COMPETE 2020), consisting of a steering committee and a technical secretariat (OECD, 2020[4]).

Table 4.2. Implementing agencies in Portugal: comparative overview

Policy domain	Innovation	SME development	FDI promotion	Regional development
Implementing agency	**ANI**	**IAPMEI**	**AICEP**	**AD&C**
Date of creation	1993	1975	2007	2013
Ministry in charge	Ministry of Economy and Digital Transition and Ministry of S&T and Higher Education	Ministry of Economy and Digital Transition	Ministry of Foreign Affairs	Ministry of Planning
Legal form	Autonomous agency	Autonomous agency	Autonomous agency	Ministry department
Mandate	Support technological and business innovation and promote partnerships	Promote the innovation, competitiveness, and growth of Portuguese SMEs	Attract and facilitate FDI and support the internationalisation of domestic companies	Implement regional development policies and coordinate the EU Structural and Investment Funds
Target population	All firms, research institutions	SMEs	SMEs for internationalisation support and large companies or large investment projects for investment support	All firms
Sectoral focus	All sectors	All sectors except tourism	All sectors	All sectors
Related national strategies	Technological & Business Innovation Strategy (2018-2030)	Industry 4.0 National Strategy (2017)	2030 Economic Internationalisation Programme (2020)	Portugal 2020 Partnership Agreement, Portugal 2030 Strategy
Main instruments	SIFIDE R&D tax incentives	SME Academy	Portugal 2020 grants & tax incentives for productive and R&D investment	Portugal 2020 Partnership Agreement

Source: OECD elaboration.

When compared to other EU countries, it becomes clear that Portugal's FDI-SME diffusion governance system is segmented along lines reflecting different policy domains. Governance systems within the EU vary, ranging from deeply centralised frameworks where FDI-SME diffusion policies are the responsibility of a single line Ministry; to balanced institutional set-ups where policy formulation in the areas of FDI, SMEs, innovation and regional development is shared among a small number of institutions; and to segmented governance systems where several line ministries and implementing agencies are involved in policy formulation and implementation.

For instance, Slovenia's Ministry of Economic Development and Technology is responsible for all FDI-SME diffusion policy areas (Figure 4.2). Policy implementation is entrusted to one single implementing agency, SPIRIT Slovenia, which is responsible for FDI, SMEs, innovation and tourism promotion, while regional development policy is coordinated through the Ministry's Regional Development Directorate. In Ireland, recent institutional reforms have led to a rather balanced governance framework. FDI-SME diffusion policy areas are split across three Ministries, with the Department of Enterprise, Trade and Employment bearing responsibility for FDI and SME policy, while innovation policy sits with the newly established Department of Further and Higher Education, Research, Innovation and Science.

Institutional settings like Portugal's are not necessarily less effective in the implementation of FDI-SME diffusion policies as long as inter-institutional coordination mechanisms are in place to overcome policy silos. Given the high transaction costs associated with the segmentation of governance systems, the cost effectiveness of Portugal's institutional setting should be ultimately weighed against the quality of coordination and the potential benefits of a more centralised approach. For instance, an assessment of policy coordination mechanisms is conducted in the next section, pointing towards weaknesses in inter-ministerial collaboration across the areas of investment promotion, innovation, entrepreneurship and regional development.

Figure 4.2. Institutional arrangements for FDI-SME diffusion policy areas in Slovenia and Ireland

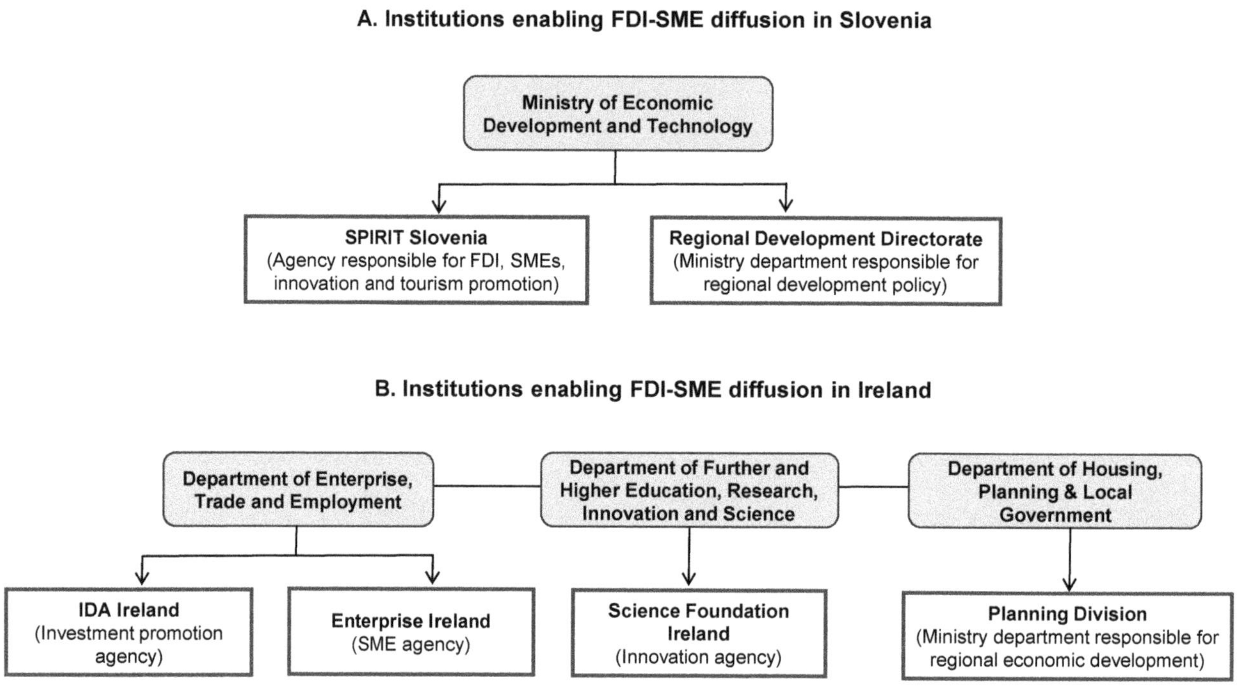

Source: OECD elaboration based on EU/OECD Survey on Policies enabling FDI spillovers to domestic SMEs (2021).

The regional footprint of national implementing agencies varies with the Norte and Centro regions receiving increased policy attention

Proximity could be a strong enabling factor of efficient policy delivery. Recent findings from EU countries show that FDI responds better to the activity of Investment Promotion Agencies (IPAs) operating in closer proximity to investors' operations (Crescenzi, Di Cataldo and Giua, 2019[5]). Similarly, the availability of appropriate business development services is a local issue because SMEs and entrepreneurs generally access the services within a narrow local area (e.g. approximately 50 kilometres) and are therefore dependent on the quality of local supply (OECD, 2019[6]). In addition, a local presence is often necessary to ensure programmes and policies are aligned with each region's economic and market characteristics.

There are, however, wide cross-country disparities in the way national agencies operate at the subnational level. In some countries where inter-institutional coordination is limited, local presence in the form of secondary offices may be crucial to ensure that businesses in all regions can benefit from tailored support. In other cases, national agencies coordinate activities with regional actors such as local governments and regional development agencies, who possess knowledge of the local context. For instance, Belgium, Denmark, Latvia, and Poland largely deliver business development services through subnational governments and actors (OECD, 2019[6]). Likewise, in France, the national IPA collaborates with local autonomous agencies that provide aftercare services to foreign firms while they set up their operations in specific regions (OECD, 2018[7]).

Given their economic and political importance, the Lisbon and Porto metropolitan areas host the primary offices of the main implementing agencies. AICEP, IAPMEI and ANI have their headquarters in Porto while they also maintain offices in Lisbon, the country's administrative capital. In contrast, AD&C has a single office in Lisbon only, reflecting its legal status as a department within the Ministry of Planning.

Beyond the two metropolitan areas, the regions of Centro and Norte host the largest number of subnational offices, reflecting the increased policy attention that they receive due to their status as two of Portugal's least developed regions (Figure 4.3). In fact, the two regions accounted for around 80% of the total direct financial support for business investment that was allocated to domestic firms under the Portugal 2020 Incentive Schemes (IS), which are financed by the European Regional Development Fund (EDRF) and the European Social Fund (ESF) (AD&C, 2019[8]). The regional footprint of national agencies is very limited in the regions of Algarve and Alentejo, and completely absent in the two autonomous regions of Madeira and Azores due to their special political and administrative status.

Figure 4.3. The regional presence of national implementing agencies in relation to FDI flows, SME population, and business innovation intensity

Number of agency offices, share of FDI, SMEs, and business R&D in NUTS 2 regions of continental Portugal

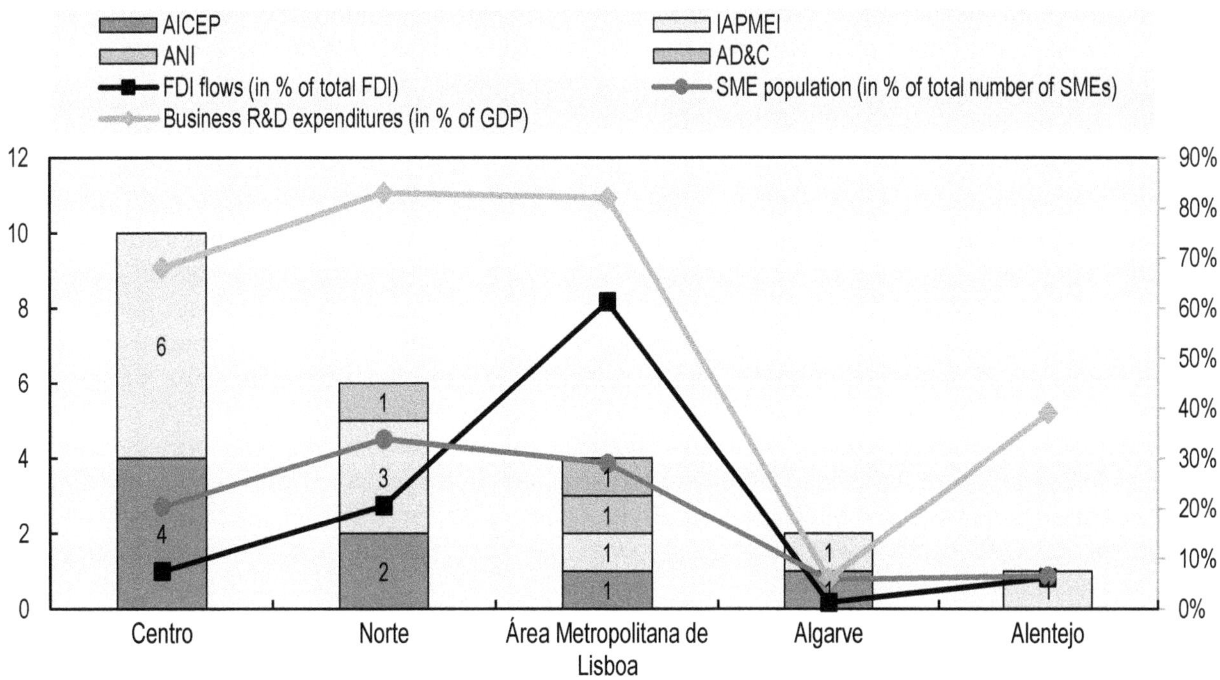

Source: EU/OECD Survey on Policies enabling FDI spillovers to domestic SMEs (2021), Financial Times fDi Markets database and Refinitiv, Pordata database, and OECD Regional Statistics.

The increased policy attention that the Norte and Centro regions receive compared to Algarve and Alentejo is also explained by their business demographic characteristics. The large majority of SMEs is located in Centro, Norte and the Lisbon area, while a similar picture emerges when looking at the geographic distribution of FDI flows, with Centro and Norte attracting a fair share of foreign firms compared to the rest of Portugal, excluding the Lisbon area (see Chapter 2). The increased presence of both domestic and foreign firms in these regions means that the demand for business support services is high and therefore requires government agencies to allocate significant human and financial resources for the implementation of their policies and the dissemination of their activities to wider target audiences.

Portuguese institutions follow various approaches with regard to implementing their policies and programmes at the local level. IAPMEI has the largest network of local offices and a decentralised governance structure, which aims to ensure, on the one hand, that SMEs will have access to tailored technical support in the region they operate; and on the other hand that valuable information about market conditions and the actual needs of local businesses will reach the agency's headquarters. A dedicated Regional Proximity Directorate ensures IAPMEI's regional presence and coordination with local governments, while subnational offices in twelve cities across all regions of Portugal (Lisbon, Porto, Faro, Evora, Leiria, Coimbra, Aveiro, Covilha, Viseu, Guarda, Braga, and Braganca) provide information and business consulting services to local SMEs.

AICEP's governance structure favours the establishment of overseas investment promotion offices (currently in 52 countries), rather than subnational offices. AICEP has a limited regional footprint with a small number of representatives based in six cities (Aveiro, Braga, Faro, Coimbra, Leiria, and Viseu) across continental Portugal. The agency has also partnered with the Azores Business Development Society, to ensure local presence in the Azores autonomous region (Ponta Delgada, Angra do Heroismo). This is in line with recent OECD findings that show that only 38% of OECD IPAs have subnational offices while 75% of them have their own offices abroad with dedicated personnel working on investment promotion (OECD, 2018[7]). AICEP's subnational representatives are administratively located in the same offices with other public agencies, including IAPMEI, and provide mostly services aimed at the internationalisation of local firms, including their integration in the supplier networks of foreign investors. FDI facilitation and aftercare services are generally coordinated at central level by staff based in AICEP's offices in Lisbon and Porto, and provided in collaboration with the agency's subnational representatives, municipalities and local IPAs (e.g. Invest Porto, Invest Lisbon, Invest Braga).

Historical estimates (Riccardo Crescenzi, 2019[9]) modelled for Europe suggest that in the right combinations, regional IPAs could increase investment and jobs by up to 25%. For FDI spillovers to occur, IPAs have to strike the right balance between headquarter vs. local presence. This means that they often have to supplement the mandate of subnational institutions by engaging themselves in investment facilitation locally, providing aftercare services, and helping foreign firms navigate local administrative procedures. AICEP's presence at the subnational level helps improve the interconnection between national, regional and local delivery of investment facilitation services. Moving forward, further policy consideration should be given to balancing national and local priorities and strengthening collaboration with subnational governments, which have been given enhanced responsibilities in the area of investment attraction following recent territorial government reforms (see next section). Although such collaboration already exists in large cities and regions where FDI is concentrated, more efficiencies could likely be found through enhanced cooperation with economically weaker regions that may face challenges in mobilising public and private actors in support of local FDI-SME ecosystems. Such an approach would also support ongoing efforts by the Portuguese government to tailor national programmes to the particular needs of local areas, including less developed regions (see chapter 5). Chapter 6 provides further insights into the regional aspects of FDI-SME diffusion policymaking, focusing on the regions of Norte and Alentejo.

Portugal's multilevel governance system appears centralised compared to other EU and OECD countries

While regulations are set at a national level, policies that strengthen FDI diffusion on domestic SMEs can be introduced by various levels of government; many of these policies are designed and executed at the subnational level. Effective multilevel governance reduces the burden on foreign and domestic firms to understand and coordinate across different layers of administration (OECD, 2019[10]).

Portugal is one of the least decentralised countries among EU and OECD countries (OECD, 2020[4]). Portuguese municipalities, parishes (*freguesias*) and inter-municipal councils that currently form the subnational government in the country have much less spending and revenue powers than most of their peers in other EU countries. Another characteristic of Portugal is the absence of a regional government level, which is instead a frequent feature of EU countries of similar population size (OECD, 2020[4]). Although the 1976 Constitution introduced a legal framework to establish administrative regions with elected councils and own budget, regional level problems have been tackled mainly through five regional planning and coordination entities, the Commissions for Coordination and Regional Development (CCDRs). The CCDRs are responsible for the territorial coordination of central government services in each region, and their presidents have been appointed directly by the government until recently. In addition, Portugal has established 21 Inter-municipal Communities and 2 Metropolitan Areas (CIMs and MAs in Portuguese, which correspond to the NUTS 3 level[2]) that aim to reinforce inter-municipal cooperation and fulfil tasks beyond the borders of single municipalities. Portugal also has two autonomous regions that include the Azores and Madeira islands. In these two regions, regional governments have general administrative, political and legislative powers, except for the functions of sovereignty and national representation, including responsibilities for regional development. The regional governments participate in national strategic exercises (e.g. the National Tourism Strategy and the National Strategy for the Sea), but also develop their own regional strategies determined by regional political priorities.

Most regional policy approaches undertaken by subnational governments are related to the use of cohesion policy funding from the EU Structural and Investment Funds (OECD, 2019[11]). The scope for fiscal action is also uneven across regions. Municipalities differ considerably in their capacity to generate own revenues (OECD, 2020[4]). Lisbon and Porto have the highest levels of own revenues per inhabitant, followed by municipalities in the coastal area. Inland municipalities are instead very dependent on intergovernmental transfers. Inter-municipal cooperation remains limited, as only a fraction of local spending has been assigned to the CIMs and metropolitan areas so far. The role of CIMs in the design and implementation of FDI-SME diffusion policies varies but overall has remained limited due to the lack of inter-municipal cooperation over matters related to investment attraction and their reliance on the priorities of the municipalities that make up their membership. In most cases, CIMs contribute to ad hoc collaborative programmes that are implemented by multiple regional and local actors.

Since 2019, a new decentralisation programme is being gradually implemented (OECD, 2019[12]). Within the scope of the territorial governance reforms, the Portuguese government passed a new framework act for the transfer of public competences to the municipalities and CIMs. It involves an extensive delegation of competences to the municipalities and parishes in several policy areas, such as education, welfare, health, transport, civil protection, cultural heritage and housing. It also aims to increase the share of resources spent at local level and includes the possibility of municipal delegation to the CIMs, which can now be also responsible for investment attraction. The transfer of new powers to the CIMs is still ongoing, and not all of them have incorporated these additional mandates into their work programmes. The transfer of mandates to the CIMs should be further encouraged, in particular in the areas of investment attraction and SME development. Getting the CIMs more involved in the formulation and implementation of inter-municipal investment promotion and SME development initiatives could help complement policy efforts undertaken at the local level by AICEP and IAPMEI and contribute to further tailoring national programmes and policies to local needs.

Moreover, strengthening the capacities and operational autonomy of regional administrations has been a key priority for the Portuguese government (OECD, 2020[4]). In 2020, the presidents and vice-presidents of the CCDRs were elected for the first time by an electoral college made up of mayors, municipal councillors, and presidents of municipal assemblies. Given the crucial role of regional administrations in the management of EU funds and the implementation of smart specialisation strategies, these reforms go in the right direction and could help CCDRs improve their legitimacy, clarify their mission and responsibilities, create a culture of collaboration with other local government actors, and devise comprehensive regional development strategies that take into account FDI and SME policy issues.

4.3. Policy coordination across institutions and tiers of government

Actions to improve the impact of FDI on the productivity and innovation of domestic SMEs need to be aligned with the objectives and priorities set by government across different sectors and policy areas. This often entails cooperating with a number of government institutions dealing with FDI attraction, promotion and facilitation as well as SME innovation and internationalisation, and maintaining very strong ties with institutions operating at national and subnational levels.

Although coordination is a fundamental and longstanding problem for public administrations, there is still no standardised method for approaching coordination issues, and much of the success or failure of attempts to coordinate appear to depend upon context. Instruments of coordination can be formal or informal; based on regulation, incentives, norms and information sharing; top-down relying on the authority of a lead actor, or bottom-up and emergent. (Box 4.1). Overall, coordination approaches and instruments may vary depending on the context, country and policy area.

High-level advisory councils lack a clear mandate and resources to facilitate inter-ministerial collaboration and policy coordination

Mechanisms that ensure horizontal policy coordination between Ministry departments dealing with SME and innovation policies and those responsible for investment promotion and broader economic and regional development policies are not sufficiently developed in Portugal. The divide between these policy domains becomes clear from the co-existence of distinct high-level councils for different policy areas. These councils bring together the Centre of Government (i.e. Prime Minister's office), line Ministries, implementing agencies as well as representatives from the private sector and the Portuguese innovation ecosystem to identify priority areas where cross-ministerial planning and decision-making is required.

- The **National Council on Entrepreneurship and Innovation** (*Conselho Nacional de Empreendedorismo e Inovação, CNEI*) is chaired by the Prime Minister and composed of representatives from government, academia and the private sector. Its mission is to ensure inter-ministerial coordination and define priority areas and sectors for the implementation of Portugal's innovation and entrepreneurship policy (Government of Portugal, 2012[13]). Together with the National Council for Science and Technology (*Conselho Nacional de Ciência e Tecnologia, CNCT*), which focuses on science and applied research policy issues, the CNEI is part of the governance structure of the Portuguese Smart Specialisation Strategy (S3) (Government of Portugal, 2014[14]).
- The **Strategic Council for the Internationalisation of the Economy** (*Conselho Estratégico de Internacionalização da Economia, CEIE*) is chaired by the Prime Minister and composed of the ministers responsible for finance, foreign affairs and the economy, as well as representatives of Portuguese business associations (Government of Portugal, 2011[15]). Its mission is to provide advice to government on foreign investment and international trade issues and contribute to the development of national strategies on the internationalisation of the Portuguese economy in collaboration with AICEP and the Ministry of Foreign Affairs.
- The **Inter-ministerial Coordination Commission for Portugal 2020** (*Comissão Interministerial de Coordenação, CIC*), consists of several government members and is headed by the Minister responsible for regional development. It is in charge of political coordination for the Portugal 2020 Partnership Agreement, Portugal's strategic framework for the implementation of the 2014-2020 EU Structural and Investment Funds (Government of Portugal, 2014[16]).

Box 4.1. Policy coordination : principles, instruments and benchmarking

Coordination occurs when decisions made in one programme or organisation consider those made in others and attempt to avoid conflict (*negative coordination*) or seek to cooperate on solutions that can benefit all the organisations and their clients (*positive coordination*) (Scharpf, 1994[17]). *Strategic coordination* involve the coordination of programmes around broad strategic goals of government, such as the Sustainable Development Goals (SDGs) (Peters, 2018[18]). Co-ordination relies upon a mix of interactions, with both vertical and horizontal aspects, the former ones referring to co-ordination between a ministry and its delivery agencies, and the latter covering for instance inter-ministry relations (OECD, 2012[19]). Co-ordination can be fostered at different points in the policy cycle, from policy design to implementation to evaluation.

(Metcalfe, 1994[20]) proposes a policy coordination scale as a method for comparing coordination capacities in governments. The components of policy coordination capacity are cumulative in the sense that higher-level coordination functions depend on the existence and reliability of the lower ones. From almost total independence of programmes (1) to very close policy integration (9): (1) Independent Decision-Making by Ministers; (2) Communication with other Ministers (Information Exchange); (3) Consultation with other Ministers (Feedback); (4) Avoiding Divergences Among Ministers; (5) Search for Agreement Among Ministers; (6) Arbitration of Policy Differences; (7) Setting Limits on Ministerial Action; (8) Establishing Central Priorities; and (9) Government Strategy.

Instruments of co-ordination can be based on regulation, incentives, norms and information sharing. They can be top-down and rely upon the authority of a lead actor or bottom-up and emergent (Peters, 2018[18]). They include (OECD, 2012[19]):

- *National strategies and action plans* typically involve wide consultation and deliberation, provide diagnostic overviews of what the strengths-weaknesses-opportunities-threats of an SME/innovation/local ecosystem could be, and set a shared vision of the goals pursued.
- Closely related, *policy evaluations and reviews* are a source of strategic intelligence, and a means for promoting greater co-ordination.
- *Dedicated agencies or ministries* assume the leadership of the national policy agenda in some policy domains (e.g. FDI/SME/innovation/regional) and often responsibility of coordination. At the same time, *inter-agency joint programming* can facilitate co-ordination and other aspects of governance as agencies share agenda and action.
- The *Centre of government (*CoG), e.g. the President's or Prime Minister's Office, can bridge interests and bureaucratic boundaries. *High-level policy councils*, can also deal with aspects of policy coordination although they often have variable roles and composition across countries.
- Finally, *informal channels of communication between officials* or *job circulation* (of civil servants, but also experts and stakeholders) can play a role and suggest a relatively well-developed culture of inter-agency trust and communication.

Although coordination is a fundamental and longstanding problem for public administration and policy, there is still no standardised method for approaching related issues, and much of the success or failure of attempts to coordinate appears to depend upon context (Peters, 2018[18]). Coordination approaches and instruments need to be matched to circumstances, so does the need to coordinate across countries and policy areas. Some policy domains may work well with minimal attempts to coordinate with others, but others may require substantial policy integration and coordination. Likewise, some political systems may emphasise coordination and government more strongly than others (Hayward and Wright, 2002[21]).

Although horizontal policy coordination in the areas of innovation and entrepreneurship could theoretically be driven by the CNEI, in practice, over the past few years, the council has rarely held any meetings, and lacks a clear mandate, sufficient financial resources and dedicated staff to support its work. Its activities often depend on ad hoc requests from government and does not have a permanent function that would allow it to establish its legitimacy as an independent advisory and coordination body (OECD, 2019[2]). The CEIE, on the other hand, has been actively involved in the formulation of national strategies on the internationalisation of the Portuguese economy, and is responsible for monitoring the execution of the recently launched 2030 Economic Internationalisation Programme.

Institutional silos are less prominent in the management of the EU Structural and Investment Funds, which require a higher degree of collaboration between ministries, agencies, national and subnational operational bodies for their disbursement and allocation towards policy priorities identified by the government. While political coordination is ensured by the CIC, coordination at the technical level is entrusted to AD&C, which cooperates with the managing authorities of the four thematic and seven regional operational programmes. AD&C ensures coordination by issuing technical guidance notes on the implementation of the EU funds, by participating in working groups dealing with policy design and implementation, and by leading or participating in functional networks in areas such as the Portugal 2020 incentive schemes, regional dynamics, smart specialisation and science, technology and innovation support, where various agencies share their experiences and ensure operational alignment.

Overall, Portugal appears to lack an overarching high-level coordination body with a broad remit to ensure cross-ministerial planning and decision-making across the FDI, SME, innovation and broader economic and regional development policy agendas. While policy silos are common in many countries, the rise of multi-dimensional issues which require whole-of-government responses has led the Centres of Government to take a more active role in aligning multi-department workplans to government actions. In Latvia, for instance, a collegial advisory authority chaired by the Prime Minister was established in 2014 to facilitate planning and evaluation of the country's long-term development objectives, initiate structural reforms and ensure coherence of national and local government policy (OECD, 2019[22]). This was complemented by a Cross-sectoral Coordination Centre that reports directly to the Prime Minister and aims to foster collaboration and joint actions between ministries. Portugal could consider strengthening the role that the Centre of Government plays in coordinating multi-dimensional issues throughout the policy cycle, including across FDI-SME diffusion policy areas.

The implementation of national strategies and action plans is often driven by EU programming and funding conditionalities

National strategies and action plans can be important instruments for policy coordination as they are cross-cutting in nature and often require whole-of-government responses to ensure their effective implementation. Portugal has adopted a number of strategic documents to articulate priorities in FDI-SME diffusion policy areas (Table 4.3). For instance, the Technological and Business Innovation Strategy sets out national priorities for the consolidation of the Portuguese research and innovation ecosystem, while the Action Plan for the Digital Transition involves several Ministries and agencies in the implementation of targeted measures to improve digital skills and promote the digitalisation of SMEs (Government of Portugal, 2018[23]). A national Economic Internationalisation Programme (*Programa Internacionalizar 2030*) was also launched in 2020, outlining areas where inter-institutional action is needed to increase FDI flows to Portugal and enable more Portuguese companies to export and invest abroad.

Although Portugal does not have a dedicated SME strategy, workstreams targeting SMEs have been integrated into several national strategies and action plans, making SME policymaking a cross-cutting issue that brings together various Ministries and implementing agencies (OECD, 2021[24]). This is a common practice in EU and OECD countries. SME policy considerations are increasingly mainstreamed in other policy agendas and are often combined with place-based or sector-wide approaches. The national internationalisation strategies of Norway, Spain, Slovenia and the UK include specific measures aimed at encouraging SMEs to consider exporting, while the Czech Republic's National Research, Development and Innovation Policy Strategy (2016-20) foresees new services to help SMEs become more involved in R&D (OECD, 2019[25]).

The establishment of government task forces to coordinate the implementation of national strategies and ensure inter-institutional collaboration is also common in Portugal. Startup Portugal, a public-private entity in which IAPMEI and ANI participate as partners, was established to coordinate the implementation of the National Strategy for Entrepreneurship. Another example is the Digital Transition Action Plan, whose implementation is coordinated by the Digital Portugal Task Force, while the Capitalise programme, which aims to improve access to finance conditions for Portuguese SMEs, is managed by the Task Force for the Capitalisation of Companies (EMCE).

Table 4.3. National strategic frameworks in Portugal

Strategic frameworks	Timeframe	Description	Responsible organisations
Portugal 2020	2014-2024	Strategic framework for the implementation of the 2014-20 European Structural and Investment Funds, focusing on competitiveness and internationalisation through i) increased technology and knowledge intensity, ii) enhanced export-orientation of Portuguese companies; iii) SMEs pursuing more advanced business strategies; iv) improved financing conditions to the economy.	AD&C
Technological and Business Innovation Strategy	2018-30	Main reference for innovation policy. Promote innovation-focused growth and investment, and the improvement of employment, income and quality of life of all Portuguese. Among other targets, the strategy aims to strengthen the attraction of innovation-oriented FDI.	ANI
National Strategy for Entrepreneurship	Since 2016	National Strategy for Entrepreneurship built around three pillars: i) ecosystem (e.g. accelerators, incubators), ii) funding (equity funding, alternative sources) and iii) internationalisation (e.g. attract foreign start-ups, investors, incubators etc.).	Startup Portugal
Action Plan for the Digital Transition	Since 2020	Support the digital transformation of businesses, with focus on AI, 5G, cloud, and the Internet of things. Includes an e-Residency Programme, Technological Free Zones (e.g. special regulatory regimes), a Digital Qualification Program for SMEs in the Countryside and the creation of Digital Innovation Hubs for Entrepreneurship.	Digital Portugal Task Force
Industry 4.0 National Strategy	Since 2017	Accelerate technology adoption by Portuguese businesses, create a favourable context for the development of i4.0 start-ups, and make Portugal an attractive location to invest in Industry 4.0.	Ministry of Economy and Digital Transition; IAPMEI
2030 Economic Internationalisation Programme	2020-30	Sets the priorities for the Portuguese economy's internationalisation, attraction of FDI, and the strengthening of Portuguese direct investments abroad	Ministry of Foreign Affairs; AICEP
National and Regional Smart Specialisation Strategies	2014-20	Improve the performance of the national and regional innovation systems and the competitiveness and internationalisation of the economy, supported by its competitive and comparative advantages and local capabilities and competences.	Ministry of Economy and Digital Transition; Ministry of Science, Technology and Higher Education; Ministry of Planning; Ministry of Territorial Cohesion; CCDRs
Portugal 2030 Strategy	2020-30 (ongoing)	Four pillars: i) promote a more inclusive society, while also responding to the challenges of demographic transition and ageing; ii) address the skills and competitiveness bottlenecks; iii) promote climate transition and the sustainability and efficient use of resources; and iv) boost territorial cohesion and reduce regional disparities while promoting ecological and digital transitions.	AD&C
Recovery and Resilience Plan	2020-30 (ongoing)	Strategy for the implementation of the EU Recovery and Resilience Facility, focusing on the green and digital transformation of the economy.	Recover Portugal Task Force, AD&C, Ministry of Finance/GPEARI

Source: Compiled based on (EC/OECD, 2021[26]); (Startup Portugal, 2021[27]); (EC, 2021[28]) and national documentation.

A key finding from both survey data and in-person meetings with Portuguese officials is that Portugal's national strategy setting and priorities for several key policy areas have been driven by the conditionality associated with obtaining external funding sources, namely EU funds. The Portugal 2020 Partnership Agreement between the Government of Portugal and the European Commission, which was adopted in 2014, outlines the national policy priorities across key thematic domains, including competitiveness and internationalisation, employment, human capital and sustainability, and how they can contribute to regional, urban and rural development

The implementation of Portugal 2020 relies upon both horizontal coordination between different ministries, agencies and thematic Operational Programmes; as well as vertical coordination between AD&C, the CCDRs and seven regional Operational Programmes, one for each NUTS 2 region. The most important strategic documents guiding the allocation of the EU funds in policy areas related to FDI-SME diffusion are the national and regional Smart Specialisation Strategies, which are a prerequisite for Portugal to access EU funding. The alignment with these strategies is mandatory in the implementation of Portugal 2020 investments in research and innovation and is a priority in other areas, such as the support to SME competitiveness. A comprehensive framework for inter-institutional coordination has been also set out in Portugal's 2020-2030 Recovery and Resilience Plan, which lays out the country's national priorities for the use of the Next Generation EU fund, the EU's landmark financial instrument for recovery from the Covid-19 pandemic. The governance model of the strategy includes the establishment of an inter-ministerial commission and a national monitoring committee while technical coordination is ensured by the Recover Portugal Task Force, AD&C and the Office for Economic Policy and International Affairs (GPEARI) of the Ministry of Finance. The policy priorities and measures set out in the Portugal 2030 Strategy will be mainly supported by the EU funds.

As Portugal enters a new policy cycle, the large number of thematic and cross-cutting national strategies and actions plans means that FDI-SME diffusion policy objectives are addressed across several strategic documents. This increases the risk of policy overlaps and contradictions and could lead to ambiguity about the pursued policy objectives and the responsibilities of various institutions. Their implementation will therefore require increased attention on the issues of policy alignment and coordination as well as the use of robust monitoring tools to identify policy inefficiencies and take corrective action.

Inter-agency policy coordination takes place through both formal and informal channels

At the agency level, inter-institutional coordination is frequent, although the extent of it varies from one agency to another. Horizontal coordination mechanisms are primarily formalised by laws and regulations, which often describe the role and responsibilities of each institution, their internal management processes, and the policy areas where inter-institutional collaboration is required (Figure 4.4). For instance, the 2012 Law, which approved AICEP's latest by-laws (amended in 2015 and 2020 but still in force) requires that AICEP collaborates with IAPMEI and the national tourism authority, *Turismo de Portugal*, to support the internationalisation of Portuguese firms and the promotion of their brands abroad. Similarly, the participation of FCT and IAPMEI in the joint board overseeing ANI under a "hybrid" governance structure entrenched in legislation aims to remove policy silos in the areas of innovation and entrepreneurship and allow for some coordination between the Ministry of Science, Technology and Higher Education and the Ministry of Economy and Digital Transition.

Joint programming, whether for entire workstreams or targeted actions, is also used to foster greater collaboration between Portuguese implementing agencies. For instance, coordination on SME and entrepreneurship policy issues takes place across the board between AICEP, IAPMEI and ANI, with AICEP focusing on projects strengthening the internationalisation of Portuguese companies, and IAPMEI and ANI on their innovation and technological capabilities. For joint programming to work a clear distribution of roles and responsibilities, shared monitoring tools and a code of conduct are often needed to ensure the effective implementation of joint actions. Findings from the OECD-IDB survey confirm the large number of formal and informal relationships that public agencies develop with their broader institutional framework. 74% of IPAs' strategic relationships in the OECD area are relationships with public and semi-public institutions (OECD, 2018[7]).

Figure 4.4. Policy coordination in Portugal by policy domain and type of coordination instrument

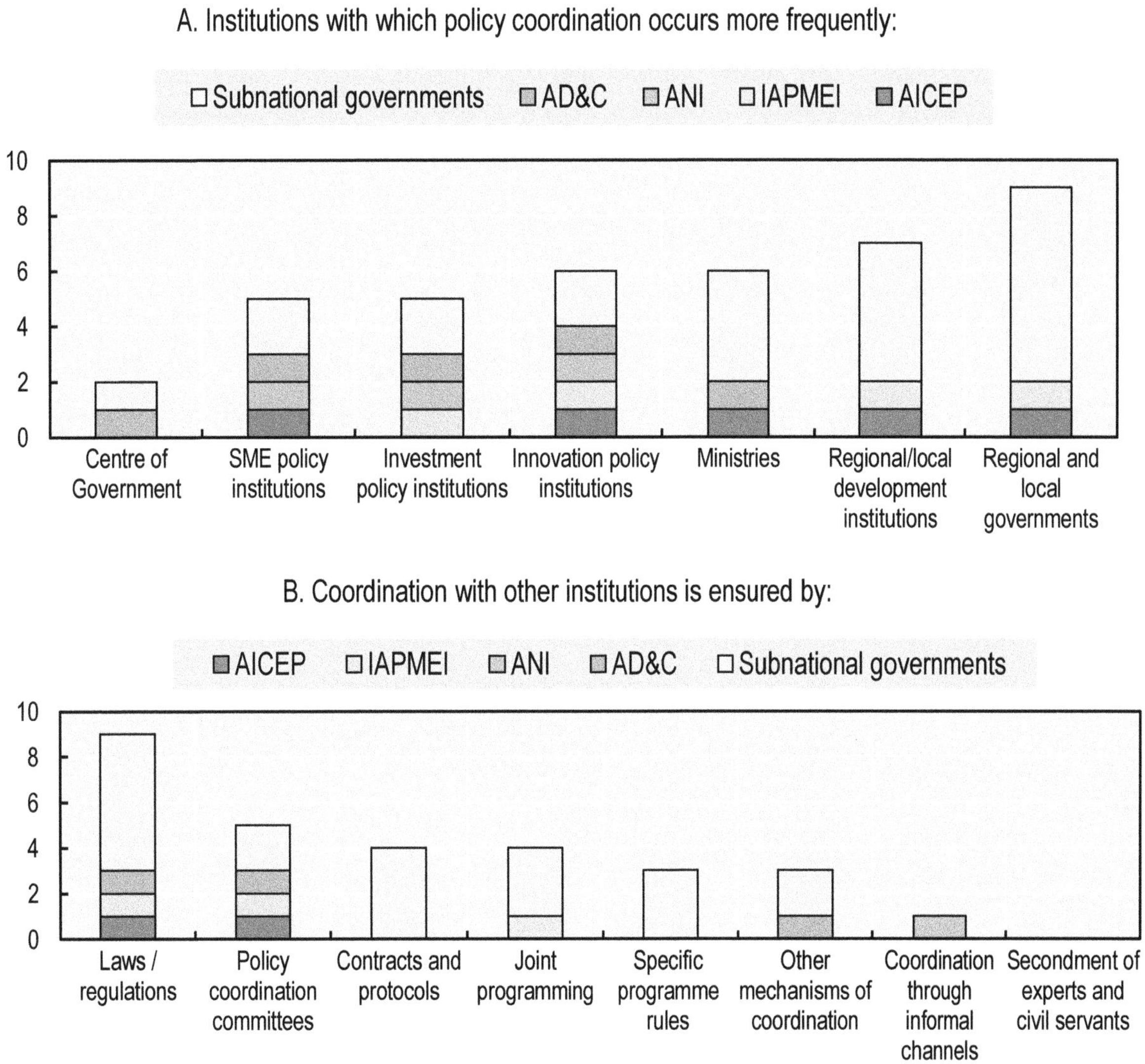

Note: The following national and subnational institutions are included in this figure: AICEP, IAPMEI, ANI, AD&C, CCDR Norte, CCDR Alentejo, Porto Metropolitan Area, CIM Alentejo Litoral, CIM Central Alentejo, CIM Alto Minho, CIM Cavado, CIM Alto Alentejo.
Source: EU/OECD Survey on Policies enabling FDI spillovers to domestic SMEs (2021).

Inter-institutional committees have been also set up for the implementation of specific policy workstreams that require a whole-of-government approach. Inter-agency coordination on investment matters takes place through the Permanent Commission for Investor Support (*Comissão Permanente de Apoio ao Investidor, CPAI*), which is managed by AICEP and gathers representatives from different public institutions, including IAPMEI, Turismo de Portugal, the Portuguese Environment Agency, the Tax and Customs Authority, the Ministry of Economy and Digital Transition and the CCDRs. The CPAI is responsible for ensuring a close follow-up of investment projects of potential national interest by monitoring administrative procedures applicable to the issuance of licenses, permits and other approvals, thus ensuring faster responses.

Many FDI-SME diffusion policies (52%) involve an element of collaboration in their formulation and implementation (Figure 4.5). This includes initiatives and programmes that are designed and implemented jointly by multiple agencies or strategies and action plans that require a whole-of-government approach to be executed. Among the institutions that are most cited in the implementation of joint programmes, the main implementing agencies (AICEP, IAPMEI, ANI), the Ministry of Economy and Digital Transition and the Ministry of Foreign Affairs stand out given the crucial role they play in supporting FDI and SME policies. The Operational Programme for Competitiveness and Internationalisation (COMPETE 2020) as well as the Regional Operational Programmes of the EU Structural and Investment Funds are also involved in many policy initiatives that are funded through the Portugal 2020 Partnership Agreement.

Figure 4.5. Collaborative policy design and implementation in Portugal

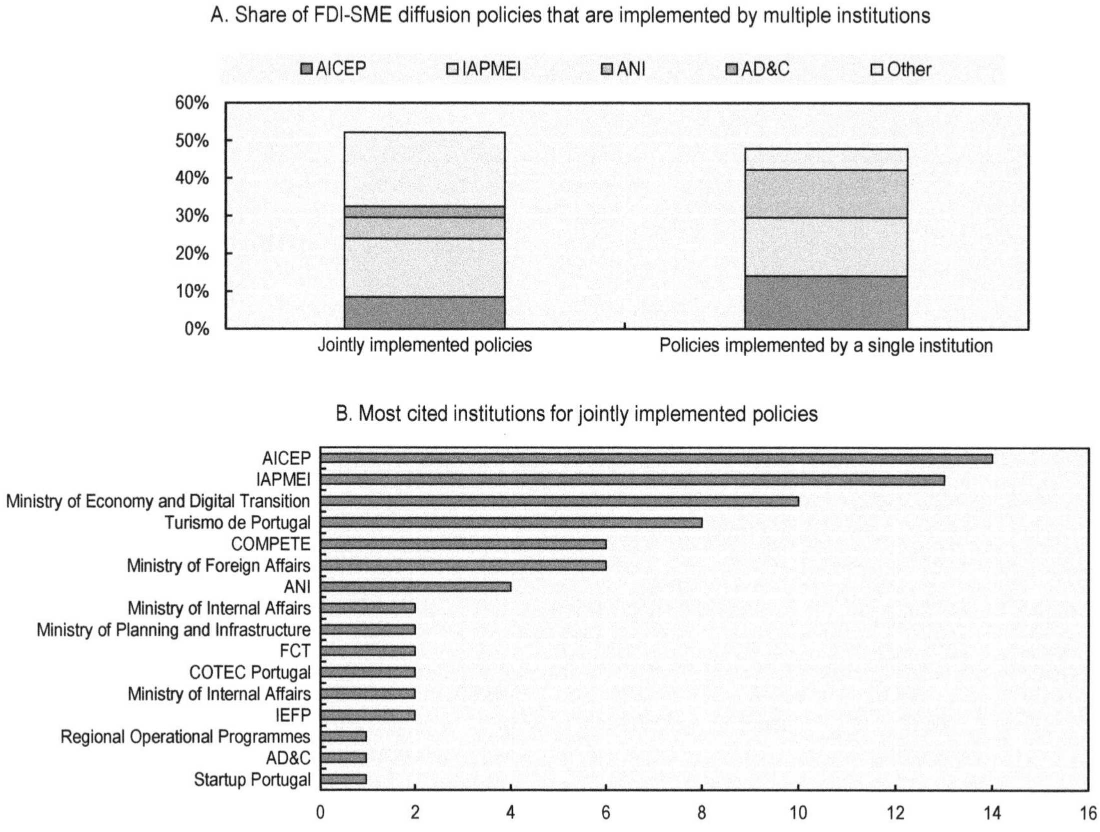

Source: EU/OECD Survey on Policies enabling FDI spillovers to domestic SMEs (2021).

At the subnational level, coordination can take various forms and involve both formal and informal channels of communication. AICEP collaborates with regional IPAs such as Invest Lisbon, Invest Porto and Invest Braga, to accompany investors on the ground and provide aftercare services. The value that these collaborations bring to investor support services can however be limited due to the competition arising among subnational IPAs in attracting FDI projects to their regions. Regarding the role of regional and local governments, Portugal's regional administrative authorities (CCDRs) do not have competences for attracting investment, and therefore any collaboration with them is limited to the provision of SME support services. In contrast, policy coordination between AICEP, inter-municipal councils (CIMs) and municipalities is more frequent, although this is done informally and on a case-by-case basis. Interviews conducted among agency staff tend to show that in most cases CIMs and municipalities know better the local context but do not have experience dealing with foreign investors. Portugal could consider further strengthening the mandate and capacities of the CIMs in order to enable them to be more involved in investment promotion in collaboration with AICEP.

Contractual partnership agreements are also used at the agency level to put forward joint policy actions. For instance, AICEP has signed cooperation protocols with the Azores Business Development Society (*Sociedade para o Desenvolvimento Empresarial dos Açores, SDEA*), which is responsible for supporting business development and attracting foreign investment in the autonomous region of Azores. The protocols have fostered collaboration between the two entities on issues relating to the internationalisation of Azorean companies, and facilitated the inclusion of Azores in AICEP's site selection platform, which helps investors identify the best location within Portugal to set up their business.

4.4. Evaluation of policy impact and engagement with stakeholders

Policy learning and adaptation are hindered by limited evaluation capacities at the agency level

Policy evaluation aims to inform about the appropriateness and effectiveness of public policy interventions. Evaluations take place at different stages of the policy cycle (ex ante, mid-term, ex post); target specific projects, organisations, programmes, policies or the overall policy system; are implemented as part of a contract or enforced by law; are process- or impact-oriented; and serve learning or accountability purposes. Assessment methods and criteria vary accordingly. A comprehensive monitoring and evaluation (M&E) framework for assessing FDI-SME diffusion policies could play a crucial role as an "early warning mechanism" to identify potential system failures and take corrective action.

In Portugal, the use of comprehensive M&E frameworks is limited to government institutions involved in the implementation of policies supported by the EU Structural and Investment Funds. With the exception of AD&C and the managing authorities of the operational programmes of the EU funds, none of the other implementing agencies, whose role is crucial in enabling FDI-SME diffusion, have a dedicated unit or internal capacity to systematically evaluate the impact of their policy initiatives. The OECD/EC survey findings show that only half of the FDI-SME diffusion policies implemented in Portugal have been evaluated, of which 68% are policies implemented under the EU-funded Portugal 2020 Partnership Agreement (Figure 4.6).

Although Portugal 2020 incentive schemes are managed by various government agencies (including AICEP, IAPMEI and ANI), their evaluations are coordinated by AD&C and the managing authorities of the EU-funded operational programmes. A set of programme, financial and operational indicators is used to assess progress on the execution of Portugal 2020 actions and measure their impact on beneficiaries. A Monitoring and Evaluation Network (*Rede M&A*) has been also established between the technical coordination bodies of the EU Structural and Investment Funds and the management authorities of the operational programmes. The network promotes M&E activities and the exchange of good practices among members. Practically, it prepares an evaluation plan for review by the Inter-ministerial Coordination Commission (CIC), creates instruments to monitor the implementation of recommendations, and ensures organisational learning and training on M&E practices.

Figure 4.6. Share of FDI-SME diffusion policies that have been evaluated in Portugal

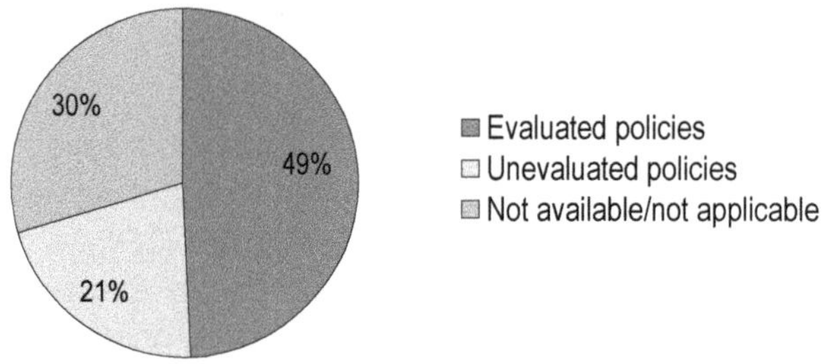

Source: EU/OECD Survey on Policies enabling FDI spillovers to domestic SMEs (2021).

The evaluation of policies that are not backed by EU funding instruments is less systematic and does not allow for strategic foresight and planning. The main criticism relates to the skills and internal capacities of implementing agencies and to the scope of evaluations, which is often procedural and centred on implementation issues rather than on results and impact (OECD, 2019[2]). This is in line with evidence from other government institutions in EU Member States that implement policies linked to the EU's smart specialisation strategy. In a 2020 survey conducted by the EU's Joint Research Centre (JRC), half of the national and regional implementing authorities considered their capacity to collect and analyse data inadequate, with potential negative consequences on the process of policy learning and adaptation (Hegyi et al., 2021[29]).

The M&E capacities of the main Portuguese implementing agencies vary. AICEP does not have a dedicated evaluation unit and relies on ad hoc meetings and consultations with its clients and other stakeholders to collect feedback after a project is implemented. Although stakeholder consultations can be more or less formal, frequent and standardised, they are a common evaluation instrument that IPAs use to assess their performance and impact in attracting inward FDI. Recent OECD findings show that OECD IPAs favour qualitative evaluation methodologies – such as benchmark comparisons (78% of IPAs), client surveys (75%), and stakeholder consultations (69%) – over quantitative ones (e.g. quality control assessments, cost benefit analyses, and econometric assessments) (OECD, 2018[7]). The main challenge that AICEP and other OECD IPAs have to overcome is the partial information and incomplete or ambiguous results that qualitative evaluations often provide. Qualitative tools should ideally be complemented by more quantitative and systematic approaches, whenever possible.

A similar picture emerges when looking at the M&E capacities of IAPMEI. Monitoring frameworks and requirements for frequent policy evaluations have been introduced in the implementation cycle of recent policy initiatives. For instance, two annual monitoring exercises have been conducted for IAPMEI's sectoral clustering programme (the 2017 Competitiveness Clusters initiative) while a triennial evaluation is currently underway to assess the performance of clusters. A monitoring committee has been also established to collect information on the implementation of the Startup Visa programme, which allows entrepreneurs from outside the EU to set up their startup in Portugal.

ANI has a dedicated innovation policy monitoring unit, which compiles and makes available indicators to measure Portugal's innovation performance. Granular data are also collected on the implementation of several innovation support programmes in which ANI is involved. However, fewer resources are dedicated to the evaluation of policy impact. The SIFIDE R&D tax incentive scheme is the only policy instrument under ANI's remit for which a comprehensive evaluation exercise has been carried out so far (Government of Portugal, 2019[30]). This became possible with the establishment of an external Working Group of experts, which carried out a systematic survey of tax incentive schemes in Portugal and developed an impact assessment methodology for future evaluations of tax incentive schemes.

Although the practice of policy impact assessments is rather limited, the evaluation of overall institutional performance is more systematised. Since 2007, all Portuguese public institutions are obliged to use the Evaluation and Accountability Framework (QUAR), which is the public administration's main management tool to evaluate the performance of public bodies and to raise the accountability of their top managers. The framework looks at the institution's mission, strategic and operational objectives, performance indicators, as well as at how human and financial resources are allocated to the pursuit of their objectives. The annual QUAR assessment can influence the budget allocated or the policy priorities pursued. For instance, consecutive insufficient performance can lead to services being discontinued and priorities adjusted. However, these evaluation exercises do not assess the impact and effectiveness of specific policy interventions.

Overall, Portugal could benefit from the establishment of a comprehensive horizontal M&E framework that covers all major policy fields and goes beyond satisfying the monitoring requirements of the EU Structural and Investment Funds. This would involve mapping various sources of indicators and placing emphasis on measuring results and impacts rather than implementation issues. The recently launched Action Plan for the Digital transition includes a comprehensive M&E framework, which relies upon approximately 100 indicators from various sources including the EU's Digital Economy and Society Index (DESI). In the selection of monitoring tools priority was given to indicators covering areas where Portugal's performance gap is wider compared to other EU countries (Government of Portugal, 2020[31]). Efforts to identify appropriate monitoring frameworks and systematically collect and analyse data in other policy areas should continue.

Apart from the use of quantifiable outcome-based performance indicators, reliable evaluations of individual policy actions will require strong internal capacity to plan, prepare and execute ex ante and ex post evaluations. The experience that AD&C has acquired through the management of EU funds could help draw lessons on good practices and how they could be adopted by other policy delivery actors. Setting up dedicated evaluation units within each implementing agency and involving specialised staff with technical knowledge of M&E principles and implementation tools could also strengthen internal competences and improve the effectiveness of their programmes. Capacities for analysis could be supported through the provision of specialised training to raise education and awareness of public servants on the process of monitoring and evaluating policy impacts

Deliberative processes for the implementation of new policy workstreams have improved but efforts for greater stakeholder engagement should continue

Active engagement and consultation with foreign investors and local SMEs is necessary for the implementation of effective FDI-SME diffusion policies. Through their interactions with the private sector, public bodies are able to understand the challenges and expectations of foreign and domestic firms, receive feedback on the relevance of their policy programmes, and enrich policy-making processes with insights from various stakeholders. Mechanisms for regular public-private dialogue within specific sectors and supply chains are often combined with bottom-up communication processes to ensure that local level market needs and perspectives are fed into higher level policy processes.

Although public consultations are not conducted in a systematic manner by all government institutions, Portugal has recently made significant progress in the use of deliberative processes to receive feedback on prospective laws, decrees and other regulatory initiatives. In 2019, the government launched the CONSULTALEX Portal, which allows citizens and companies to participate in the legislative and regulatory procedures by consulting the draft version of laws and submitting their comments and suggestions through an online interface.

Several public consultations have been organised since 2018 on the government's strategic action plans and multi-annual work programmes for the next EU programming period (2021-27). Thematic debates took place in 2018 to inform the National Investment Programme 2030, which lays out the priorities on infrastructure investment for the next decade. In the case of the 2030 Economic Internationalisation programme, the consultation of the private sector took place in a more structured way through the CEIE. Similarly, online public consultations and stakeholder meetings were organised for the formulation of the Portugal 2030 Strategy (*Estratégia Portugal 2030*) and the 2020-2030 Recovery and Resilience Plan (*Plano de Recuperação e Resiliência*), which have both been presented to the European Commission to secure EU funding.

At the agency level, engaging with business stakeholders takes place through formal and informal channels. AICEP and ANI have advisory bodies that allow for a regular consultation of relevant communities on regulatory changes and policy programmes. AICEP's Advisory Council for Investment and Foreign Trade (*Conselho Consultivo para o Investimento e Comércio Externo*) is composed of representatives of leading investment companies and companies with significant international activities, whose role is to advise the agency on activities and programmes that contribute to strengthening Portugal's attractiveness to foreign investment. Similarly, ANI's Advisory Council is composed of independent personalities coming from the scientific and business communities, who meet at least twice a year and have the right to issue non-binding opinions on the agency's annual activity plans and reports.

Box 4.2. Policy dialogue and national strategy setting: the case of Lithuania

The government of Lithuania has engaged in an in-depth process to define its national strategy "Lithuania 2030". The State Progress Council, led by the centre of government, was responsible for the drafting process of the strategy: government authorities, business leaders, community groups and prominent public figures participated in its development.

Three working groups were set up on smart economy, smart governance and smart society. The consultation involved the national level and Lithuanians living abroad. The council also went on a road trip to discuss with mayors, municipality representatives, young people and non-governmental organisations. Innovative approaches were developed to involve harder to reach groups. Since the elderly were seen not to believe in the strategy, the council reached out to school children, who were trained to interact with the elderly. The outcome is a national strategy which is guiding the policies of the whole country and whose implementation is monitored in an inclusive process.

Source: (OECD, 2015[32])

Less systematic engagement with targeted audiences takes place through the organisation of stakeholder events, where sectoral representatives are invited, or through the organisation of ad hoc public consultations on specific workstreams. IAPMEI launched a public consultation on the simplification of the Portuguese Incentives System in 2019 in order to identify potential challenges that companies face in accessing and using financial incentive schemes. The consultation consisted of addressing a questionnaire to relevant companies and organising thematic focus groups with entrepreneurs to discuss concrete measures. The CEIE, in collaboration with AICEP, also launched a survey addressed to business stakeholders to identify barriers to the internationalisation of Portuguese companies.

Despite improvements in deliberative processes in recent years, the Portuguese government could consider re-activating the advisory role of high-level ministerial bodies, such as the CNEI, CNCT, and CEIE, and strengthening their capacity to convene stakeholders and provide input to strategy development and policymaking. Beyond their coordinating role, their mandate could be broadened to include the systematic issuing of non-binding opinions on policy initiatives that the relevant ministries bring forward, the review of consultation reports, and the outlining of proposals and options for consideration by the government.

A public dialogue culture could be also mainstreamed into the Portuguese public administration through the establishment of a comprehensive horizontal framework that would make stakeholder engagement processes part of the policy cycle across all tiers of government. In this framework, the CONSULTALEX Portal could be further consolidated as the main public online tool for citizen consultation by broadening its scope to also include strategic priority documents, action plans and multi-annual work programmes alongside laws and regulations.

References

AD&C (2019), *Evaluation of the implementation of the Incentive Schemes (IS) of the PT2020*, https://www.adcoesao.pt/sites/default/files/av_operacionalizacao_si_sex_en.pdf. [8]

Crescenzi, R., M. Di Cataldo and M. Giua (2019), *FDI inflows in Europe: does investment promotion work?*, http://www.lse.ac.uk/iga/assets/documents/research-and-publications/FDI-inflows-in-Europe-does-investment-promotion-work.pdf. [5]

EC (2021), *"President Ursula von der Leyen welcomes the first official submission of a recovery and resilience plan by Portugal"*, https://ec.europa.eu/commission/presscorner/detail/en/ip_21_1869. [28]

EC/OECD (2021), *STI Policy Compass*, https://stip.oecd.org/stip.html. [26]

Government of Portugal (2020), *Action Plan for the Digital Transition (Plano de Ação para a Transição Digital)*, https://dre.pt/application/conteudo/132133788. [31]

Government of Portugal (2019), *Os Benefícios Fiscais em Portugal: Conceitos, metodologia, e prática, Grupo de Trabalho para o Estudo dos*, https://www.portugal.gov.pt/download-ficheiros/ficheiro.aspx?v=%3d%3dBAAAAB%2bLCAAAAAAABACzMDQwAgCG5%2bMmBAAAAA%3d%3d. [30]

Government of Portugal (2018), *Technological and Business Innovation Strategy for Portugal 2018-2030*, https://dre.pt/home/-/dre/114832287/details/maximized. [23]

Government of Portugal (2014), *Decree-Law n.º 11/2014 of 22 January*, https://dre.pt/application/conteudo/571030. [1]

Government of Portugal (2014), *Decree-Law No. 137/2014*, Official Journal, https://dre.pt/web/guest/legislacao-consolidada/-/lc/123915613/201912081649/73740716/diploma/indice. [16]

Government of Portugal (2014), *Estratégia de Investigação e Inovação para uma Especialização Inteligente (EI&I)*, https://www.compete2020.gov.pt/admin/images/RIS3_Nacional_ENEI_Especializacao-Inteligente.pdf. [14]

Government of Portugal (2012), *Resolution of the Council of Ministers n.º 45/2012*, https://dre.pt/application/file/553320. [13]

Government of Portugal (2011), *Council of Ministers no. 44/2011*, https://dre.pt/web/guest/pesquisa/-/search/146923/details/normal?l=1. [15]

Government of Portugal (2011), *Decree-Law n.º 121/2011 of 29 December*, https://www.portaldiplomatico.mne.gov.pt/images/LeiOrganicaMNE.pdf. [3]

Hayward, J. and V. Wright (2002), *Governing from the Centre: Core Executive Coordination in France*, Oxford University Press. [21]

Hegyi, F. et al. (2021), *The Smart Specialisation Policy Experience: Perspective of National and Regional Authorities*, Publications Office of the European Union, Luxembourg, http://dx.doi.org/doi: 10.2760/554632. [29]

Metcalfe, L. (1994), "International Policy Co-ordination and Public Management Reform", *International Review of Administrative Sciences*, Vol. 60/2, pp. 271–290, https://doi.org/10.1177/002085239406000208. [20]

OECD (2021), *Stocktake of existing SME policy frameworks in OECD countries. An OECD Strategy for SMEs.* [24]

OECD (2020), *Decentralisation and Regionalisation in Portugal: What Reform Scenarios?*, OECD Multi-level Governance Studies, OECD Publishing, Paris, https://dx.doi.org/10.1787/fea62108-en. [4]

OECD (2019), *"Business Development Services for SME Productivity Growth – International Experience and Implications for Local Economic Policy ", report to the OECD Co-operative Action Programme on Local Economic and Employment Development.* [6]

OECD (2019), *Latvia - Good institutional practices in promoting policy coherence for sustainable development*, https://www.oecd.org/governance/pcsd/toolkit/goodpractices/. [22]

OECD (2019), *Making Decentralisation Work: A Handbook for Policy-Makers*, OECD Multi-level Governance Studies, OECD Publishing, Paris, https://dx.doi.org/10.1787/g2g9faa7-en. [10]

OECD (2019), *OECD Regional Outlook 2019: Leveraging Megatrends for Cities and Rural Areas*, https://oe.cd/pub/2vq. [11]

OECD (2019), *OECD Review of Higher Education, Research and Innovation: Portugal*, OECD Publishing, Paris, https://dx.doi.org/10.1787/9789264308138-en. [2]

OECD (2019), *OECD SME and Entrepreneurship Outlook 2019*, OECD Publishing, Paris, https://dx.doi.org/10.1787/34907e9c-en. [25]

OECD (2019), *World Observatory of Subnational Government Finance and Investment - Portugal*, https://www.sng-wofi.org/country-profiles/Fiche%20PORTUGAL.pdf. [12]

OECD (2018), *Mapping of Investment Promotion Agencies in OECD Countries*, http://www.oecd.org/investment/Mapping-of-Investment-Promotion-Agencies-in-OECD-Countries.pdf. [7]

OECD (2015), *Lithuania: Fostering Open and Inclusive Policy Making*, OECD Public Governance Reviews, OECD Publishing, Paris, https://dx.doi.org/10.1787/9789264235762-en. [32]

OECD (2012), *STI governance structures and arrangements*, OECD Publishing, Paris, https://doi.org/10.1787/sti_outlook-2012-9-en. [19]

Peters, G. (2018), "The challenge of policy coordination", *Policy Design and Practice*, Vol. 1/1, pp. 1-11, http://dx.doi.org/DOI: 10.1080/25741292.2018.1437946. [18]

Riccardo Crescenzi, M. (2019), *FDI inflows in Europe: does investment promotion work?.* [9]

Scharpf, F. (1994), “Games Real Actors Could Play: Positive and Negative Coordination in Embedded Negotiations”, *Journal of Theoretical Politics*, Vol. 6/1, pp. 27-53, https://doi.org/10.1177/0951692894006001002. [17]

Startup Portugal (2021), *Web site*, https://startupportugal.com/. [27]

Notes

[1] The promotion and funding of academic research is under the responsibility of the Foundation for Science and Technology (*Fundação para a Ciência e a Tecnologia, FCT*).

[2] Nomenclature of Territorial Units for Statistics.

5 The policy mix for FDI diffusion on Portuguese SMEs

This chapter reviews the mix of policies in place for fostering FDI spillovers on the productivity and innovation of Portuguese SMEs. It identifies the FDI-SME diffusion channels and enabling factors that are effectively supported by Portugal's policy framework, and the policy instruments used to promote FDI-SME linkages, noting areas for further policy development or a shift in the policy mix. It also conducts an assessment of various aspects of regulation impacting the diffusion of knowledge from foreign to domestic firms, focusing on investment and trade openness, competition and labour market regulations.

5.1. Summary of findings and recommendations

The quality of the legal and regulatory environment can determine whether a country can attract productivity-enhancing and innovation-oriented FDI, and whether spillovers on domestic SMEs can occur. A number of more targeted policies at the intersection of investment, SME and entrepreneurship, innovation and regional development areas can also further boost FDI-driven knowledge diffusion and its impact on domestic economies. These laws, regulations and policy initiatives cannot be considered in silos but in the framework of an adequate and coherent policy mix. The main challenge for governments is ensuring that the policy mix is aligned with the country's economic structure, policy priorities, and economic geography.

This chapter reviews the policy mix for FDI spillovers on Portuguese SMEs and identifies areas in which it can be strengthened (Table 5.1). Based on an assessment of 72 policy initiatives, it identifies the main FDI-SME diffusion channels and enabling factors that are supported by Portugal's policy framework, and draws comparisons with and examples from other EU countries, in particular Ireland and Lithuania, which offer significant opportunities for mutual learning. These comparisons are complemented with a discussion on Portugal's strategic policy priority to support the internationalisation of SMEs and use FDI as an important channel for improving the productivity and innovation of the domestic economy.

Table 5.1. Findings and recommendations on Portugal's policy mix for FDI-SME diffusion

Findings	Recommendations
Enabling conditions for FDI diffusion on Portuguese SMEs	
Portugal has one of the most open FDI market access regimes in the OECD area. FDI promotion policies exhibit a consistent targeting of innovative and knowledge-intensive activities and include mainly regulatory and financial incentives.	Avoid potential inconsistencies and redundancies arising from operating too many regulatory incentives at too small a scale.
	Structure FDI promotion policies into clearly articulated support packages that are sufficiently differentiated to target different types of FDI (e.g. large investors, start-ups, R&D, etc.)
Public financial support to R&D and business innovation is above the OECD average and on par with top innovators such as the USA and Canada.	Re-balance the policy mix towards skills upgrading programmes that could help SMEs access qualified human capital.
A large number of publicly supported credit lines and co-investment programmes are in place to facilitate SME access to finance. However, inefficiencies in the judicial system, deficiencies in collateral and bankruptcy laws and the balance sheet constraints of Portuguese banks create tight SME lending conditions.	Address the vulnerabilities of the banking sector in order to free up capital for new lending to SMEs.
	Remove bottlenecks in judicial efficiency so that banks can enforce collateral without going through long court proceedings.
	Leverage the new National Promotional Bank to promote access to equity capital and alternative financing instruments for SMEs.
The availability and quality of the knowledge transfer infrastructure has improved (e.g. Collaborative Laboratories), however regional disparities are observed in SME support services.	Expand the presence of knowledge transfer organisations to less developed regions, and ensure that they have adequate financial and human resources to implement SME support activities.
FDI-SME diffusion channels	
Portugal has a comprehensive set of policies (e.g. Suppliers Clubs, matchmaking platforms, collaborative R&D incentives, Internationalisation Academy, etc.) to foster FDI-SME linkages and strategic partnerships.	Expand the Suppliers Clubs to additional sectors of strategic importance for the Portuguese economy. Assess whether SMEs continue to benefit from supply chain linkages with foreign affiliates after public support is phased out.
The scope of incentives for R&D collaborations is often limited to collaborations between domestic actors only.	Prioritise the selection of innovative foreign affiliates in the collaborative R&D incentive schemes administered by ANI.
Stringent employment protection regulations may hinder labour mobility from foreign to domestic firms in sectors and regions with low absorptive capacities.	Reform labour market rules to reduce hiring costs for SMEs and enable them to retain and attract highly skilled workers.
A limited number of targeted policies is in place to foster greater labour mobility from foreign MNEs to the domestic entrepreneurial ecosystem (e.g. *INOV Contacto, Tech Visa*).	Build on the success of the *INOV Contacto* programme and broaden the range of policies available to encourage labour mobility (e.g. corporate spin-outs, payroll tax incentives for highly skilled workers, employee exchange programmes, etc.).
Regulatory barriers to competition are on par with the OECD average. However, the competition channel may be hindered by barriers to entry and conduct restraints in professional services and retail trade.	Ease entry and conduct requirements for certain professional services and retail trade, to improve competition and ensure a level playing field for foreign and domestic firms.

5.2. Overall balance of the policy mix for FDI diffusion on domestic SMEs

Strengthening SME absorptive capacities and encouraging strategic partnerships appear to be the main objectives pursued by Portugal

In Portugal, FDI spillovers on domestic SMEs are supported by a variety of policy initiatives that are designed and implemented by government agencies, Ministry departments, inter-institutional committees and Task Forces responsible for the coordination of national strategies. The policy mix relies mostly on measures that aim to strengthen the broader enabling environment for FDI-SME diffusion rather than the direct channels through which productivity and innovation spillovers occur (Figure 5.1)[1]. More than 60% of the policy initiatives assessed for the purpose of this study target the absorptive capacity of local SMEs through measures that aim to upgrade entrepreneurial skills, support SME innovation and facilitate the acquisition of new technologies. A large number of policy initiatives (31%) also targets the attraction of FDI into productivity-enhancing and R&D-intensive activities, while a few initiatives (15%) are in place to promote agglomeration effects by exploiting the potential of spatial and network linkages as sources of productivity and innovation for Portuguese regions (i.e. economic geography factors).

Targeted public action is also undertaken to strengthen FDI-SME diffusion channels, although not all channels are supported to the same extent. Value chain linkages (26%) and strategic partnerships (36%) are supported through financial incentives for R&D and technology collaboration, matchmaking services bringing together foreign investors with Portuguese SMEs, as well as supplier development programmes aimed at supporting the internationalisation of small firms. In contrast, a small number of policy initiatives (14%) is in place to promote competition and knowledge exchange between foreign and domestic firms, and little is done to facilitate the mobility of skilled workers in the domestic labour market (3%).

Figure 5.1. Portuguese policies and the FDI-SME diffusion channels and factors they act upon

In % of policy initiatives

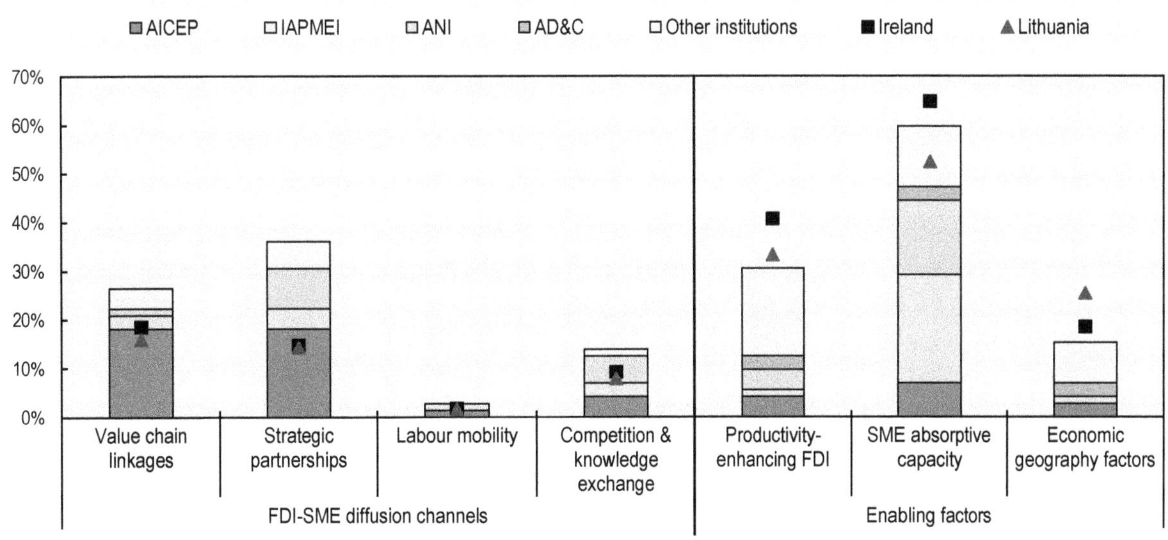

Source: EU/OECD Survey on Policies enabling FDI spillovers to domestic SMEs (2021).

Preliminary findings from the OECD/EU Survey on Policies enabling FDI-SME linkages and productivity and innovation spillovers to domestic SMEs show that Portugal's policy mix does not substantially diverge from other EU countries with similar economic and market conditions. Policies targeting SME absorptive capacities tend to dominate the policy mix of EU Member States, while the labour mobility and competition channels receive less attention from policymakers.

Nevertheless, the Portuguese policy mix does reflect differences in policy priorities and institutional arrangements. When compared to Ireland and Lithuania, two countries with open economies driven in large part by foreign investors and EU membership, Portugal appears to implement a wider range of policy initiatives to promote FDI-SME linkages and strategic partnerships. This can be partly due to AICEP's dual mandate to attract FDI and support the internationalisation of Portuguese firms, which allows for greater alignment of resources and synergies between the two very distinct work-streams – i.e. the aftercare services provided to foreign investors and the supplier development programmes targeting domestic firms. In fact, merging inward investment promotion and trade promotion into a single agency is a common practice among OECD governments, with 56% of OECD IPAs being responsible also for activities that support the internationalisation of their domestic economies (OECD, 2018[1]). IDA Ireland and Invest Lithuania, the Irish and Lithuanian investment promotion agency (IPA) respectively, are notable exceptions to this trend as they focus on investment promotion only.

Differences in the policy mix are also observed regarding productivity-enhancing FDI and the consideration of economic geography factors in policymaking. As outlined in the following sections, IDA Ireland promotes a more diverse range of policies than AICEP to attract and facilitate productivity-enhancing investment, including by targeting small multinationals and giving them access to SME support instruments implemented by Enterprise Ireland, the Irish SME agency. Regarding economic geography factors, Portugal has placed particular emphasis on attenuating regional disparities through targeted territorial enhancement measures, regional smart specialisation strategies, and action plans tailored to the economic and market specificities of less developed regions. Considerable policy attention has also gone into strengthening agglomeration economies through the recognition of industrial clusters and the provision of technical and financial support to promote the internationalisation of local entrepreneurial ecosystems.

Financial support schemes dominate the policy mix, followed by technical assistance, information and facilitation services

Policies that aim to strengthen FDI spillovers on SMEs can involve various types of support (e.g. financial support, regulatory incentives, technical assistance, facilitation services, governance frameworks), reflecting the plethora of strategic objectives they may seek to fulfil as well as the many pathways to achieving policy outcomes (Box 5.1). Achieving coherence and balance in the mix of policy instruments is an important goal.

The Portuguese government relies mainly on financial incentives and to a lesser extent on other measures to strengthen FDI spillovers on domestic firms (Figure 5.2). Significant variation is, however, observed in the type of support used to achieve different policy objectives (Figure 5.3). Whereas most of Portuguese policies supporting the absorptive capacity of domestic SMEs make use of financial instruments (e.g. grants for SME innovation, R&D tax credits), the attraction of knowledge-intensive FDI is pursued primarily through regulatory incentives (e.g. fast-track licensing regimes). Similarly, technical assistance, information and facilitation services are usually offered to promote value chain linkages and strategic partnerships. Many of these policies provide additional support for economic activities that involve business-to-business (B2B) and science-to-business (S2B) collaboration, reflecting the importance that the national policy system ascribes to the role of networks in creating, accessing and sharing new knowledge. Linked to the role of networks is the availability and efficiency of the country's knowledge transfer infrastructure (e.g. networking facilities, technology transfer offices, science and technology parks) which has been significantly improved to allow foreign affiliates, SMEs and domestic R&D institutions to collaborate on the development of new products and services.

Box 5.1. The policy mix for FDI-driven productivity and innovation diffusion on domestic SMEs: a typology of policy instruments

The policy mix concept refers to the set of policy rationales, arrangements and instruments implemented to deliver one or several policy goals, as well as the interactions that can possibly take place between these elements (Meissner and Kergroach, 2019[2]). Many of the policies that strengthen the diffusion of knowledge and technology from FDI to domestic SMEs are implemented by multiple institutions and belong to different policy domains (e.g. innovation, investment, entrepreneurship, science and technology, regional development). These "policy systems" can support the channels through which FDI spillovers occur (i.e. value chain relationships, labour mobility, competition and imitation) or the enabling factors that affect their magnitude (i.e. FDI characteristics, SME absorptive capacity, economic geography). A policy initiative can, however, act upon several channels and enabling factors and make use of various policy instruments, reflecting the plethora of policy goals it may seek to achieve as well as the many pathways to achieving productivity and innovation diffusion from foreign firms to local SMEs.

An analysis of the policy mix for FDI-SME diffusion goes beyond the characteristics of policy formulation and implementation, and focuses more on the areas where the different policy mix components are used in complementary and mutually reinforcing ways to achieve desired outcomes. It places emphasis on questions of completeness, balance and interaction among strategic objectives, policy goals, instruments, sectors and populations targeted, and institutional actors involved. Ideally, the policy mix will take into account interactions among these elements and ensure balanced support to enhance the contribution of FDI to the productivity and innovation of SMEs. Based on the type of instrument used, such policies can be classified into:

- *Governance frameworks,* such as national strategies and action plans that lay out policy priorities and define the framework within which policy action on FDI, SMEs and innovation is organised;
- *Regulatory standards and incentives*, which define the framework within which foreign and domestic firms operate and often use legal rules to encourage or discourage different types of business activities (e.g. lighter administrative and licensing regimes for certain types of investments, local content *requirements* for foreign firms and labour mobility incentives);
- *Financial support schemes* in direct (e.g. grants, loans) or indirect form (e.g. tax relief) to encourage or discourage certain types of business activities (e.g. investment tax incentives, R&D vouchers, wage subsidies for skilled workers).
- *Technical assistance, information and facilitation services*, which aim to encourage the uptake of knowledge (e.g. skill and supplier development programmes) and facilitate interactions between foreign and domestic firms (e.g. matchmaking services and networking events);
- *Agglomeration and collaboration networks*, which refers to platforms, facilities and infrastructures that enable spatial and network-related knowledge diffusion.

Source: Authors based on (Meissner and Kergroach, 2019[2]).

Figure 5.2. Policy instruments used in Portugal, Ireland and Lithuania to enable FDI-SME diffusion

In % of policy instruments

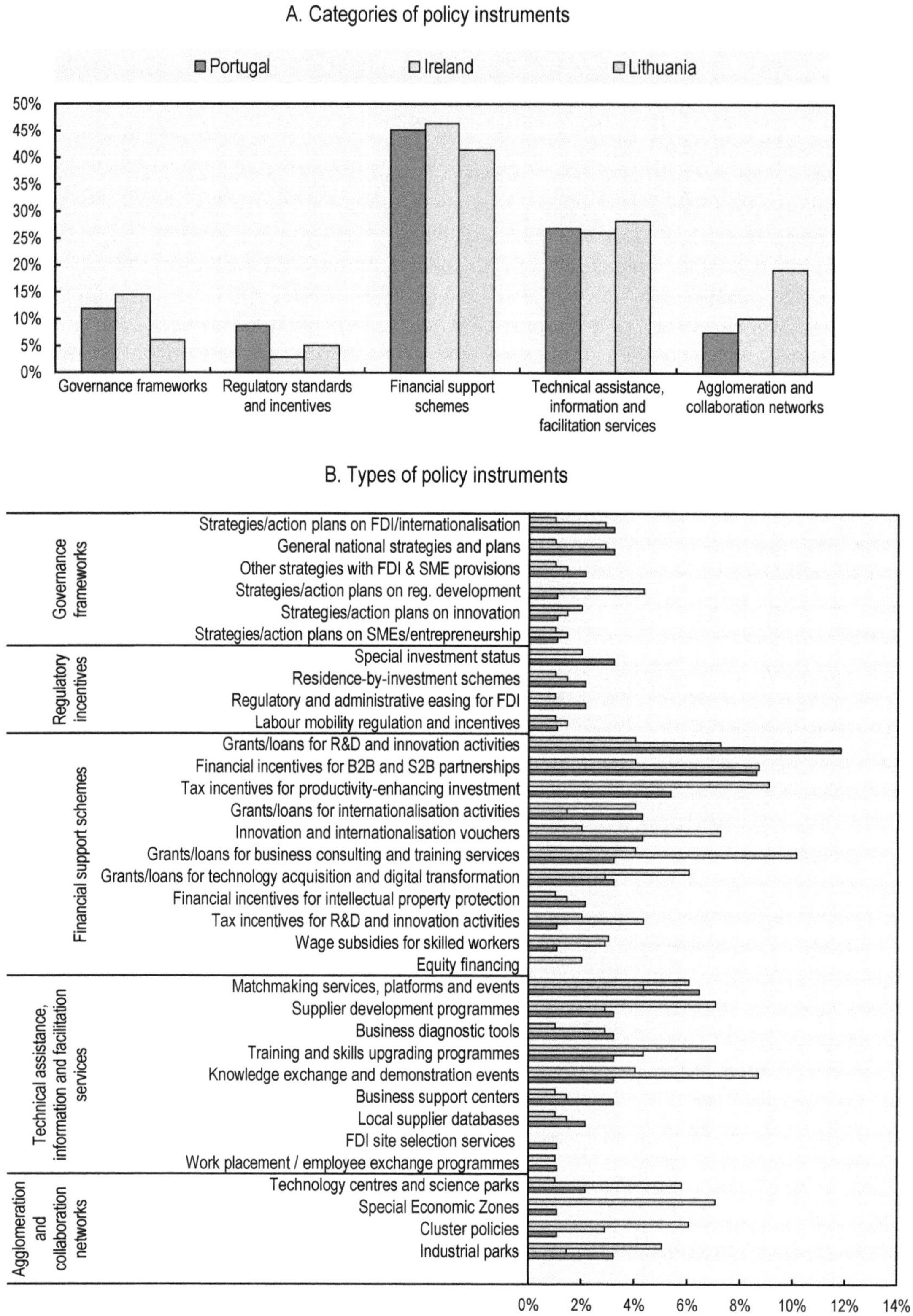

Source: EU/OECD Survey on Policies enabling FDI spillovers to domestic SMEs (2021).

One of the major factors influencing the current mix of policies is the desire and necessity of Portugal to hasten its transition to a knowledge-based economy. Being a small and open economy on the periphery of the EU, the policy priority of recent governments has been to move the economy towards knowledge-intensive and high-technology sectors. Another factor reflected in the chosen policy mix lies in the availability of the EU Structural and Investment Funds, which have been used since 2014 to finance the government's policy priorities in the areas of investment, entrepreneurship, innovation and smart specialisation through the Portugal 2020 Partnership Agreement. With the exception of the tax incentive schemes, all other financial instruments available to domestic firms are implemented in the framework of the EU-funded Portugal 2020 Incentive Schemes. This explains the large number of financial support measures that are currently in place to support the innovation and internationalisation of the Portuguese economy.

Portugal's policy mix also presents a relatively high degree of selectivity, which is driven by the national and regional smart specialisation strategies. Many policies target specific types of firms (e.g. SMEs), priority sectors and value chain activities, as well as specific geographic areas. A more targeted approach is consistent with wider industrial and innovation policy frameworks aimed at smart specialisation, and with current development thought about the role of selective policy interventions in designing industrial policies for sustainable growth. As international competition grows, selective targeting can play an important role in developing critical mass in innovation, knowledge creation and technology-based industrial production, particularly in the case of smaller economies with limited available (financial) resources.

Figure 5.3. Policy instruments used in Portugal to support FDI-SME diffusion channels and enabling factors

In number of policy initiatives

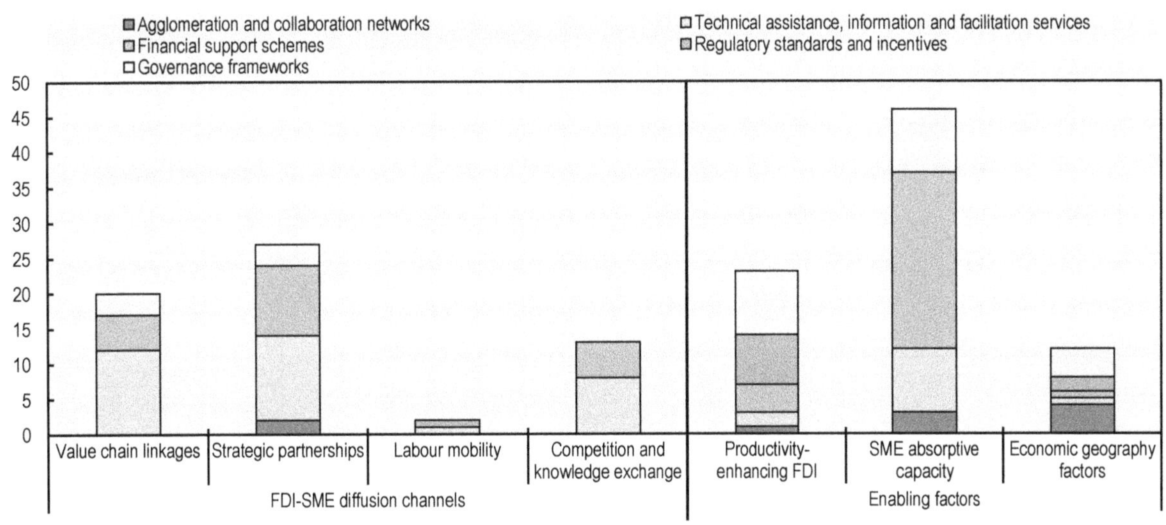

Source: EU/OECD Survey on Policies enabling FDI spillovers to domestic SMEs (2021).

Portugal's market openness may facilitate productivity-enhancing FDI, but certain regulatory restrictions could hinder the competition and labour mobility channels

In addition to targeted measures to encourage knowledge and technology diffusion from FDI to SMEs, the broader regulatory conditions matter for the direction and magnitude of FDI spillovers. Host country factors such as openness to international investment and trade, competition rules that facilitate market entry and exit, and a balanced labour market policy regime can influence the performance and market behaviour of SMEs in downstream sectors that could benefit from the presence of foreign affiliates.

Portugal has one of the most open FDI market access regimes in the OECD area, reflecting its strategic choice to use FDI for productivity growth, job creation and regional development. Regulatory barriers to competition are on par with the OECD average following several reforms in product market regulations that took place in recent years to create a lighter licensing regime and reduce red tape. More could be done, however, to ease certain competition-distorting restrictions in professional services and the retail trade sector, which are faced with considerable barriers to entry and conduct restraints. There is also scope to further improve Portugal's performance in the area of simplification and evaluation of regulations. The quality of public services and coherence and transparency of regulations are factors that significantly influence competition and the investment climate more broadly. Finally, labour mobility, an important channel through which productivity spillovers from foreign to domestic firms occur, may be also limited in sectors with low SME absorptive capacities as a result of the stringent employment protection regulations that are currently in place. Overly restrictive labour market regulations may have adverse impacts on SMEs' capacity to retain and attract highly skilled workers as SMEs are often unable to match the wage rates of foreign –typically larger– affiliates (see Chapter 3).

Figure 5.4. Portugal's performance in key regulatory areas

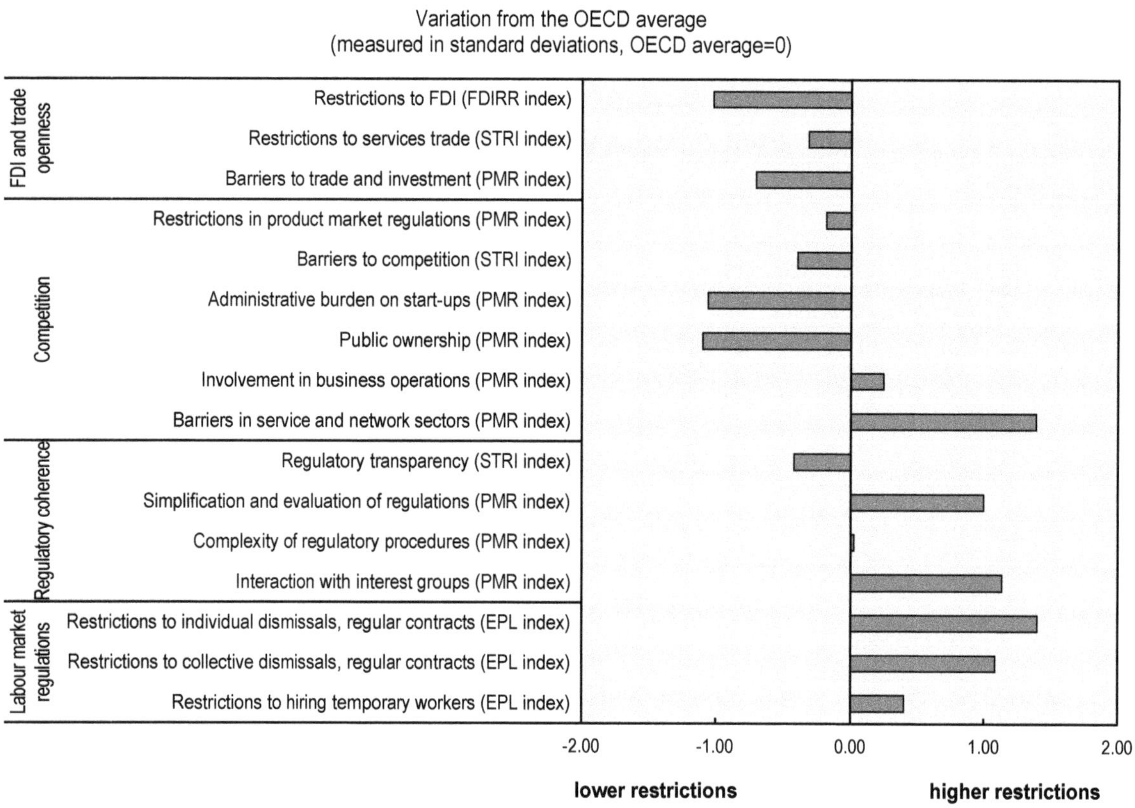

Note: Data bars pointing left show lower regulatory restrictions than the OECD average, and data bars pointing right show higher restrictions.
Source: OECD elaboration based on the FDIRR, STRI, PMR and EPL indices.

The COVID-19 pandemic has led to adjustments in policy design and implementation

The COVID-19 pandemic has forced many governments to take extraordinary measures to limit the impact of the containment measures on their economies. Preliminary findings from the EU/OECD survey on policies enabling FDI diffusion on SMEs show that government institutions involved in investment promotion, SME support, innovation and regional development had to change objectives and re-arrange workstreams, instruments and budgets due to the COVID-19 pandemic. Some digitalised their activities, e.g. by organising site visits, meetings or events online, adopting customer relationship management systems and marketing automation tools (e.g. Lithuania), or launching online platforms for sharing information (e.g. Bulgaria).

Similar trends are observed among the main Portuguese agencies. Most of the assessed FDI-SME diffusion policies have not been impacted by the COVID -19 pandemic but many have been adjusted (Figure 5.5). Among these, half entailed adjustments to the timeframe of their implementation and one third adjustments to their objectives. For certain policies the budget was increased to finance new actions or provide additional financial support to business enterprises, while other programmes were adjusted to target the sectors that were most affected by the containment measures such as tourism, hotels and restaurants, and commercial activities.

Portuguese agencies also had to adjust their workstreams and prioritise new funding schemes. The approval of payments to eligible businesses was prioritised, and in the case of reimbursable financial incentives a deferral period of 12 months was automatically applied. Additional budgets were also allocated to finance public health-related R&D activities and help companies shift their production lines towards goods aimed at combatting the pandemic. Finally, the mode of delivery of certain programmes had to change to accommodate the new market conditions created by the containment measures. Several policies that were previously delivered in person such as skills upgrading programmes for SMEs, matchmaking services and networking events for foreign and domestic firms, had to move online. For instance, AICEP created task forces to respond more quickly to requests from companies operating in the most affected sectors and sectors of significant importance for the Portuguese economy (e.g. agrifood, logistics, health, and construction materials). Several webinars were also organised to inform Portuguese companies about the impact of the Covid-19 pandemic on foreign markets. More than 400 online meetings between companies and AICEP's overseas offices were organised during the first month of the lockdown.

Figure 5.5. The impact of the Covid-19 pandemic on Portugal's FDI-SME diffusion policies

In % of policy initiatives

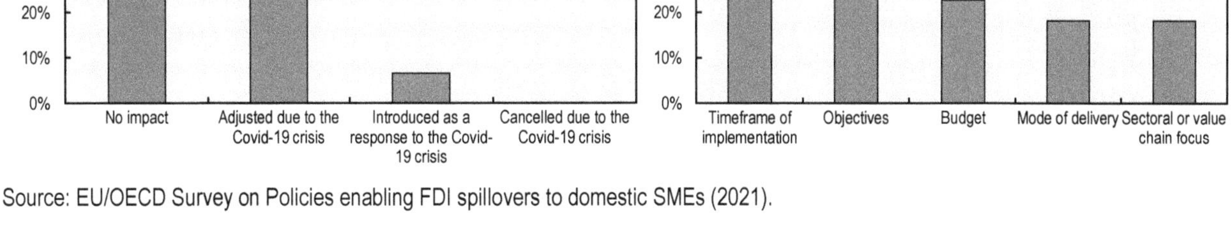

Source: EU/OECD Survey on Policies enabling FDI spillovers to domestic SMEs (2021).

5.3. Policies acting upon the enabling environment for FDI diffusion on SMEs

Attracting and facilitating productivity-enhancing FDI

The type of FDI that a country attracts and the extent to which foreign firms create linkages with the local economy depend on the regulatory environment for FDI and the legal framework for market entry and conduct, amongst other factors. Openness to FDI may not only affect productivity in industries that get market access, but also those in downstream sectors that benefit from potentially better access to high quality inputs and services domestically. Targeted regulatory and financial incentives as well as information and facilitation services can also play a crucial role in channelling FDI into more productive and knowledge-intensive activities with higher spillover potential for domestic SMEs.

Portugal has one of the most open economies to foreign investment

According to the OECD FDI Regulatory Restrictiveness (FDIRR) index, Portugal is one of the most open economies in the OECD area and the third most open among OECD EU countries (Figure 5.6). Portuguese law prohibits any market access discrimination based on nationality, and foreign investors enjoy the same conditions and rights as domestic companies with regard to the incorporation of their companies, mergers and acquisitions, taxation, social security contributions, the liability of shareholders and their day-to-day business activities. At the sectoral level, fisheries, transport, the air and maritime sectors, and financial services are the sectors where most restrictions are found; however, these are still significantly lower than the OECD average (Figure 5.7). For instance, government approval is required for foreign and domestic investments in defence, water management, public telecommunications, maritime and air transport. The establishment of a credit institution or insurance undertaking is also subject to authorisation by the Bank of Portugal for EU firms or the Ministry of Finance for non-EU firms (US Department of State, 2020[3]).

An investment screening framework is in place for investments undertaken by companies from outside the EU/EEA that intend to acquire direct or indirect control over strategic assets related to defence, national security, energy, transportation and communication services. Decree-Law No. 138/2014 lays out the screening mechanism, which allows the Portuguese Council of Ministers to oppose acquisitions of strategic assets when these are deemed to threaten national security or the provision of essential services (Government of Portugal, 2014[4]). Since October 2020, the EU FDI Regulation entered into force, which automatically applies to Portugal and broadens the sectoral scope of national screening mechanisms within the EU to include critical infrastructures such as healthcare, media and data processing.

Figure 5.6. Portugal has very few statutory restrictions to foreign investment

OECD FDI Regulatory Restrictiveness Index, 2019 (open=0; closed=1)

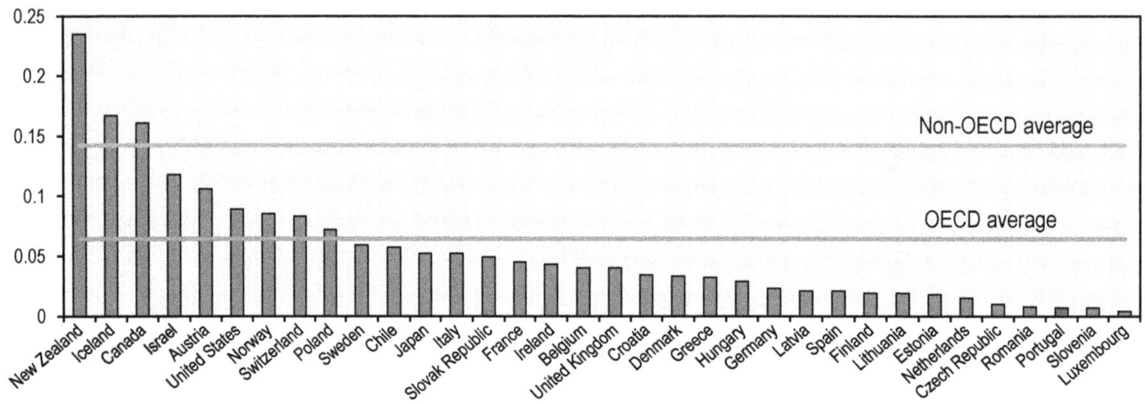

Note: The OECD FDI Regulatory Restrictiveness Index only covers statutory measures discriminating against foreign investors. Source: OECD FDI Regulatory Restrictiveness Index (database), www.oecd.org/investment/fdiindex.htm

Figure 5.7. FDI restrictions are limited to only a handful of sectors

OECD FDI Regulatory Restrictiveness Index, overall and sector-specific, 2019

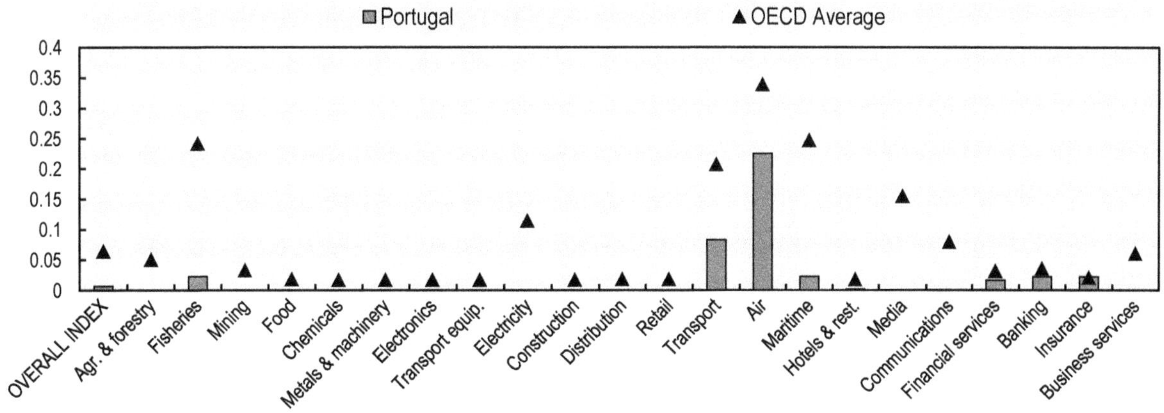

Source: OECD FDI Regulatory Restrictiveness Index (database), www.oecd.org/investment/fdiindex.htm

Together with FDI restrictions, other behind-the-border regulations, including barriers to trade, barriers to competition and other discriminatory measures, affect the degree of local embeddedness of foreign affiliates and shape market access conditions in downstream sectors that could benefit from their presence. Given the important role that services play for Portugal's position in GVCs and its upgrading potential, examining non-FDI market access conditions in the services sector could provide a better understanding of the potential for FDI-SME diffusion in a large part of the domestic economy.

According to the OECD Services Trade Restrictiveness Index (STRI), Portugal has one of the most favourable regulatory environments for services trade in the OECD area, with lower than the average STRI score in 18 out of 22 services sectors in 2020 (Figure 5.8). While in certain sectors such as engineering services, the STRI of Portugal increased significantly between 2014 and 2016 due to a tightening of the rules concerning the licence to practice, steps towards greater openness to services trade were recorded in several other sectors in recent years. Higher than average restrictions are found only in legal, accounting, architecture and engineering services. This is largely due to behind-the-border regulation in the form of tight immigration policies and other restrictions on the movement of people and foreign entry. For instance, commercial presence and citizenship of an EEA country or a country that has signed a reciprocal agreement with Portugal is required to practice engineering and architecture services. For accounting services, at least 51% of the equity shares must be held by licensed accountants, while statutory auditors must own at least 51% of the equity shares of an audit firm (OECD, 2019[5]).

Regulatory and financial incentives are the main policy instruments used to attract foreign investment into productivity-enhancing and R&D-intensive activities

Portugal's strong performance on FDI and trade openness reflects the country's strategic policy priority to improve economic conditions by keeping markets open for Portuguese and foreign firms and attracting FDI that contributes to productivity growth. In recent years, the internationalisation of the economy has become a major policy priority for the Portuguese government (Table 5.2). A national Internationalisation Programme (*Programa Internacionalizar*) was launched in 2017, outlining areas where public action is needed with the aim to increase FDI inflows and enable more Portuguese companies to expand, export and invest abroad. The programme was updated in 2020 (*Programa Internacionalizar 2030*) to reflect the government's policy priorities for the next decade and take into account the impact of the Covid-19 pandemic on the economy. Efforts have been also made to mobilise FDI from foreign firms that are part of the Portuguese diaspora. The *National Diaspora Investment Support Programme* (PNAID) was approved in 2020 and a specialised Diaspora Investor Support Office (*Gabinete de Apoio ao Investidor da Diáspora*) operates within the Ministry of Foreign Affairs to support investments of Portuguese communities and companies located abroad.

Figure 5.8. Portugal's overall STRI score is in line with the OECD average

OECD Services Trade Restrictiveness Index, 2020 (open=0; close=1)

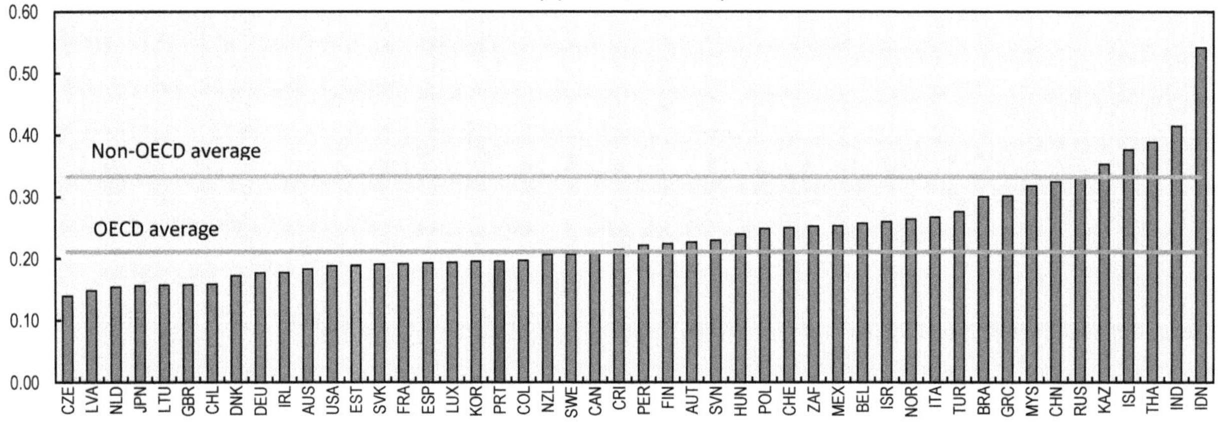

Note: The OECD STRI indices take values between zero and one, one being the most restrictive. The STRI database records measures on a Most Favoured Nations basis. Preferential trade agreements are not taken into account. Air transport and road freight cover only commercial establishment (with accompanying movement of people). The indices are based on laws and regulations in force on 31 October 2019.
Source: OECD STRI database, 2020.

Overall, Portugal exhibits a consistent targeting of innovative and knowledge-intensive activities across all the FDI promotion policies assessed for the purpose of this study. The policy mix for the attraction of knowledge-intensive FDI relies heavily on regulatory incentives (Figure 5.9). The government has introduced four special investment regulatory regimes for different types of investments, including large-scale projects, investments in less developed regions, as well as diaspora investments. These regulatory schemes allow investors to benefit from simplified and expedited licensing and administrative procedures – and in the case of diaspora investments financial support – under certain conditions. These include, amongst others, the requirement to introduce technological processes in cooperation with domestic R&D institutions and to demonstrate the potential for spillover effects on Portuguese SMEs.

Investing in R&D and innovation activities is also one of the eligibility criteria for the granting of business investor visas. In order to encourage different types of entrepreneurs to establish their operations in the Portuguese market, the government operates two residence-by-investment schemes, which allow individuals to obtain residence rights through investments in certain sectors and types of assets. The recently launched Startup Visa programme is addressed to innovative start-ups while the Residence Permit for Investment (ARI) scheme targets large investors. Several tax incentives are also available to foreign investors – however these also apply to domestic firms on equal terms. Apart from the SIFIDE II scheme, which has been the main instrument used by government to support business R&D for both domestic and foreign firms, a set of contractual tax benefits apply to large investments that promote technological innovation and attenuate regional disparities.

Recent government efforts to tap into the spillover potential of different types of FDI and pursue broader developmental objectives by diversifying the support available to foreign investors are a step in the right direction. Moving forward with the implementation of these measures, it will be important to avoid potential inconsistencies and redundancies arising from operating too many regulatory schemes at too small a scale and in different parts of government (e.g. AICEP, IAPMEI, Ministry of Economy and Digital Transition, Ministry of Foreign Affairs). Greater coordination among the relevant actors, better communication of the available public support, and clarity about how different policies can meet the needs of different types of investors could ensure policy coherence and improve the uptake of recently introduced measures.

Figure 5.9. Policy instruments for productivity-enhancing and knowledge-intensive FDI

In % of policy instruments

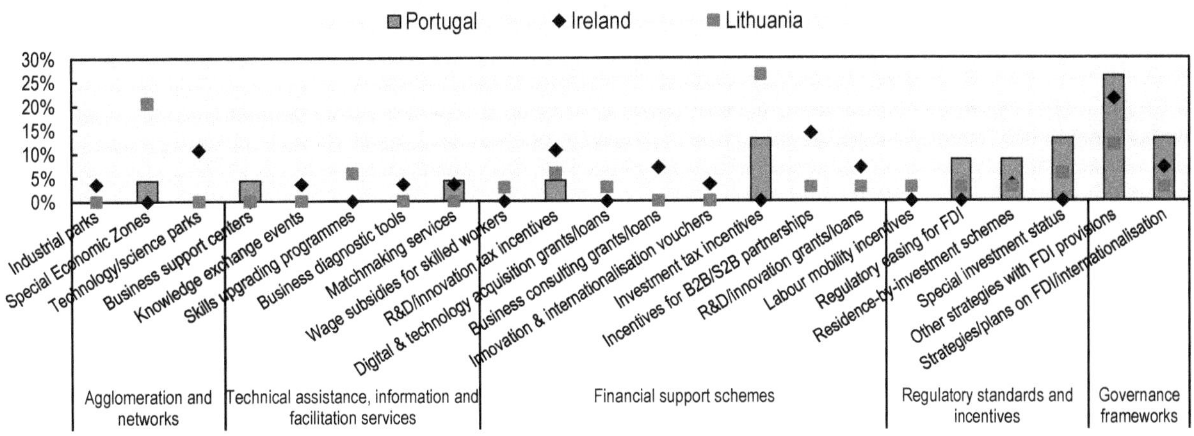

Source: EU/OECD Survey on Policies enabling FDI spillovers to domestic SMEs (2021).

Ultimately, regulatory incentives (e.g. PIN and PII status, Diaspora Investor status, ARI scheme, Startup Visa programme) will have to be structured into clearly articulated packages of support that also combine financial support (e.g. Portugal 2020 grants, SIFIDE II) and technical assistance (e.g. access to networks and clusters) and are sufficiently differentiated to target a variety of foreign firms and investment projects. For instance, Lithuania recently launched the "Green Corridor for Large-Scale Investment Projects" initiative, which provides a comprehensive package of support to large investments of national significance, including tax incentives, grants, fast-track licensing procedures, access to dedicated land plots, streamlined migration processes for foreign employees, and training programmes tailored to the needs of large-scale investors. IDA Ireland has partnered with Enterprise Ireland, the Irish SME agency, to provide a package of technical and financial support for small foreign-owned multinational companies to help them grow and expand their R&D activities in the Irish market.

Further exploiting the potential of small high-growth multinational companies that often drive job creation and innovation in knowledge-intensive sectors is an area that Portugal could prioritise. These innovative firms have different needs from large investors that cannot be addressed solely through regulatory incentives. The uptake of the Startup Visa programme, which grew from 34 recipients in 2018 to 89 in 2020, demonstrates the great potential that innovative startups present for the Portuguese market. AICEP and IAPMEI could further leverage their respective expertise on investment promotion and SME development to create a distinct support package for small high-growth companies, and ensure that these firms are aware of and have access to the SME support services provided by the Portugal 2020 Incentives Schemes.

Table 5.2. Main policies for productivity-enhancing and knowledge-intensive FDI

Main policies	Description	Implementing institution
National Diaspora Investment Support Programme	The programme aims to take advantage of the potential of Portuguese communities living abroad to support the internationalisation of the economy through diaspora investments.	Ministry of Foreign Affairs
Investment Monitoring System	The Permanent Investor Support Commission is responsible for monitoring and facilitating investment projects of both domestic and foreign firms that fulfil certain criteria, including producing innovative and tradable goods and services, and having spillover effects on Portuguese SMEs. The monitoring regime streamlines all administrative and licensing procedures as well as procedures for granting financial incentives.	Permanent Investor Support Commission
Investment of Potential National Interest (PIN) Status and Investment for the Interior (PII) Status	The PIN status is granted to projects of more than 25 million euro that create 50 or more jobs, while the PII status is granted to projects of more than 10 million euro that create at least 25 jobs and take place in Portugal's interior areas. Projects granted the PIN and PII status benefit from a priority assessment and simplification of licensing and administrative procedures. Projects that do not fulfil the conditions can still benefit if they undertake R&D and innovation activities, are export-oriented and produce tradable goods/services.	Permanent Investor Support Commission
Diaspora Investor Status	The Diaspora Investor Status is granted to members of the Portuguese diaspora who undertake an investment project in Portugal either individually or through a company. The status gives access to a set of financial incentives with additional benefits if the investment project is located in the interior of the country.	Ministry of Foreign Affairs
Residence Permit for Investment (ARI)	The Residence Permit for Investment Activity (ARI) enables third country nationals to obtain a temporary residence permit to conduct business in Portugal. There is a minimum amount that should be invested, which ranges depending on the type of activities involved, including investing in research activities conducted by Portuguese public or private R&D entities.	Foreigners and Borders Service
Startup Visa	The Startup Visa programme targets entrepreneurs from outside the EU's Schengen Zone who already own or consider launching a startup, but aim to set it up in Portugal. For the visa to be granted, solid business and financial plans are required demonstrating that the startup will undertake innovative activities and contribute to job creation.	IAPMEI
Contractual Tax Benefits for Productive Investment	The Contractual Tax Benefits for Productive Investment apply to investments of at least 3 million euro that take place in specific sectors (e.g. manufacturing, accommodation, filmmaking, computer programming, business services, R&D activities) and are deemed of strategic importance for the national economy, the reduction of regional disparities and the promotion of technological innovation.	Investment Tax Incentive Coordination Council
Tax Regime for Investment Support (RFAI)	The RFAI includes several tax benefits upon income and real estate taxes for investments in the extractive and manufacturing sectors, tourism, IT services and technologies, shared services centres as well as defence, energy and telecommunications.	Tax Authority
SIFIDE II	SIFIDE II has been the main instrument used by government to support business R&D since its establishment in 1997. SIFIDE consists of a credit against the corporate tax liability for expenditures incurred on R&D activities.	ANI
Diaspora Investor Support Office (GAID)	The Diaspora Investor Support Office is a facilitation platform aimed at supporting micro and small investment projects from Portuguese diaspora communities.	Ministry of Foreign Affairs

Source: EU/OECD Survey on Policies enabling FDI spillovers to domestic SMEs (2021).

Strengthening the absorptive capacity of Portuguese SMEs

Policies targeting the absorptive capacity of local SMEs can take many forms (e.g. subsidies, grants, loans, tax relief, infrastructures, training programmes) and target various aspects of SME performance (e.g. access to innovation assets, access to skills, access to finance).

In Portugal, SME absorptive capacities are supported primarily through financial incentives and technical assistance programmes (Figure 5.10). Policy targeting of SMEs is also very common. More than 58% of the policies assessed for the purpose of this study target Portuguese SMEs only or provide some sort of preferential treatment to them in the form of additional financial support, more lax requirements and conditionalities, and prioritisation in their selection as recipients of public support (Figure 5.11). The significant targeting of SMEs observed in the current policy mix reflects to a large extent the strategic choice of the Portuguese government to mainstream SME issues into national development frameworks.

Non-corporate entities such as research centres, higher education institutions and technology transfer offices are also involved in several programmes. Portuguese policymakers increasingly recognise the role that these institutions can play in bridging the gap between science and industry, creating new knowledge and facilitating the commercialisation of R&D. Non-corporate entities are mostly involved in policies of collaborative nature that are implemented by ANI and focus on R&D and innovation activities. On the other hand, very few initiatives apply exclusively to foreign firms. Most policies (61%) are open to all firms irrespective of their origin while several programmes supporting SME absorptive capacities naturally target domestic firms only (33%).

Figure 5.10. Policy instruments for SME absorptive capacities in Portugal

In % of policy instruments

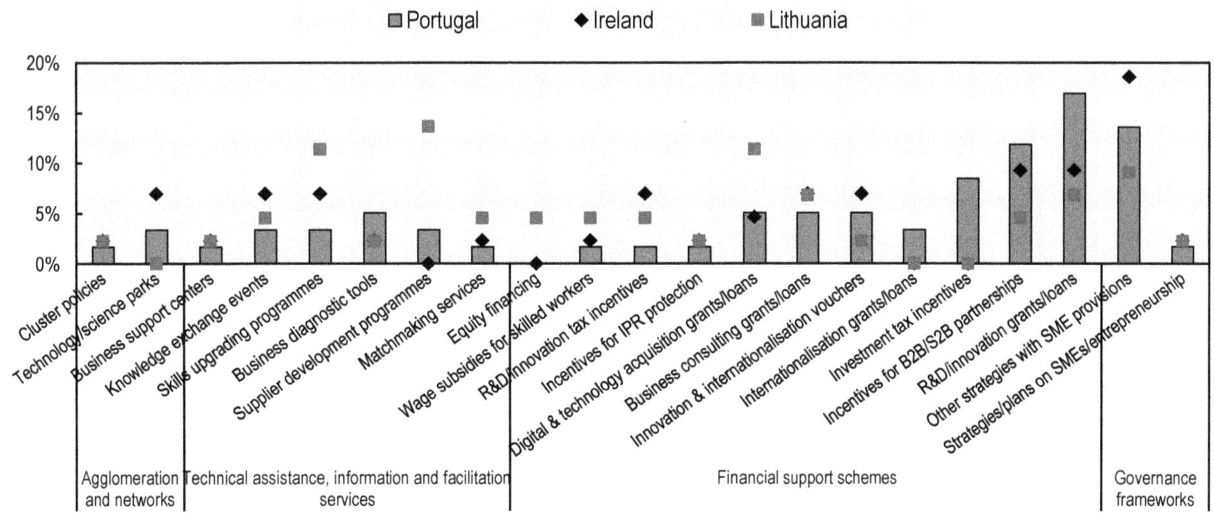

Source: EU/OECD Survey on Policies enabling FDI spillovers to domestic SMEs (2021).

Figure 5.11. Policies targeting SMEs versus generic policies

In % of policy initiatives

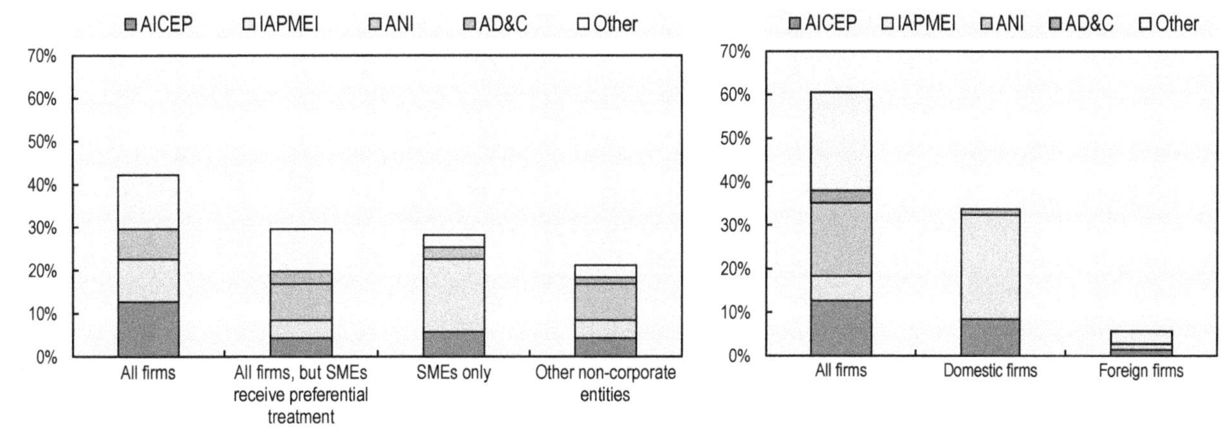

Source: EU/OECD Survey on Policies enabling FDI spillovers to domestic SMEs (2021).

The policy mix for business research and innovation relies on financial incentives

Governments worldwide increasingly rely on direct and indirect financial support measures to promote business R&D and encourage innovation, in particular among SMEs. According to the OECD R&D tax incentives database, in 2018, Portugal was placed above the OECD and EU average in terms of total government support to business R&D (BERD), at a rate equivalent to 0.21% of GDP (Figure 5.12) – on par with top innovators such as the US and Canada.

Direct funding in the form of grants and loans represents only a limited share of the total government expenditure. The Tax Incentives System for Research and Business Development (SIFIDE II) has instead been the main instrument used by the Portuguese government to support business innovation since its establishment in 1997. In 2018, the tax scheme accounted for 81% of total public support for R&D (OECD, 2020[6]). The increasing reliance on fiscal incentives rather than direct funding is consistent with trends in other developed economies. Across the OECD area, tax support represented around 56% of total government support of business R&D in 2018 compared to 36% in 2006. The shift in the policy mix has been more pronounced among EU Member States, with tax support doubling from 26% of total government support in 2006 to 57% in 2018.

Figure 5.12. Direct government funding and tax support for business R&D

OECD R&D Tax Incentive Database, 2018

As a percentage of GDP

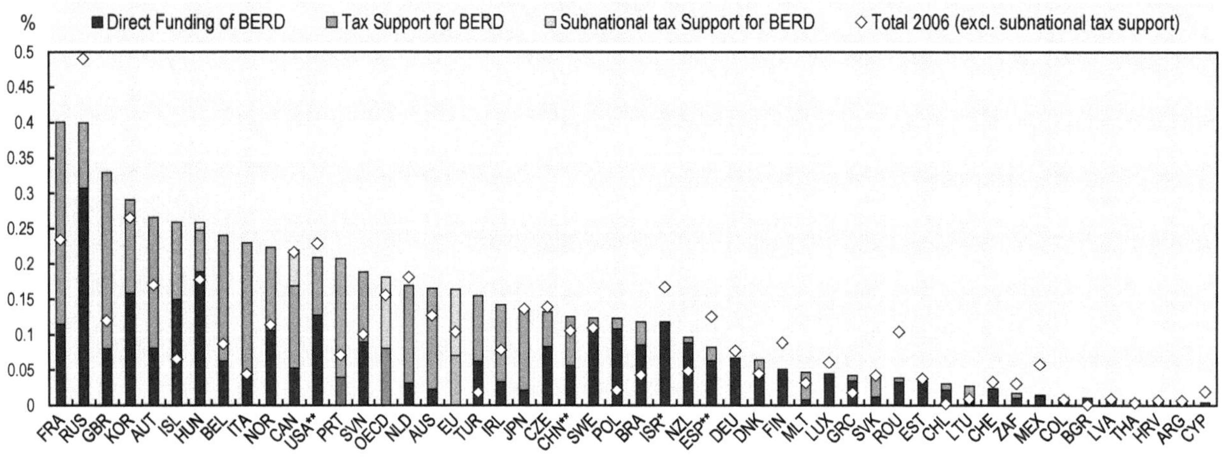

* Data on tax support not available, ** Data on subnational tax support not available

Source: OECD R&D Tax Incentive Database, http://oe.cd/rdtax, December 2020

Direct support measures for SME research and innovation activities are administered through the Business Investment Incentive Schemes of the Portugal 2020 strategic framework, which lays out the policy priorities that govern the use of the EU Structural and Investment Funds for the period 2014-2020. The Competitiveness and Internationalisation (COMPETE 2020) Operational Programme and the Regional Operational Programmes are responsible for allocating grants and loans to domestic firms through three sets of financial instruments; namely incentives for business innovation and entrepreneurship, which aim to support investments in productive innovation and creative entrepreneurship; incentives for the qualification and internationalisation of SMEs, which aim to strengthen the competitiveness of SMEs and their expansion to global markets; and incentives for research and technological development, which aim to increase business investment in technological R&D.

Other initiatives called collective actions (*Sistema de apoio a ações coletivas)* as well as scientific and technological research projects (*Sistema de apoio à investigação científica e tecnológica*) provide financial support to non-corporate actors such as universities and research centers to strengthen knowledge transfers. The most important strategic documents guiding the allocation of funds under the COMPETE 2020 and Regional Operational Programmes are the national and regional smart specialisation strategies. The alignment with these strategies is mandatory in the implementation of Portugal 2020 investments in research and innovation and a priority in other areas, such as the support to SME competitiveness.

Portuguese SMEs make up the majority of recipients of both direct and indirect financial support schemes. The number of the SIFIDE II recipients has steadily increased over the past decade from around 400 recipients in 2006 to close to 2000 in 2019. Most of this increase is attributable to SMEs, which accounted for more than 81% of R&D tax relief recipients and 46% of the total allocated tax support over the period 2006-2019 (Figure 5.13). Similarly, SMEs accounted for more than 73% of the total number of enterprises that benefitted from the Portugal 2020 Research and Technological Development funds over the period 2014-2020.

Figure 5.13. Direct and indirect financial support allocated to SMEs for business research and innovation activities

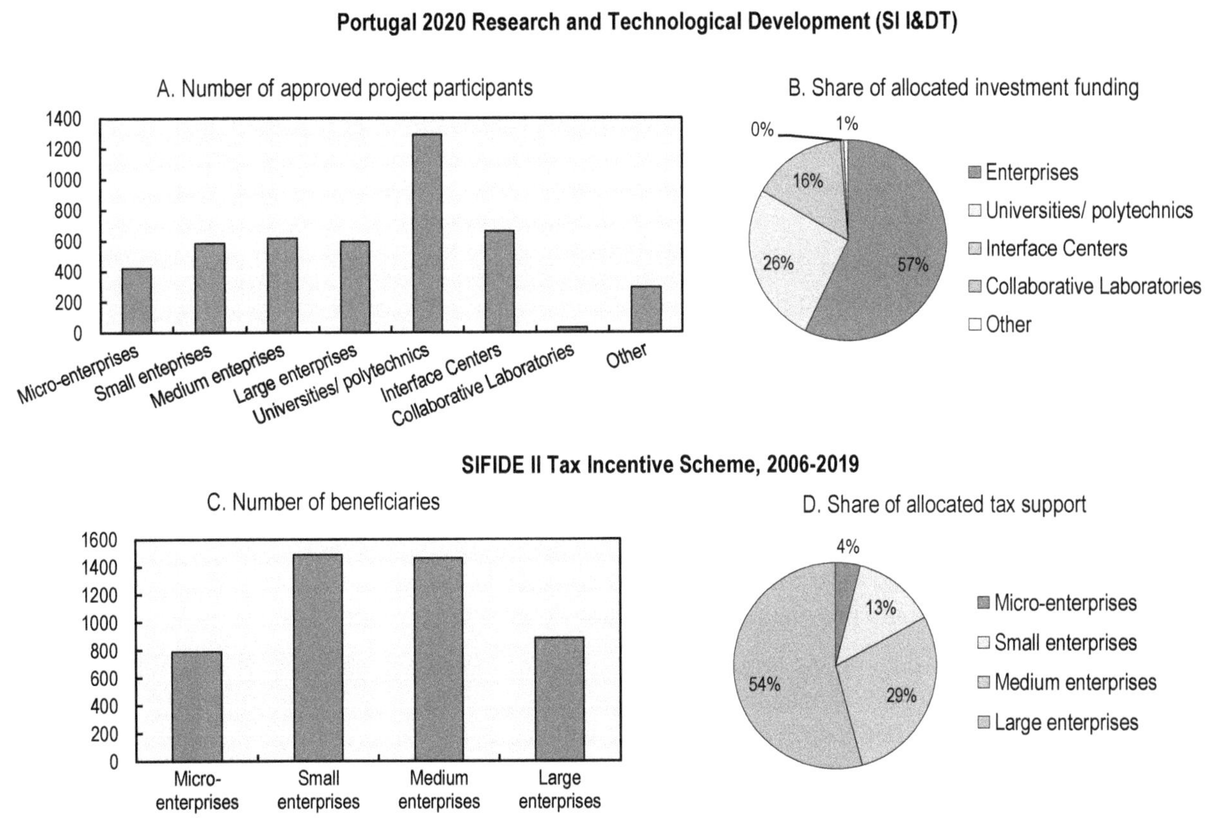

Source: ANI Activity Indicators, accessed on 23 May 2021.

Efforts to remove bottlenecks in judicial efficiency and strengthen financial stability should continue in order to improve SME access to finance

For many SMEs, the high fixed costs of establishing a distribution network and adjusting their products for overseas standards, often require external finance. Well-functioning financial markets can strengthen the absorptive capacity of domestic SMEs by providing the liquidity that they need to develop new products and invest in technology upgrading (Farole and Winkler, 2014[7]).

The ease of getting credit is an area where Portugal ranks worst according to the EU's Small Business Act (SBA) 2019 performance assessment, reflecting deficiencies in credit reporting systems and collateral and bankruptcy laws (European Commission, 2019[8]). The willingness of banks to provide a loan and the rate of rejected loan applications have deteriorated to below the EU average, while there has been an increase in the average time it takes for a company to get its invoices paid. Over the period 2010-2018, SME lending declined by almost 35% and total business loans dropped by 38% due to the balance sheet constraints of Portuguese banks and a less favourable perception of risk which led to stricter credit standards and tighter lending conditions (OECD, 2020[9]). Overall, the stability of the Portuguese banking sector has steadily improved following the 2008 global financial crisis and the subsequent euro area debt crisis; however banks are still highly exposed to sovereign debt and bank profitability is among the lowest in the EU (OECD, 2021[10]).

Portugal's underperformance in these areas can be partially attributed to weak contract enforcement procedures because of inefficiencies in the judicial system. According to the EU Justice Scoreboard 2020, Portugal performs poorly with regard to resolving civil and commercial legal cases due to significant bottlenecks in some court districts (European Commission, 2020[11]) (OECD, 2019[12]). Banks should be better able to enforce collateral without going through long and uncertain court proceedings. To address these issues, the Portuguese government has put forward targeted measures through the *Programa Capitalizar*, which aims to foster the use out-of-court restructuring mechanisms, promote efficient and transparent court proceedings, and establish an early warning mechanism that informs companies of their financial situation. Due consideration on improving judicial efficiency is also given in the recently launched Recovery and Resilience Plan, which focuses on the simplification and modernisation of insolvency procedures and reforms in the operation of Administrative and Tax Courts (Government of Portugal, 2021[13]).

Despite challenges with bank-based SME financing, access to public financial support and the availability of venture capital for new and growing SMEs is well above the EU average, reflecting the large number of publicly supported credit lines and co-investment programmes that the government has introduced as part of the *Startup Portugal* strategy. The strategy aims to promote alternatives to bank loans such as equity finance, crowdfunding, peer-to-peer lending and co-investment. These financing schemes are channelled to the Portuguese market through several state-owned institutions. A National Promotional Bank (*Banco Português de Fomento, BPF*), was established in 2020 to support SMEs, midcaps and large companies through targeted funding, equity, guarantees and other hybrid instruments. The participation of IAPMEI, AICEP and Turismo de Portugal in BPF's corporate governance as shareholders can help further expand credit supply for foreign and domestic firms that want to engage in innovative activities and allow for greater synergies across the investment promotion and SME development policy agendas.

PME Investimentos, a public company regulated by the Bank of Portugal, also serves as a fund-of-funds that facilitates the lending activity of national financial services providers. *PME investimentos* manages the 200M Fund and the *Portugal TECH* co-investment fund, which provide venture capital to support innovative projects developed between companies, universities, research centres and incubators. The *Capitalizar* credit line was also launched by IAPMEI in partnership with *PME Investimentos* to support SMEs in the adoption of Industry 4.0 solutions (i.e. automation, cloud computing, internet of things) (PME Investimentos, 2018[14]).

The emphasis that the government has placed on strengthening the availability of publicly supported financing instruments is a step in the right direction given the challenges that the Portuguese bank-based financial system has faced over the past decade. The establishment of a National Promotional Bank is expected to play a crucial role in attracting foreign investment and financing innovation. SMEs should be further encouraged to source finance from equity markets and exploit the potential that these new sources of financing can provide. Such an approach should rely on measures that facilitate market-based long-term debt financing, increase the availability of alternative financing, and promote access to equity capital through the stock market. Meanwhile, efforts to reduce the vulnerabilities of the banking sector and free up capital for new lending to SMEs should continue. The 2021 OECD Economic Survey of Portugal stresses the need to further improve financial stability by developing distressed debt markets and introducing new tools to ensure timely recognition of bank losses and debt restructuring (OECD, 2021[10]).

Efforts to address skill shortages in local labour markets should continue

Skill shortages and mismatches undermine the ability of the economy to increase productivity and upgrade into knowledge-intensive sectors. The skills of the local labour force are an important determinant of SME absorptive capacity and can significantly influence the potential for knowledge spillovers from foreign to domestic firms (Farole and Winkler, 2014[7]). Education and skills policies therefore play a crucial role in helping domestic firms meet the requirements of foreign investors.

In Portugal, the strategic objective of improving the skills of the workforce has been mainstreamed in several national strategies that identify new areas of policy action, placing particular emphasis on digital skills. The Digital Transition Action Plan includes a skills workstream, focusing on actions related to formal education, vocational training and digital literacy. Similarly, the National Strategy for Artificial Intelligence 2030 (*Estratégia Nacional de Inteligência Artificial*) outlines specific objectives and measures with regard to fostering AI skills and digital qualifications. Digital skills have been also addressed through the *INCoDe.2030* initiative, which aims to improve digital literacy and the production of new knowledge through the use of digital technologies (Government of Portugal, 2017[15]). Portugal's Recovery and Resilience Plan, has also prioritised public investments in upgrading the skills of adults and young students and increasing the number of STEM graduates (Government of Portugal, 2021[13]).

IAPMEI implements various training programmes for Portuguese SMEs through its *SME Academy*, which aims to improve the managerial and organisational skills of employees through vocational training activities and other forms of learning experiences aligned with sectoral needs. A *National Mentors Network* has been established to support entrepreneurs in the development of their business ideas and projects. In order to address the problems of low educational attainment, the government has also placed particular emphasis on increasing the offer of vocational education and training (VET) opportunities to its workforce (OECD, 2020[16]). Launched in 2017, the *Qualifica* programme, is the country's flagship initiative to improve the training and qualifications of adults. During 2018-2020, more than 300 *Qualifica* centres were established across all Portuguese regions to provide support for the recognition and certification of prior learning acquired in formal and non-formal contexts and to refer adults to education and training pathways, in particular less qualified adults, unemployed people and people not in education, employment or training (NEET).

To address skill shortages a whole-of-government approach is required given the cross-cutting nature of the skills agenda. Linkages with other policy areas should be strengthened to ensure that educational, vocational and training programmes are not implemented in silos but are aligned with Portugal's national strategies for smart specialisation, innovation and entrepreneurship. The programming of the EU funds for the period 2021-2027 and the launch of new action plans that lay out policy priorities for the next decade offer a great opportunity to raise the effectiveness of related measures and ensure policy coordination between different initiatives and implementing actors. The Portugal Digital Task Force, which was set up to coordinate the implementation of the Action Plan for Digital Transition, can play a key role in coordinating and facilitating synergies between existing and new skills upgrading initiatives. A horizontal alignment of policy priorities and actions will be needed to address skills shortages.

Furthermore, IAPMEI's *SME Academy* and AICEP's *Internationalisation Academy* could be leveraged to re-balance the policy mix for SME absorptive capacity towards skills upgrading programmes that could help SMEs access qualified human capital. Shifting the focus from financial support schemes to technical assistance and training programmes could address the underlying causes of low absorptive capacities in specific regions and sectors.

Expanding the presence of knowledge transfer infrastructure in Portugal's least developed regions is crucial to overcome the lack of absorptive capacities of traditional SMEs

Apart from financial support and skills development programmes, the Portuguese government has placed particular emphasis on strengthening the availability of knowledge transfer services and bridging the gap between SMEs and other actors of the Portuguese innovation ecosystem. SME absorptive capacities are influenced strongly by the local knowledge transfer infrastructure, which may include technology transfer offices, applied research centres, universities and other facilities that contribute to the creation and diffusion of knowledge.

The gradual expansion of intermediary organisations over the past decade has led to the establishment of a diverse network of technology transfer offices, R&D centres and science and technology parks. The 2017 Interface Programme provided financial and technical support for the establishment of Technological Interface Centres (CITs) and Collaborative Laboratories (CoLabs). The centres play the role of an innovation broker and, together with SMEs, implement a wide range of technology-oriented projects. Since the launch of the initiative in 2017, there have been 31 entities across Portugal recognised as CITs and 35 entities recognised as Collaborative Laboratories, operating in various thematic areas, including digital technologies, nanotechnologies, production technologies, energy and sustainability, biotechnology, mobility and transport services.

However, there are significant regional disparities in the availability of support services. Most CITs and CoLabs are concentrated in the Norte and Centro regions as well as the coastal areas of Portugal, leaving inland areas and least developed regions without the necessary infrastructure to support SME innovation and business growth. Efforts to expand their presence across Portugal should continue and be coupled with a needs assessment of local business innovation ecosystems. As suggested by the 2019 OECD Higher Education, Research and Innovation Review of Portugal and planned by the Portuguese government in its recently launched Recovery and Resilience Plan, the presence of these intermediary organisations could be further consolidated by ensuring adequate financial and human resources to maintain and expand their networks (OECD, 2019[17]). The government's commitment to continue supporting CITs and CoLabs will allow them to further consolidate their presence in local entrepreneurial ecosystems and improve their business advisory activities.

Mainstreaming economic geography factors into FDI-SME diffusion policies

Clusters embed characteristics such as industrial specialisation and geographical proximity that make knowledge spillovers more likely to happen. From a policy perspective, this means that FDI attraction policies, SME policies and cluster development policies could go hand in hand to increase the potential of FDI for SME productivity. Moreover, informing investors about the investment potential of regions and improving the local business climate by adapting policies to the economic and market characteristics of local economies could prove effective.

Economic geography considerations have been mainstreamed into key FDI-SME diffusion policy areas

The government of Portugal has made the strategic choice to use FDI promotion and SME support policies to attenuate regional disparities. Economic geography factors are addressed through agglomeration instruments, regulatory and tax incentives as well as several strategic governance frameworks that touch upon regional development issues (Figure 5.14).

The Interior Enhancement Programme was launched in 2018, outlining a set of measures to support the country's interior territories, which are characterised by weak economic activity and demographic decline. The programme shaped the framework for the establishment of several FDI- and SME-related initiatives, including the *PII investment status* (described in the previous section) for investments undertaken in

Portugal's interior territories, the *Tax Benefits for Portugal's Interior Areas* for SMEs operating in the agricultural, commercial, industrial and services sectors, and the Advanced Internationalisation programme implemented by AICEP for companies located in Portugal's least developed municipalities. As is the case in other EU Member States, the regional smart specialisation strategies are also key elements of Portugal's regional development policy framework. Many initiatives implemented by national government agencies rely on the strategic priorities, actions and specialisation fields identified in these strategies to improve the competitiveness and internationalisation of regional economies. As described in Chapter 4, the CCDRs play a crucial role in operationalising these measures at the local level and integrating smart specialisation considerations into broader regional strategies and action plans.

Overall, Portugal's policy mix exhibits some degree of spatial differentiation in the formulation and implementation of policies enabling FDI diffusion on domestic SMEs (Figure 5.15). Although most policies apply to all Portuguese regions on equal terms, a large number of them (45%) involves a place-based approach to the eligibility conditions and the amount of support provided to firms. Many financial support schemes provide higher co-financing rates for investments undertaken by firms located in Portugal's less developed (Norte, Centro, Alentejo and Açores) and transition (Algarve) regions. A place-based approach is also pursued in the granting of investment tax incentives; investments undertaken in less developed regions benefit from higher tax relief.

Figure 5.14. Policy instruments for agglomeration and economic geography factors

In % of policy instruments

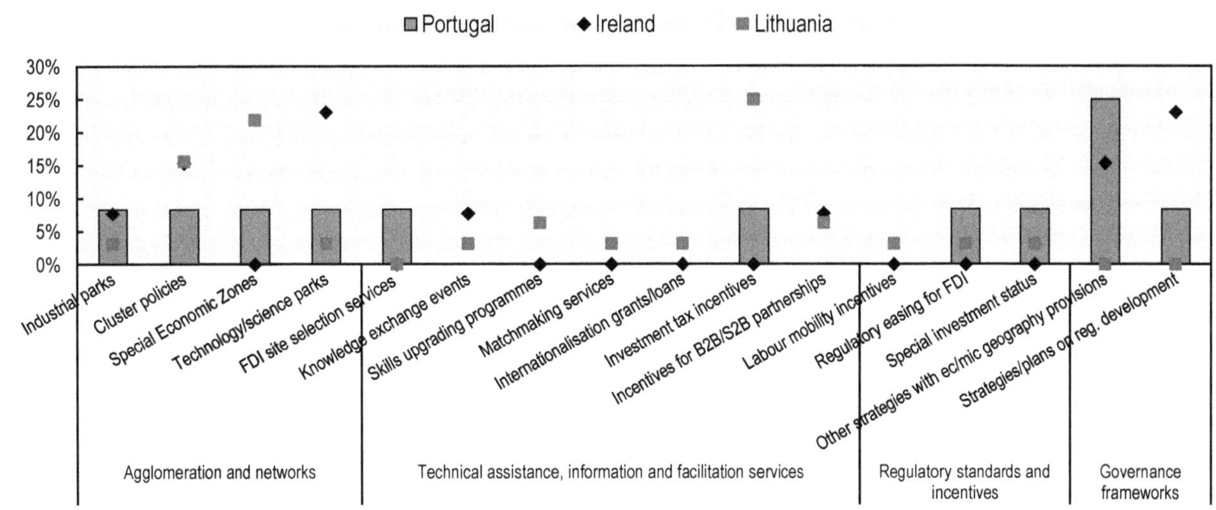

Source: EU/OECD Survey on Policies enabling FDI spillovers to domestic SMEs (2021).

Figure 5.15. Place-based targeting of FDI-SME diffusion policies

In % of policy initiatives

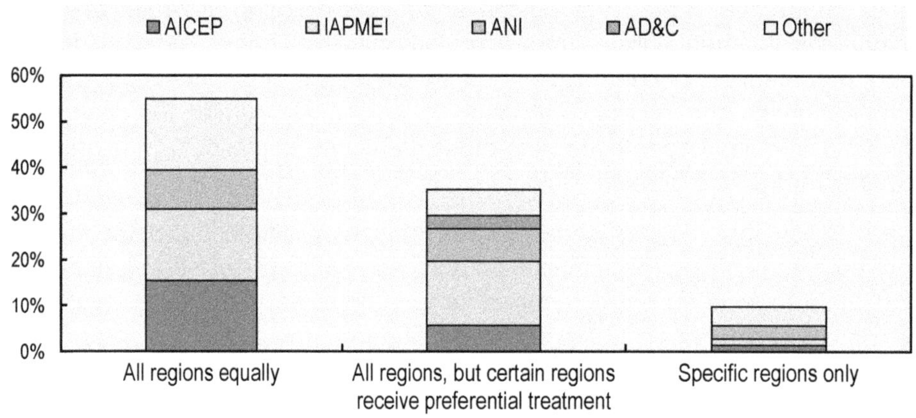

Note: The Autonomous Regions of Acores and Madeira are excluded from this analysis. "All regions" refers to the NUTS 2 regions of continental Portugal. Source: EU/OECD Survey on Policies enabling FDI spillovers to domestic SMEs (2021).

Agglomeration policies are driven by geographic and sectoral priorities identified in Portugal's smart specialisation strategy

Recent policy initiatives aimed at supporting clusters, industrial parks and business networks have been successful in mobilising the public and private sectors and providing them with the necessary technical and financial support to foster greater collaboration. Since 2017, IAPMEI has coordinated the recognition and establishment of 18 industrial clusters covering various sectors of the economy and involving companies, business associations, public institutions and non-corporate entities of the Portuguese research and innovation ecosystem. The clusters play an important role in supporting SMEs to implement smart specialisation strategies, assess bottlenecks in their performance, and provide feedback to government agencies on the implementation of effective SME policies. In 2019, several agreements ("*Sectoral Pacts for Competitiveness and Internationalisation*") were signed between the Ministry of Economy and some of the recognised clusters, whereby they commit to a set of collaborative actions in line with smart specialisation, including training and skills development programmes, measures to promote industry 4.0 practices, innovation activities, and targeted reforms in the regulatory environment to address barriers to innovation and internationalisation in specific sectors and value chains (IAPMEI, 2021[18]).

AICEP is also increasingly taking into account agglomeration economies when supporting foreign firms in their FDI location decisions. *AICEP Global Parques*, a subsidiary of AICEP, operates three industrial parks in different locations across Portugal that both domestic and foreign firms can use to set up their business. The parks are able to host any kind of business activity, but depending on their location they tend to attract companies undertaking activities in line with the sectoral make-up of local economies. For instance, the Zils park attracts companies operating in the energy, agribusiness, logistics, technology and services sectors; the BlueBiz park focuses on office centres, aeronautics, industrial, agribusiness, logistics, and automotive sectors; while the Albiz park hosts companies operating in the industrial, logistics and services sectors. An online *Site Selection Platform* was also recently launched to help foreign investors find the best business location within Portugal that meets their requirements.

Portuguese cluster policies rely on sectoral considerations and priorities identified in the national and regional smart specialisation strategies. The strategies identify several priority areas that should be targeted by public action, such as the transport and environmental industries, health and life sciences, tourism, the creative and cultural sectors, ICTs, fisheries, the agro-food industry, energy, and industrial production technologies (Government of Portugal, 2014[19]). In fact, these sectoral considerations are also reflected in other policy initiatives (Figure 5.16). Many Portuguese policies focus on supporting firms in tradable sectors that are exposed to international competition, while pre-production activities such as basic and applied R&D receive increased policy attention. For instance, the EU-funded Portugal 2020 incentive schemes are open to firms operating in all economic activities with the exception of financial services, the defence sector and betting games. However, only investments aimed at the production of tradable goods and services can receive financial support, a condition assessed on the basis of several criteria including the amount of direct and indirect exports in a given sector, the provision of services to non-residents, as well as the degree of import substitution observed in a given sector over time. In the case of investment tax incentives, mostly firms operating in the agricultural, industrial, and commercial and services sectors can benefit from tax relief for their investments, although certain tax schemes (e.g. RFAI, Contractual Tax Benefits) apply to a wider range of sectors.

Figure 5.16. Sector-specific versus sector-neutral policies

In % of policy initiatives

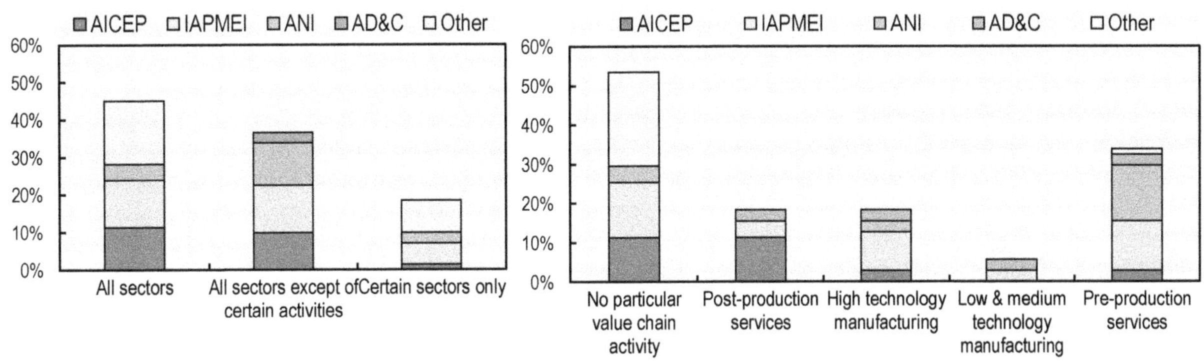

Note: The following value chain activities are considered: i) Pre-production services: R&D, concept development, design, patents; ii) Low and medium-technology manufacturing: production of simple, relatively unsophisticated goods such as basic metals, plastic products, food, textiles, etc; iii) High-technology manufacturing: production of highly specialised, technologically sophisticated goods such as computer and electronic products, pharmaceuticals, chemicals, medical products, etc; iv) Post-production services: marketing, sales, logistics, brand management, distribution and customer services.
Source: EU/OECD Survey on Policies enabling FDI spillovers to domestic SMEs (2021).

5.4. Key policies acting upon FDI-SME diffusion channels

Promoting FDI-SME linkages and strategic partnerships

Matchmaking services and financial incentives for R&D collaboration dominate the policy mix for value chain linkages and strategic partnerships

Portugal has a comprehensive policy framework to foster collaboration between foreign firms and domestic SMEs (However, financial incentives for R&D collaborations do not necessarily always involve foreign affiliates and their scope can be limited to collaborations between national actors only. The Suppliers Clubs programme has helped channel Portugal 2020 funding into collaborative R&D projects involving foreign affiliates and domestic firms; however more could be done to broaden their use for FDI-SME partnerships as well as partnerships between foreign affiliates and domestic R&D institutions. ANI, as the main agency responsible for collaborative R&D incentives, could encourage R&D-intensive foreign affiliates that do not participate in a Suppliers Club to engage in collaborative projects by prioritising their selection as recipients of financial support. Moreover, the success of the Suppliers Clubs programme could be further consolidated with the establishment of additional FDI-SME supplier networks in sectors of strategic importance for the Portuguese economy. Due consideration should be also given to monitoring the impact of the programme in the longer term to assess whether SMEs continue to benefit from supply chain linkages after the end of each project implementation cycle. The alignment of SME capacities with the needs of foreign investors will ensure that supplier networks are maintained after public support is phased out.

Figure 5.17; Table 5.3). As part of its aftercare services, AICEP implements two programmes that help foreign investors identify local suppliers, targeting traditional SMEs as well as young innovative start-ups. Several matchmaking platforms and local supplier databases are also in place to bring down information barriers and allow foreign and domestic firms to identify local sourcing and partnership opportunities. For instance, AICEP has developed a new platform, which relies on AI technology to deliver customised matchmaking services, while ANI operates the Business and Technology Exchange platform, which serves as a single access point for Portuguese technology offers and requests.

The Suppliers Clubs programme, which is AICEP's flagship initiative for the integration of Portuguese companies into global value chains, has been successful in mobilising a variety of public and private actors and delivering a package of support services to help local SMEs collaborate with foreign affiliates. The programme combines matchmaking services to help foreign and domestic firms identify collaboration opportunities and agree on jointly-implemented projects; business consulting and training programmes provided by foreign affiliates to their suppliers based on an assessment of their performance; and financial support through the Portugal 2020 incentive schemes to help SMEs upgrade their technological capabilities and respond to the needs of foreign firms. Such a comprehensive approach to supply chain development can help SMEs increase their chances of becoming partners and suppliers of foreign firms.

Many trade promotion policies provided by IPAs and SME agencies are also important for enabling SMEs to acquire new skills and upgrade their capabilities in various aspects of their performance – management, production, sales, innovation – and provide coaching and training in quality control and product certification. AICEP's *Internationalisation Academy* offers training programmes and online courses developed in partnership with Portuguese universities and business schools to help companies acquire knowledge of certification standards and processes. An *Online Exports Programme* also provides tailored consulting services on issues related to e-commerce and digital transformation. Financial incentives for internationalisation activities are another type of support that Portuguese SMEs can receive. For instance the *SME Internationalisation vouchers and grants* help SMEs acquire consulting services from international market experts and receive technical assistance for the implementation of export-oriented projects, including product certification.

Regarding strategic partnerships, the Portugal 2020 Incentives System for Research and Technological Development (SI I&DT) supports industrial research and experimental development activities implemented in partnership between companies or between companies and non-corporate entities of the Portuguese research and innovation ecosystem. ANI is responsible for the management and evaluation of applications submitted for these schemes, which cover various collaborative activities. For instance, the *Co-promotion R&D Centres* incentive provides financial support to a group of companies and non-corporate entities, who are led by an SME and aim to jointly develop innovative products, conduct technological feasibility studies, and share resources on the basis of a shared activity plan. Similarly, several other financial support schemes such as the *Mobiliser Programme* and the *Enterprise R&D* incentive provide higher co-financing rates when R&D activities are undertaken in a collaborative way among various companies.

However, financial incentives for R&D collaborations do not necessarily always involve foreign affiliates and their scope can be limited to collaborations between national actors only. The Suppliers Clubs programme has helped channel Portugal 2020 funding into collaborative R&D projects involving foreign affiliates and domestic firms; however more could be done to broaden their use for FDI-SME partnerships as well as partnerships between foreign affiliates and domestic R&D institutions. ANI, as the main agency responsible for collaborative R&D incentives, could encourage R&D-intensive foreign affiliates that do not participate in a Suppliers Club to engage in collaborative projects by prioritising their selection as recipients of financial support. Moreover, the success of the Suppliers Clubs programme could be further consolidated with the establishment of additional FDI-SME supplier networks in sectors of strategic importance for the Portuguese economy. Due consideration should be also given to monitoring the impact of the programme in the longer term to assess whether SMEs continue to benefit from supply chain linkages after the end of each project implementation cycle. The alignment of SME capacities with the needs of foreign investors will ensure that supplier networks are maintained after public support is phased out.

Figure 5.17. Policy instruments for value chain linkages and strategic partnerships

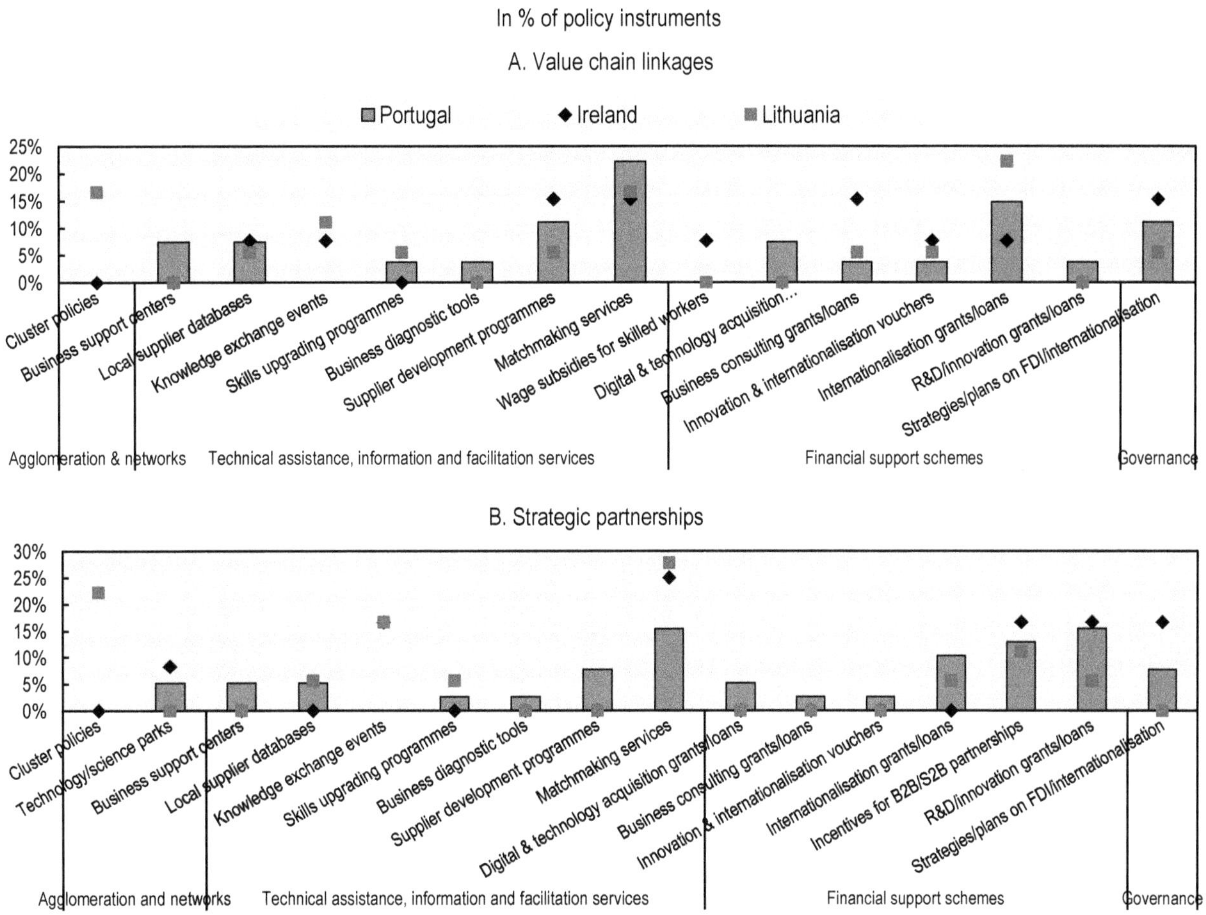

Source: EU/OECD Survey on Policies enabling FDI spillovers to domestic SMEs (2021).

Table 5.3. Main policies for value chain linkages and strategic partnerships

Main policies	Description	Implementing institution
Suppliers Network – Sourcing in Portugal Initiative	It involves B2B meetings and short business trips during which foreign investors meet Portuguese suppliers to evaluate the potential of their products and services and explore opportunities for collaboration.	AICEP
Startups Connecting Links programme	It introduces Portuguese startups to foreign multinationals and promote the products and services of young innovative firms with potential for growth.	AICEP
National Manufacturers Catalogue	IAPMEI maintains a *National Manufacturers Catalogue*, which contains information on products manufactured by Portuguese companies across different sectors	IAPMEI
Business Matchmaking platform	AICEP is currently developing a new Business Matchmaking platform, which will rely on AI technology, including machine learning and big data, to deliver customised services to	AICEP

	companies, including matching with investors, information on potential partners and internationalisation plans.	
Business and Technology Exchange platform	ANI operates a *Business and Technology Exchange platform*, which serves as a single access point for Portuguese technology offers and requests, allowing companies to receive information on collaborative R&D projects and identify opportunities for business partnerships.	ANI
Suppliers Clubs	Groups of Portuguese suppliers collaborate with foreign multinationals and other non-corporate entities of the Portuguese research and innovation ecosystem for the development of new products, services and technologies	AICEP, IAPMEI, ANI
Internationalisation Academy	AICEP's *Internationalisation Academy* offers training programmes and online courses developed in partnership with Portuguese universities and business schools to help companies diversify the markets in which they operate and acquire knowledge of certification standards and processes	AICEP
Export Offices	They are jointly operated by AICEP and IAPMEI in 10 different locations across Portugal, and provide information on available training programmes and help SMEs build business networks and approach foreign firms in domestic and international markets.	IAPMEI, AICEP
PT2020 SME Qualification and Internationalisation Incentives	The Portugal 2020 Incentives System for SME Qualification and Internationalisation includes a set of financial incentives to support companies in the development and promotion of their brand, the expansion of their business activities to international markets, the certification of products based on international standards, the setup of e-commerce platforms, and the introduction of new organisational and commercial business models	AICEP, IAPMEI
PT2020 R&D Collaboration Incentives	The Portugal 2020 Incentives System for Research and Technological Development (SI I&DT) supports industrial research and experimental development activities implemented in partnership between companies or between companies and non-corporate entities of the Portuguese research and innovation ecosystem	AICEP, ANI

Source: EU/OECD Survey on Policies enabling FDI spillovers to domestic SMEs (2021).

Facilitating the mobility of workers from foreign MNEs to the domestic entrepreneurial ecosystem

Productivity spillovers from labour mobility depend on the quality of labour market regulations and the availability of policies and programmes that encourage workers to move from foreign firms to the domestic entrepreneurial ecosystem. Striking the right balance between employment protection and adaptable labour markets, while incentivising the mobility of skilled workers in sectors with considerable FDI presence through targeted measures can contribute to greater spillovers on local economies.

Portugal's stringent employment protection regulations may hinder labour mobility in sectors and regions with low SME absorptive capacities

According to the OECD indicators of Employment Protection Legislation (EPL), in Portugal, rules for individual and collective dismissals of regular workers are significantly stricter than the OECD average (Figure 5.18). The regulatory setting for hiring temporary workers is, however, less strict than the rules for regular workers, but still significantly above the OECD average. Limits on dismissals can contribute to maintaining incomes in times of economic crisis, but overly restrictive regulations can reduce firms' survival chances. Restrictions in the hiring and firing of workers may also discourage Portuguese SMEs, which cannot easily match the wage rates of larger –often foreign– firms, from offering employment to highly skilled workers. As seen in Portugal and other EU countries (e.g. Netherlands, Sweden) relatively low regulation of temporary contracts in situations of high regulation of regular contracts can lead to strong labour market segmentation between highly protected regular workers and weakly protected temporary workers (OECD, 2014[20]). This dualism has deterred many employers from offering permanent contracts, leading to Portugal having one of the highest shares of workers on temporary employment in the EU (20.4% in Q2 2019, well above the EU average of 12.6%) (European Commission, 2020[21]).

Figure 5.18. Portugal has stricter regulations on employment protection than other OECD countries

OECD Employment Protection Legislation Indicators, 2019 (most strict = 6, least strict = 0)

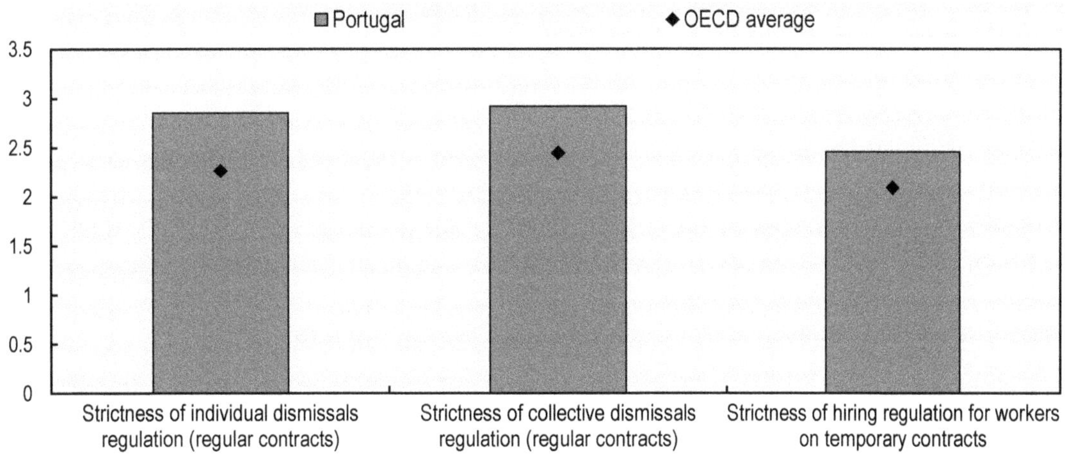

Note: The OECD indicators of employment protection are synthetic indicators of the strictness of regulation on dismissals and the use of temporary contracts. For each year, indicators refer to regulation in force on the 1st of January. Range of indicator scores: from 0 (low regulatory protection) to 6 (high regulatory protection).
Source: OECD Employment Protection Legislation Database, 2019

The overall restrictiveness of the Portuguese labour market policy regime points towards potential weaknesses in the diffusion of productivity and innovation through labour mobility, in particular in regions and sectors with low absorptive capacities. Recent evidence from EU countries shows that the benefits for a local economy from FDI are lowest where there exist a combination of stringent employment protection legislation and low absorptive capacity of domestic firms (Becker et al., 2020[22]). This is because foreign firms seek to attract local talent by offering higher wages that domestic firms with low absorptive capacity are unable to match. Increased wage disparities coupled with rigid labour market conditions limit the ability of domestic firms to retain and attract skilled workers, leading to a significant crowding out effect that holds back labour mobility towards domestic firms.

Strict dismissal regulations may also affect Portuguese firms' incentive to invest in the human capital of their employees, which is an important component of a firm's absorptive capacity. Evidence on the impact of employment protection regulations on job training decisions shows that enforcing overly restrictive dismissal regulations combined with lower regulation of temporary contracts (as is the case in Portugal) may lead to reduced investment by firms on improving the skills of their employees (Almeida and Aterido, 2011[23]). This is mainly due to the increased firing costs that firms have to face and the relative ease of offering temporary employment, which does not involve long-term skills enhancement opportunities. Recent labour policies in Portugal have focused on disincentivising the use of temporary contracts. The 2019 labour market reform reduced the maximum duration of temporary contracts from 3 to 2 years and introduced a requirement for firms to justify their use. The *Contrato-Geração* measure was also implemented with the aim to promote permanent employment for both first-time jobseekers and the long-term unemployed (European Commission, 2020[21]). These measures have not, however, addressed the overall restrictiveness of the regulatory framework.

In line with recommendations from the 2021 OECD Economic Survey of Portugal, the government should consider reforming certain labour market rules to strike the right balance between employment protection and adaptable labour markets – for instance, by allowing dismissals for performance-related reasons while maintaining strong protection against arbitrary dismissals (OECD, 2020[24]; OECD, 2021[10]). Labour market regulations and their role in FDI-SME diffusion should be also considered in the context of other drivers of labour mobility, including the absorptive capacity of domestic SMEs and the availability (or lack) of skills in the local labour force (see section on SME absorptive capacities). Portuguese SMEs will also need to have access to technical and financial support to provide on-the-job training to their employees. Measures that strengthen their competitiveness and productivity can help them compete effectively with foreign affiliates, offer better wages and attract highly skilled workers.

The labour mobility channel receives less policy attention in the overall policy mix

The main Portuguese government agencies do not implement many targeted policies that could contribute to greater labour mobility between foreign and domestic firms. In fact, this is not unusual among EU Member States. Preliminary findings from the OECD/EU Survey on Policies enabling FDI spillovers to domestic SMEs show that the labour mobility channel receives less attention from policymakers. In many EU countries, labour mobility schemes are linked to broader skill development strategies that aim to reduce skill mismatches and shortages in sectors where FDI activity is concentrated.

AICEP implements the *INOV Contacto* programme, which allows highly-skilled young graduates to conduct a short-term internship in a Portuguese company, followed by a long-term internship in a foreign multinational (Box 5.2). Since its launch in 1997, the programme has involved more than 1280 Portuguese and foreign firms and close to 6000 young employees. In the Slovak Republic, a similar internship programme for entrepreneurs is implemented by the Slovak Business Agency (SBA) whereby SME employees and individual entrepreneurs spend three months in a foreign firm, business incubator or technology park and receive counselling services from foreign experts and mentors. Although these policies do not affect the overall labour market conditions, they can provide a more targeted approach to facilitating the transfer of knowledge and skills to local labour markets.

Box 5.2. Labour mobility schemes involving foreign and domestic firms in Portugal and Slovakia

INOV Contacto programme (Portugal)

INOV Contacto is an international professional internship programme managed by AICEP that places highly qualified graduates in foreign multinationals and Portuguese firms with offices abroad for a period of 6-9 months. The programme aims to support the internationalisation of Portuguese firms through the integration of highly skilled employees in their workforce and foster links between local firms and foreign multinational companies through labour mobility. The programme is structured in three distinct parts: 1) a startup one-week course on international management; ii) short-term internship in a Portuguese company; iii) long-term internship in a multinational company abroad. Since its establishment in 1997, the programme has sent more than 5000 young professionals to work as interns in Portuguese and foreign multinational companies, allowing them to sharpen their skills in an international environment while contributing to the transfer of knowledge and skills to the Portuguese labour market.

Internship programme (Slovak Republic)

The Slovak Business Agency's (SBA) Internship Programme is designed to assist innovative companies and aspiring entrepreneurs to obtain experience in doing business in foreign markets via counselling services from foreign experts and mentors. The target group of support included companies established 3 years before at the latest (sole traders, limited liability companies, joint-stock companies) in various areas. The programme supports three types of 'internship': i) a three month stay in a business incubator, foreign firm or technology park in Israel, Singapore or the United States; ii) one week of training in the agency's National Business Centre (NBA) followed by one month abroad in another EU country; or a 5-day stay at an international conference or workshop in another EU country.

Source: EU/OECD Survey on Policies enabling FDI spillovers to domestic SMEs (2021).

Linked to domestic labour mobility schemes is the increasing number of policies adopted by OECD governments to facilitate immigration of business talent as a way to help domestic economies become more innovative and fulfil the skill needs of foreign investors. In Portugal, IAPMEI is responsible for the *Tech Visa* programme, which is addressed to companies that wish to attract highly qualified employees from outside of the EU's Schengen Zone. Only companies that demonstrate strong technological capabilities and market potential in knowledge intensive and high-technology sectors can benefit from the programme. The impact of these schemes on the productivity and innovation of domestic economies is not clear, but other factors such as labour market conditions, the presence of a thriving startup ecosystem, and the quality of the business environment are thought to be key determinants.

Portugal could build on the success of the *INOV Contacto* programme and broaden the range of policies available to encourage labour mobility between foreign and domestic firms. Incentives for corporate spin-outs could allow large firm employees, including foreign affiliates, to create their own company. Payroll tax incentives for highly-skilled or R&D workers could also encourage domestic SMEs to hire qualified employees with prior experience in multinational firms.

Creating market conditions for fair competition and knowledge exchange between foreign MNEs and local SMEs

Competition rules that ensure a level playing field for foreign and domestic firms can facilitate the entry of foreign investors and, at the same time, incentivise domestic firms to become more productive, innovate and improve the quality of their products (Lembcke and Wildnerova, 2020[25]). Policies that ensure intellectual property (IP) rights protection are also important as they guarantee the appropriability of knowledge and innovation benefits, and determine the qualities of FDI that can be attracted.

Certain product market regulations could be further streamlined to improve competition

According to the OECD Product Market Regulation (PMR) indicators, which measure the degree to which laws and policies promote or inhibit competition, regulatory barriers to competition are on par with the OECD and EU averages (Figure 5.19). Public ownership and administrative requirements on start-ups are limited while the licensing regime is very lean. Businesses can be informed about all licences and issue them through a dedicated one-stop-shop, and a 'silence is consent' rule is applied, which reduces waiting time for licence approvals. The legal framework for public procurement of goods and services is also aligned with OECD good practices. For instance, contracting authorities are obliged to make all tender documents available online and free of charge, and facilitate online tender submissions by all firms (OECD, 2018[26]).

Figure 5.19. More pro-competitive regulation is needed in certain areas

OECD Product Market Regulation, 2018 (most competitive=0; least competitive=6)

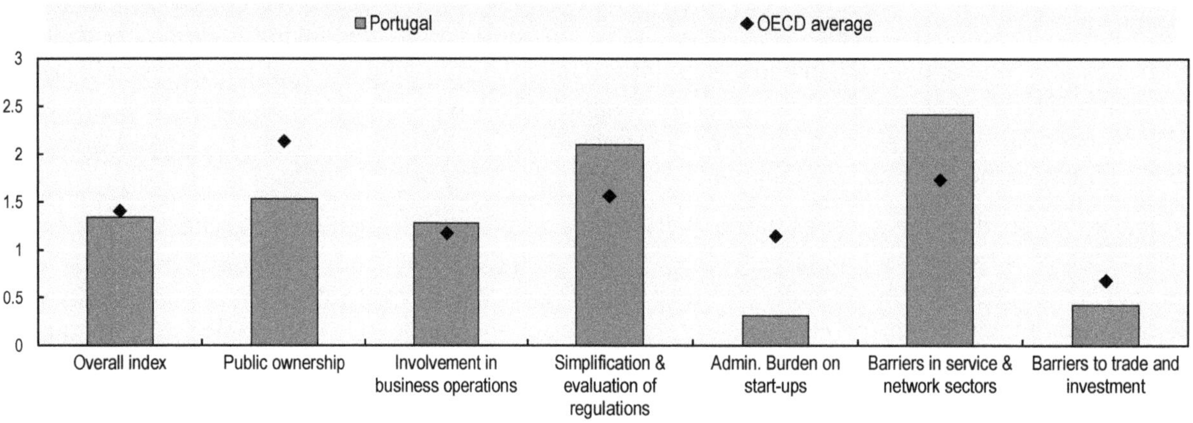

Note: The indicators refer to economy-wide regulation and are composed of the simple average of the sub-indicators on State involvement and Barriers to entry. The indicators range between 0 (most competitive) and 6 (least competitive environment).
Source: OECD PMR database, 2018.

Despite reform efforts, Portugal's PMR score indicates that there is scope to further improve its performance in the area of simplification and evaluation of regulations. The quality of public services and coherence and transparency of regulations are factors that significantly influence competition and the investment climate more broadly (OECD, 2015[27]). Several reforms have been introduced in Portugal to reduce administrative burdens for business. This included the elimination of licensing surcharges levied by municipalities, the consolidation of environmental licences, and the implementation of the Zero Authorisation initiative, which replaced various formal authorisation procedures with business making a declaration via an e-government portal. The *Simplex+* Programme was also launched in 2016 aiming to simplify laws and regulations and de-bureaucratise public services (OECD, 2019[12]). It continued efforts made by the *Simplex* programme (2006-11) and the *Simplificar* programme (2014), which focused on administrative simplification and e-government. Recent policy initiatives have increasingly focused on promoting the use of digital solutions for the simplification of public administration procedures and rules. The 2020 Action Plan for Digital Transition (*Plano de Ação para a Transição Digital*) puts forward a set of measures aiming at the digitalisation of the public administration, including the digitisation of 25 public services most used by citizens and companies and the simplification of public procurement rules. Additional measures on administrative simplification have been also included in the Strategy for Innovation and Modernisation of the State and Public Administration 2020-2023 (*Estratégia para a Inovação e Modernização do Estado e da Administração Pública 2020-2023*) (Government of Portugal, 2020[28]).

At the sectoral level, professional services (e.g. lawyers, accountants, civil engineers, etc.) and the retail sector face considerable barriers to entry and conduct restraints (Figure 5.20). Although these sectors are not FDI-intensive and therefore less relevant for FDI spillovers, they can still affect foreign affiliates' business operations in downstream sectors. When firms are subject to overly restrictive entry restrictions and onerous rules for conducting their business, a lack of competitive pressure may induce them to charge above-market prices, provide sub-optimal services and fail to adapt to market changes and innovation. The regulatory burden on these sectors could be eased by removing burdensome registration and licensing rules. These reforms are already included in the recently agreed Resilience and Recovery Plan, whereby the Portuguese government commits to streamlining the regulatory environment and removing any competition-distorting rules for highly regulated professions (Government of Portugal, 2021[13]).

Figure 5.20. Retail trade and professional services are heavily regulated

OECD Product Market Regulation, by sector, 2018

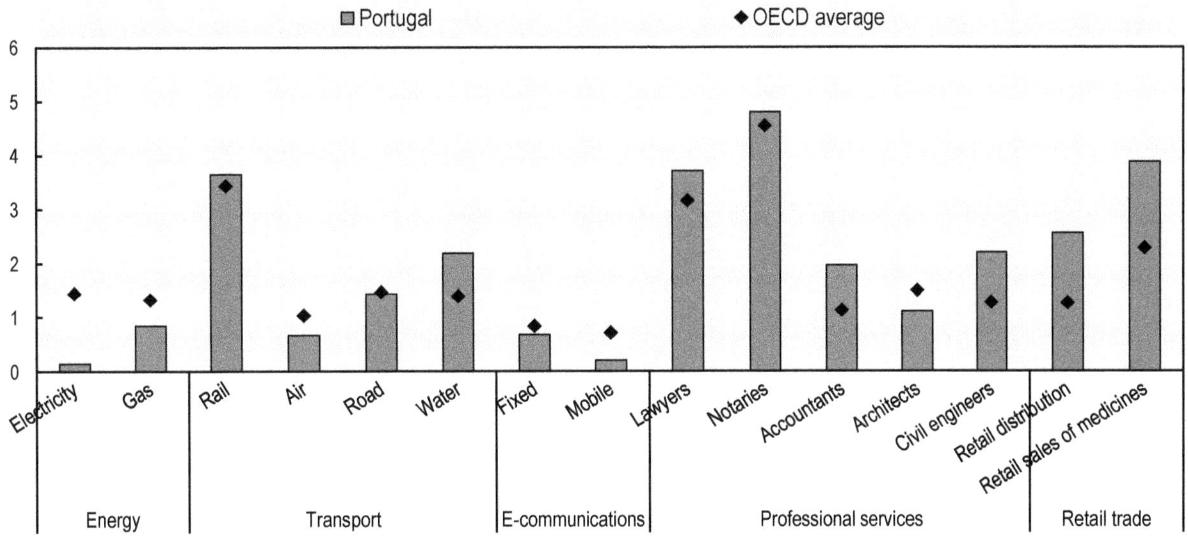

Note: Index scale 0 to 6 from most to least competition-friendly regulation.
Source: OECD 2018 PMR database

Portugal has a strong legal framework for intellectual property protection

Portugal has an extensive legal framework for IP rights protection that complies with European and international standards. It ranks 32nd out of 141 countries in terms of IP protection in the World Economic Forum's 2019 Competitiveness Report, and 31st out of 131 economies in the Global Innovation Index 2020 prepared by the World Intellectual Property Organisation (WIPO), INSEAD and Cornell University (World Economic Forum, 2019[29]; Cornell University, INSEAD, and WIPO, 2020[30]).

The registration of IP rights is done through the National Industrial Property Institute (INPI), which operates under the Portuguese Ministry of Justice. INPI organises seminars and training programmes through its Industrial Property Academy to help businesses, in particular SMEs, familiarise themselves with IP rights protection tools and processes, and makes available templates that Portuguese firms can use for technology transfer and R&D agreements. A set of financial support schemes is also available under the Portugal 2020 Incentives System for Research and Technological Development (SI I&DT) to help SMEs register their inventions, industrial designs and trademarks in Portugal and abroad.

The main legal instrument for the protection of IP rights is the Industrial Property Code (IPC), which was introduced in 2003 and covers several categories of IP rights, namely patents, utility models, trademarks, industrial designs, designations of origin and geographical indications. Over the years, the IPC has been amended and harmonised with that of other EU countries through several legal acts that incorporated EU directives on areas such as the protection of biotechnological inventions, the protection of designs, trademarks and trade secrets and the creation of supplementary protection certificates for certain products.

The enforcement of IP rights and the settlement of disputes have also significantly improved since the establishment of a specialised Intellectual Property Court in 2012. The court has jurisdiction to rule on all matters relating to industrial property rights and has contributed to more efficient litigation processes. Prior to its establishment, considerable delays in the procedural stages and decision of cases involving the enforcement of IP rights were observed in Portugal due to the backlogs of cases piled up on the calendars of civil courts (Andrade, 2015[31]). Disputes may be also settled through alternative dispute resolution such as mediation or arbitration before bringing a case before the Portuguese courts. The Arbitration Tribunal (ARBITRARE), is a state-supported arbitration centre for mediation and arbitration, which has jurisdiction to resolve solely disputes relating to industrial property between private parties and between applicants and the INPI.

The enforcement of IP rights has been further addressed since a dedicated Task Force was created to combat counterfeiting. The Anti-Counterfeiting Group aims to foster inter-institutional cooperation and strengthen the mechanisms available to address infringements of industrial property rights. The group also aims to raise awareness on IP rights, exchange statistical information on the seizure of counterfeit products and reflect on the quality of the national legal framework. The creation of specialised structures for combatting counterfeiting is common among EU Member States.

Demonstration and knowledge exchange events targeting foreign affiliates and domestic SMEs could be leveraged further to strengthen imitation effects

The organisation of networking and knowledge exchange events is a common practice among government agencies responsible for investment promotion, SME and innovation policies. For instance, Enterprise Ireland, the Irish SME agency, organises Best Practice Study Visits that allow Irish firms to visit the manufacturing plants of foreign firms and get first-hand experience on their business practices and processes.

Similarly in Portugal, IAPMEI implements the *Open Days i4.0* initiative which aims to present the technological capabilities of innovative companies during stakeholder events and promote the sharing of experiences between market actors operating in the same value chains. These public events include, in addition to moments of networking and information sharing, visits to the most advanced industrial plants in Portugal, presentations of innovative technologies, exhibitions of technology products and hands-on discussions between business representatives and other market stakeholders. The initiative is one of the measures of the Industry 4.0 Programme. Best practice demonstration events are also supported through the Portugal 2020 Incentives System for Research and Technological Development. Financial support is available to companies that want to present the outcome of their R&D activities. The public character of these demonstration actions must always be ensured for financial support to be granted.

References

Almeida, R. and R. Aterido (2011), "On-the-job training and rigidity of employment protection in the developing world: Evidence from differential enforcement", *Labour Economics*, Vol. 18, pp. S71-S82, http://dx.doi.org/10.1016/j.labeco.2011.05.001. [23]

Baechtold, R. (ed.) (2015), *Portugal*, Law Business Research Ltd, https://www.vda.pt/xms/files/v1/Publicacoes/2015/The_Intellectual_Property_Review_-_Portugal_Chapter.pdf. [31]

Becker, B. et al. (2020), "FDI in hot labour markets: The implications of the war for talent", *Journal of International Business Policy (2020)*, pp. 107–133. [22]

Cornell University, INSEAD, and WIPO (2020), *The Global Innovation Index 2020: Who Will Finance Innovation?*, https://www.wipo.int/edocs/pubdocs/en/wipo_pub_gii_2020.pdf. [30]

European Commission (2020), *Country Report Portugal 2020*, https://eur-lex.europa.eu/legal-content/EN/TXT/PDF/?uri=CELEX:52020SC0521&from=EN. [21]

European Commission (2020), *The 2020 EU Justice Scoreboard*, Luxembourg: Publications Office of the European Union, https://ec.europa.eu/info/sites/default/files/justice_scoreboard_2020_en.pdf. [11]

European Commission (2019), *2019 SBA Fact Sheet & Scoreboard*, https://ec.europa.eu/docsroom/documents/38662/attachments/1/translations/en/renditions/native. [8]

Farole, T. and D. Winkler (eds.) (2014), *Making Foreign Direct Investment Work for Sub-Saharan Africa:Local Spillovers and Competitiveness in Global Value Chains*, The World Bank, http://dx.doi.org/10.1596/978-1-4648-0126-6. [7]

Government of Portugal (2021), *Recovery and Resilience Plan*, Ministerio do Planeamento, https://dados.gov.pt/s/resources/documentacao-do-prr/20210502-190055/43-20210421-prr-finalcom.pdf. [13]

Government of Portugal (2020), *Estratégia para a Inovação e Modernização do Estado e da Administração Pública 2020 -2023*, https://www.portugal.gov.pt/download-ficheiros/ficheiro.aspx?v=%3d%3dBQAAAB%2bLCAAAAAAABAAzNDCyNAcAwYeeOwUAAAA%3d. [28]

Government of Portugal (2017), *Portugal INCoDe.2030, Iniciativa Nacional Competências Digitais, 2030*, http://www.incode2030.gov.pt/sites/default/files/incode2030_en.pdf (accessed on 11 March 2021). [15]

Government of Portugal (2014), *Decree-Law No. 138/2014 of 15 September*, https://dre.pt/pesquisa/-/search/56819089/details/maximized. [4]

Government of Portugal (2014), *Estratégia de Investigação e Inovação para uma Especialização Inteligente (EI&I)*, https://www.compete2020.gov.pt/admin/images/RIS3_Nacional_ENEI_Especializacao-Inteligente.pdf. [19]

IAPMEI (2021), *Clusters de Competitividade: Pactos para a competitividade e internacionalização*, https://www.iapmei.pt/getattachment/PRODUTOS-E-SERVICOS/Empreendedorismo-Inovacao/Eficiencia-Coletiva-e-Clusters/BrochuraClusters04052021.pdf.aspx. [18]

Lembcke, A. and L. Wildnerova (2020), "Does FDI benefit incumbent SMEs?: FDI spillovers and competition effects at the local level", *OECD Regional Development Working Papers*, No. 2020/02, OECD Publishing, Paris, https://dx.doi.org/10.1787/47763241-en. [25]

Meissner, D. and S. Kergroach (2019), "Innovation policy mix: mapping and measurement", *The Journal of Technology Transfer*, Vol. 46/1, pp. 197-222, http://dx.doi.org/10.1007/s10961-019-09767-4. [2]

OECD (2021), *OECD Economic Surveys: Portugal 2021*, OECD Publishing, Paris, https://dx.doi.org/10.1787/13b842d6-en. [10]

OECD (2020), *Financing SMEs and Entrepreneurs 2020: An OECD Scoreboard*, OECD Publishing, Paris, https://dx.doi.org/10.1787/061fe03d-en. [9]

OECD (2020), *OECD Employment Outlook 2020: Worker Security and the COVID-19 Crisis*, OECD Publishing, Paris, https://dx.doi.org/10.1787/1686c758-en. [24]

OECD (2020), *OECD R&D tax incentives database, 2020 edition*, http://www.oecd.org/sti/rd-tax-stats-database.pdf. [6]

OECD (2020), *Strengthening the Governance of Skills Systems: Lessons from Six OECD Countries*, OECD Skills Studies, OECD Publishing, Paris, https://dx.doi.org/10.1787/3a4bb6ea-en. [16]

OECD (2019), *OECD Economic Surveys: Portugal 2019*, OECD Publishing, Paris, https://dx.doi.org/10.1787/eco_surveys-prt-2019-en. [12]

OECD (2019), *OECD Review of Higher Education, Research and Innovation: Portugal*, OECD Publishing, Paris, https://dx.doi.org/10.1787/9789264308138-en. [17]

OECD (2019), *Services Trade Restrictiveness Index (STRI): Portugal 2019*, http://www.oecd.org/trade/topics/services-trade/documents/oecd-stri-country-note-portugal.pdf. [5]

OECD (2018), *Mapping of Investment Promotion Agencies in OECD Countries*, http://www.oecd.org/investment/Mapping-of-Investment-Promotion-Agencies-in-OECD-Countries.pdf. [1]

OECD (2018), *OECD Product Market Regulation (PMR) Indicators: How does portugal compare?*, https://issuu.com/oecd.publishing/docs/prt_country_note_-_tot_final. [26]

OECD (2015), *Policy Framework for Investment, 2015 Edition*, OECD Publishing, Paris, https://dx.doi.org/10.1787/9789264208667-en. [27]

OECD (2014), *OECD Employment Outlook 2014*, OECD Publishing, Paris, https://dx.doi.org/10.1787/empl_outlook-2014-en. [20]

PME Investimentos (2018), *Linha Capitalizar 2018*, https://www.pmeinvestimentos.pt/linhas-de-credito/linha-capitalizar-2018/. [14]

US Department of State (2020), *2020 Investment Climate Statements: Portugal*, https://www.state.gov/reports/2020-investment-climate-statements/portugal/. [3]

World Economic Forum (2019), *The Global Competitiveness Report, World Economic Forum, Geneva*, http://www3.weforum.org/docs/WEF_TheGlobalCompetitivenessReport2019.pdf. [29]

Note

[1] Considering the number of policy initiatives that target certain policy objectives is only a partial measure of policy focus in a given area. One policy could rely on more resources (e.g. higher budget) for its implementation, and therefore have greater impact, while several policies in another case could be underfunded and not sufficiently effective to achieve the pursued outcomes.

6 Applying a regional lens

In a world with increasingly fragmented production lines, multinational firms do not just choose countries, they select regions. Business activity and performance are also unevenly distributed within countries. As such, policies to strengthen productivity and innovation spillovers from international investments on domestic firms cannot be space blind. The regions of Alentejo and Norte are used as examples to point out how much variation can be found within a country and what can be done when developing polices and institutional frameworks to support such spillovers, including the role of subnational governments.

6.1. Summary of findings and recommendations

The productivity and innovation of local small and medium-sized enterprises (SMEs) can be enhanced through spillovers from investments and activities by foreign firms. There are several enabling factors that influence how successfully knowledge could diffuse, as well as a number of diffusion channels are at play. These enabling factors are the potential for FDI spillovers and arise from the types, motivation and origin of FDI received, the absorptive capacity of domestic SMEs to turn new knowledge into value within their operations, and the characteristics of the wider economic and geographical environment in which the firms function.

Regions can differ greatly within a country, whether because of fixed factors (such as the availability of natural resources) or policies (that affect for instance the quality of the transport network, the education system, or local governments and institutions) that in turn determine population, density of services and business activities. To this extent, the firms within regions also differ, as do trade and investment opportunities. Multinational enterprises (MNEs) increasingly consider regional rather than country-specific factors when choosing where to invest. Policies to improve spillovers from FDI to domestic SMEs are therefore more likely to be effective when these regional factors are taken into account.

This chapter focuses on these particular regional aspects factors, using the two examples of Norte and Alentejo. The two regions are distinctively different: Norte is a larger, demographically younger, more industrialised region, while Alentejo is a more remote, traditionally agricultural location, in close proximity to the capital Lisbon. This chapter explores their regional structural and economic differences, including in the types of SMEs and MNEs present. It looks into the performance of FDI-SME diffusion channels and how local policy and institutions intend to create the right economic and geographical environment for FDI-SME innovation linkages, in particular through better tailored industrial clustering and increased agglomeration benefits (Table 6.1).

Table 6.1. Findings and Recommendations Alentejo and Norte

	Norte	Alentejo
Regional characteristics	Larger, demographically younger, more industrialised region specialising in advanced manufacturing	More remote, traditionally agricultural location with technologically advanced FDI in the west (close proximity to the capital Lisbon) but regionally operating almost as 5 different entities.
Creating enabling conditions		
Increasing the potential for FDI spillovers	Successful local investment promotion agencies of Porto/Braga however wider strategic regional promotion strategy needed.	Nationally driven with some recent role from local municipalities.
Improving local SME absorptive capacity	Multiple regional agencies surveyed argue that reducing bureaucracy and better targeting could increase the number of SMEs assisted	Many types of assistance available for SMEs, particularly following COVID-19 but lack co-ordination.
Tailoring industrial clustering	Co-ordination across municipal council lead to a lack of territorial planning and difficulties building links across clusters	46 industrial parks (25% of all in Portugal) though dominated by those in Sines. Methods to improve spillovers from this area to other parts of the region to be considered.
Consolidating agglomeration benefits	Further work across agencies to capitalise on buoyant labour market and tackle high building rents	Should focus on improving internet connectivity and transportation access to Lisbon to exploit the larger good/services markets found there
Strengthening FDI-SME diffusion channels		
Building value chains linkages	IPAs link FDI with SMEs continual monitoring and mapping of regional firms could be beneficial	Regional management team capacity and capability could be enhanced with assistance from National Government.
Building strategic partnerships	High levels of joint patent applications indicating good level of partnerships despite largest domestic-FDI productivity gap in Portugal	Improve partnerships between research organisations

6.2. The differing characteristics of Norte and Alentejo

Both Portuguese regions differ substantially in their geographic characteristics, demographic structure, and level of development, economic structure and specialisation (Table 6.2). Norte is the most populous territory in Portugal and contributes almost half of all country's manufacturing activities. The southwest of the region (Área Metropolitana do Porto, Ave, Cávado) is highly industrialised, Alto Minho (Northeast) has a mixed specialisation, and Alto Tâmega and Terras de Trás-os-Montes are largely rural. Norte shows intraregional imbalances as a high proportion of its population, investment and public and private services are concentrated in the region of Porto. Alentejo has a sparsely distributed population. Its land covers around one-third of the country's territory with no metropolitan areas, though the west borders the Lisbon area. Using the OECD alternative territorial typology the TL2 region of Alentejo has over 50% of its 700 000 population with no access to any functional urban areas within a 60-minute drive (Fadic et al., 2019[1]). The region faces challenges of ageing population and rural exodus. Its endowment with vast amounts of coastland, rich soils and plenty of minerals and natural resources, facilitates agriculture, Alentejo being known as the "breadbasket of Portugal", and livestock farming, more specifically in the northern part.

Table 6.2 Summary table of regional characteristics

Characteristic	Norte	Alentejo	Portugal Average	OECD average
Portugal share of FDI	20.6%	6.2%	N/A	
Number of SMEs	86,054	430,732	N/A	
Population	3.6m	0.7m	N/A	
Share in a functional urban area	51.6%	10.2%	49.7%	58.8%
GDP per capita	USD 27,478	USD 30,141	USD 34,198	USD 44,571
Labour Productivity	USD 50,321	USD 57,493	USD 57,299	USD 72,507
Top industries by GVA share	Construction, manufacturing	Distributive trade, repairs, transport, accommodation, food service, activities in public administration	Distributive trade, repairs, transport, accommodation, food service	N/A
Employment rate	69.0%	70.2%	69.5%	66.0%
Share of population with tertiary education	12.0%	10.2%	26.3%	38.0%
Internet access	62%	46%	74%	81%

Note: Population, Employment – 2019, Productivity, GDP and Industrial specialisation – 2018, Internet access – 2016, Education – 2015,
Source: OECD (2020), OECD Regional Statistics (database) https://doi.org/10.1787/region-data-en, (PORDATA, 2021[2]), Ookla® Global Fixed and Mobile Network Performance.

Economic and industrial structure and performance

Norte's economy is dominated by manufacturing and industry sectors (excluding energy) (Figure 6.1, Panel A). Industrial production represented half of the region's gross value added (GVA) in 2018. More than one third of total employment in the region is in manufacturing and the share of jobs in industry increased by over 30 000 between 2010 and 2019. In 2020, in the context of the COVID-19 crisis, jobs fell by over 14 500, in part because of the substantial export orientation of Norte's industrial production. Manufactured products include textile and footwear, cork agglomerates, automotive parts and accessories, dairy products and wine. This reflects the diversity of the region; the southwest of the region (Porto and Braga districts) is highly industrialised, the Viana do Castelo district (Northeast) has a mixed specialisation, and the Vila Real and Bragança districts are largely rural (Figure 6.1, Panel B). Between 2004 and 2018, the sectoral composition of Norte has remained overall relatively stable, with Porto losing a number of sectors, particularly construction (Figure 6.2).

The Norte's Smart Specialisation Strategy (2014-20) focuses on improving manufacturing capabilities through increased technological adoption and human capital, and on providing specialised services (Box 6.1). It also aims to the sustainability of food, agri-environments and maritime resources, and to promote culture and creativity through tourism services. There is also a strong interest in health and life sciences.

Manufacturing in Alentejo remains limited, with 1 in every 8 people working in the sector, which is largely associated with agri-foods (e.g., cheese, wine, smoked meats) in central and inner regions of Alentejo, and a growing chemicals, transport or electronic components industry in Alentejo Litoral that hosts the petrochemical complex of Sines. Alentejo is also the largest cork-producing area in the world. Tourism plays also an important role in the region and the services represent the majority of employment – close to 60% –, although the COVID-19 has significantly affected the sector, with 16 400 fewer service jobs over 2020, particularly in hotels and restaurants (4 800 fewer) and vehicle trade and repair (2 700 fewer). At the same time fewer than 30% of jobs in the region were amenable to remote working. Between 2004 and 2018, the sectoral composition of Alentejo has changed more significantly than in Norte (Figure 6.1, Panel C) with a generalised shift in location away from Leziria de Tejo and a relocation in Baixo Alentejo, or Alto Alentejo in the case of information and communication services (Figure 6.2, Panel B).

Alentejo's strategy aims to sustainably promoting its economies related to food, forestry, minerals and other natural resources though there is a growing automotive and electronic industry –driven by the petrochemical complex of Sines in Alentejo litoral. It also aims to boost critical technologies, energy and smart mobility. Heritage, cultural and creative industries and tourism services receive particular attention, as well as specialised services of the social economy.

Norte was the region (TL2) with the lowest productivity level in 2018 in Portugal (Figure 6.3). However, GDP per capita in the metropolitan area of Porto has grown faster than in Lisbon in the most recent years. Alentejo's productivity has declined since 2015.

Box 6.1. Cluster policies and Smart Specialisation Strategy

By promoting "smart specialisation" strategies, national governments and regional authorities are attempting to enhance the competitiveness of firms and clusters. Clusters are a geographic concentration of firms, higher education and research institutions, and other public and private entities that facilitate collaboration on complementary economic activities. The main rationale for public policies to promote clusters is to increase knowledge spillovers among actors in clusters and generate a collective pool of knowledge (OECD, 2014[3]).

Smart specialisation serves an evidence-based policy framework that uses indicators, technology foresight and other priority-setting tools to help entrepreneurs and firms strengthen existing scientific, technological and industrial specialisation patterns while identifying and encouraging the emergence of new domains of economic and technological activity (OECD, 2014[3]) (OECD, 2013[4]).

The genesis of the concept can be traced back to an EU expert group who advanced that governments should focus their knowledge investments in activities – not in sectors *per se* – that reflect areas where a region or country has some comparative advantage (specialisation) or emerging areas where entrepreneurs could develop new activities (diversification) (Foray, David and Hall, 2009[5]). This connection between specialisation and technological diversification in the context of regional development has been highly influential and demonstrated that the smart specialisation as policy framework is well suited for dealing with the problems of place-based growth (McCann and Ortega-Argilés, 2013[6]).

The smart specialisation concept has been promoted at EU level through the establishment of the S³ Platform to assist regions and member states to develop regional strategies and identify the high value-added activities that offer the best chances of strengthening their competitiveness. The principles behind smart specialisation became a central element of the Europe 2020 Strategy and smart specialisation strategies have been incorporated as an *ex ante* condition to access the European Fund for Regional Development (ERDF) (OECD, 2013[4]). The same principles are also an enabling condition to be fulfilled by regions for mobilising the resources of the 2021-27 Cohesion Policy.

Key policies to support smart specialisation strategies include (OECD, 2013[4]) (OECD, 2020[7]):

- ***Policies for entrepreneurial discovery***: e.g. incentives for entrepreneurs, inter-regional linkages, new mechanisms to detect novel ideas and encourage experimentation ("self-discovery" process), and educational programmes. Smart specialisation calls for an "entrepreneurial selection" of market opportunities through a bottom-up approach.
- ***Promoting general-purpose technology platforms and networks***: e.g. technology platforms involving public and private actors, as well as standard-setting organisations.
- ***Policy intelligence and monitoring and evaluation system***: e.g. diagnostic tools, strategic analysis, mutual learning practices, or participatory foresight, and a sound monitoring and evaluation infrastructure behind, which could also involve external expertise and pilot exercises.
- ***Strategic governance for smart specialisation***: e.g. the development of local capabilities to identify local strengths and bring the results obtained from the "self-discovery" process into prioritisation; align policy actions with objectives; achieve strategic coordination, develop a vision and implementing action.

Source: (OECD, 2020[7]) Rural Wellbeing; (OECD, 2014[3]); (OECD, 2013[4]), (Foray, David and Hall, 2009[5]), (McCann and Ortega-Argilés, 2013[6]).

Figure 6.1. Regional Sectoral Concentration

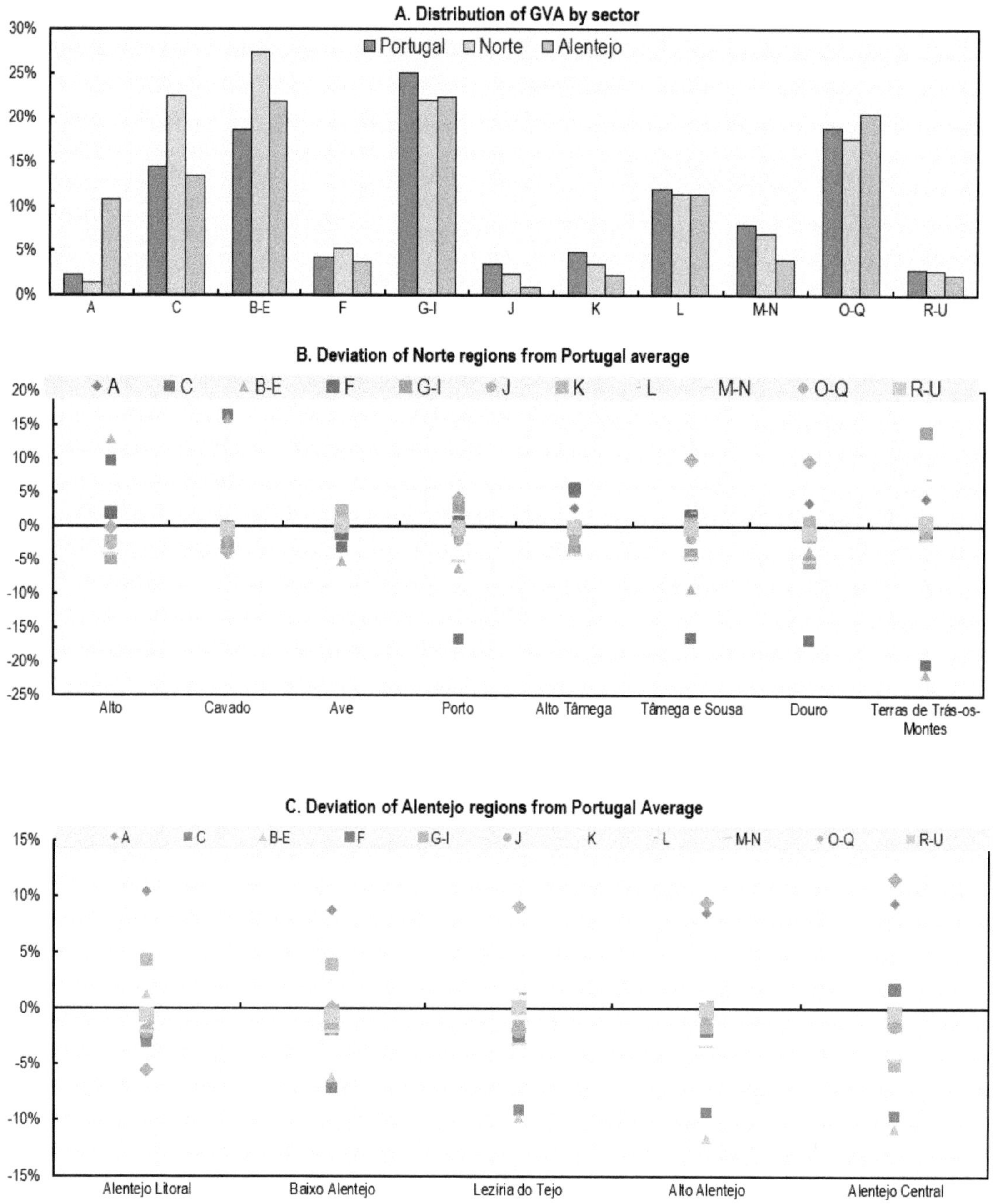

Note: Deviations are read as values e.g. in Portugal Manufacturing (C) makes up 14% of GVA (fig A), in Alto it makes up 24% i.e. 10% more than in Portugal (Fig B). A= agriculture, forestry and fishing, C= manufacturing, B-E = industry including energy, F= construction, G-I= distributive trade, repairs, transport, accommodation, food serv. Activities, J= Information and communication, K = financial and insurance activities, L = real estate activities, M-N = prof., scientific, techn. activities, admin., support service activities, O-Q= public admin., compulsory s.s., education, human health, R-U= other services.

Source: OECD (2020), OECD Regional Statistics (database), http://dx.doi.org/10.1787/region-data-en.

Figure 6.2. Change in sectoral composition over time

Percentage change in GVA, by sector and region, 2004-18

A. Norte change in sectoral share over time: 2004-2018

	Total	A	C	B-E	F	G-I	J	K	L	M-N	O-Q	R-U
Alto Minho	0%	0%	2%	2%	-1%	0%	-1%	0%	0%	0%	0%	1%
Cavado	1%	1%	0%	0%	7%	2%	2%	1%	0%	3%	-1%	1%
Ave	1%	0%	2%	1%	2%	1%	1%	0%	0%	1%	0%	2%
Porto	-2%	-2%	-5%	-5%	-11%	-4%	2%	0%	1%	-4%	1%	-7%
Alto Tâmega	0%	0%	0%	0%	0%	0%	0%	0%	0%	0%	0%	1%
Tâmega e Sousa	0%	-1%	1%	0%	3%	1%	-1%	0%	0%	1%	1%	0%
Douro	0%	1%	0%	1%	1%	1%	-2%	0%	0%	-1%	0%	1%
Terras de Trás-os-Montes	0%	2%	0%	1%	-1%	0%	-1%	0%	0%	-1%	0%	1%

B. Alentejo change in sectoral share over time: 2004-2018

	Total	A	C	B-E	F	G-I	J	K	L	M-N	O-Q	R-U
Alentejo Litoral	2%	4%	3%	-4%	5%	6%	-1%	0%	-1%	6%	0%	5%
Baixo Alentejo	16%	13%	31%	20%	7%	23%	6%	19%	16%	28%	9%	16%
Lezíria do Tejo	-21%	-21%	-28%	-24%	-31%	-28%	-22%	-20%	-17%	-32%	-9%	-12%
Alto Alentejo	7%	7%	9%	4%	6%	6%	37%	12%	7%	7%	11%	5%
Alentejo Central	-5%	-9%	-18%	5%	32%	-9%	-17%	-6%	-8%	-10%	-10%	-13%

Note: Classification based on OECD TL3 regional typology. Changes are read as values e.g. in figure A, Porto's GVA contribution/share to Norte fell by 2% between 2004-2018 driven by an 11% decrease in GVA share in construction (F). A= agriculture, forestry and fishing, C= manufacturing, B-E = industry including energy, F= construction, G-I= distributive trade, repairs, transport, accommodation, food serv. Activities, J= Information and communication, K = financial and insurance activities, L = real estate activities, M-N = prof., scientific, techn. activities, admin., support service activities, O-Q= public admin., compulsory s.s., education, human health, R-U= other services.
Source: OECD (2020), OECD Regional Statistics (database), http://dx.doi.org/10.1787/region-data-en

Figure 6.3. Norte has the lowest productivity level in Portugal although declines in other regions are closing the regional gap

Labour Productivity, Portugal TL2 regions, USD constant prices PPPs 2015, 1995-2018

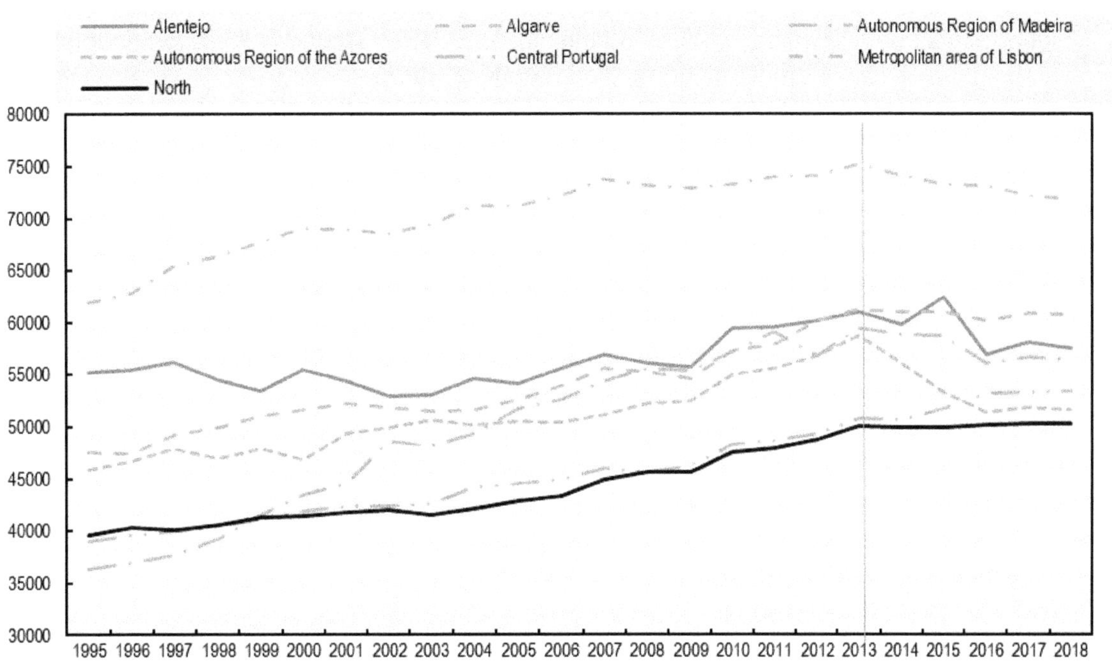

Source: "Regional Productivity", OECD (2020), OECD Regional Statistics (database), http://dx.doi.org/10.1787/region-data-en

Population, skills and labour markets

If Norte is more metropolitan than Alentejo, both regions face issues related to declining and ageing populations. Alentejo, home of 6.8% of Portugal's population, has seen its population decline by almost 7% over the last 10 years (CENSOS, 2021[8]). In comparison, Norte's population has declined by 2.7% between 2011 and 2021 (CENSOS, 2021[8]), although the population has increased in Porto's metropolitan area since 2000. In 2019, there was two elderly for every five persons of working-age in Alentejo (OECD, 2020[9]) and less than 10% aged over 75 years old in Norte (EuroStats, 2021[10]). These longer-term trends signal an ongoing decline in the pool of talents available for businesses.

Over the years, Portugal has invested heavily in education and its younger population is amongst the most educated in Europe, with a quarter of the population having attained tertiary education. However across the overall population, Portugal still shows low educational attainment, with the highest EU share at primary education level (Norte 50.8%, Alentejo 47.1%, against the EU 27 average of 20.8% in 2020). However, Norte has the highest share of students enrolled in vocational training in Portugal and ranks among one of the EU regions with the highest share of 25-64 year olds (24.9%) at tertiary education level. Alentejo's education levels are currently below the Portuguese average.

International migration is a source of talents in Portugal. Figure 6.4 illustrates that in Norte migrants were almost twice as likely to have attained higher educational qualification as a native, which is slightly more than in Portugal as a whole. Foreign-born workers were also more likely to be employed in the service sector.

Across Portugal, shortages and surpluses in a number of occupations have been identified. The European Centre for the Development of Vocational Training (Skills Panorama, 2016[11]) points to shortages in:

- **Healthcare professionals** – related to an increased demand from an ageing population and low wages/long hours leading to migration particularly of nurses. Travel links between residences and hospitals make this additionally challenging in Alentejo.
- **ICT professionals** – demand has been outstripping supply, while in both regions the number of higher education graduates in ICT is increasing. As it takes around five years to complete such a cursus, there is little room for plugging the immediate gap.
- **Technicians** – These occupations were seen as less important/prestigious and new workers in the field have been limited. In Norte, these are physical and engineering science technicians and in Alentejo process control technicians.
- **Legal, social and engineering professionals** – particularly in the public sector due to low wages and lack of public and private investment. Surveys indicate a perception of low prestige of the profession.

Surplus are also observed in other professions, including mining professionals; workers in textile, clothing and leather industries (except in the shoe industry); construct iron workers; blacksmiths, toolmakers and related trade workers; and keyboard operators. Many of these professions are facing the effects of technological change or the consequences of offshoring production in lower wage locations.

Figure 6.4. Percentage of foreign born and natives with higher education by employment sector

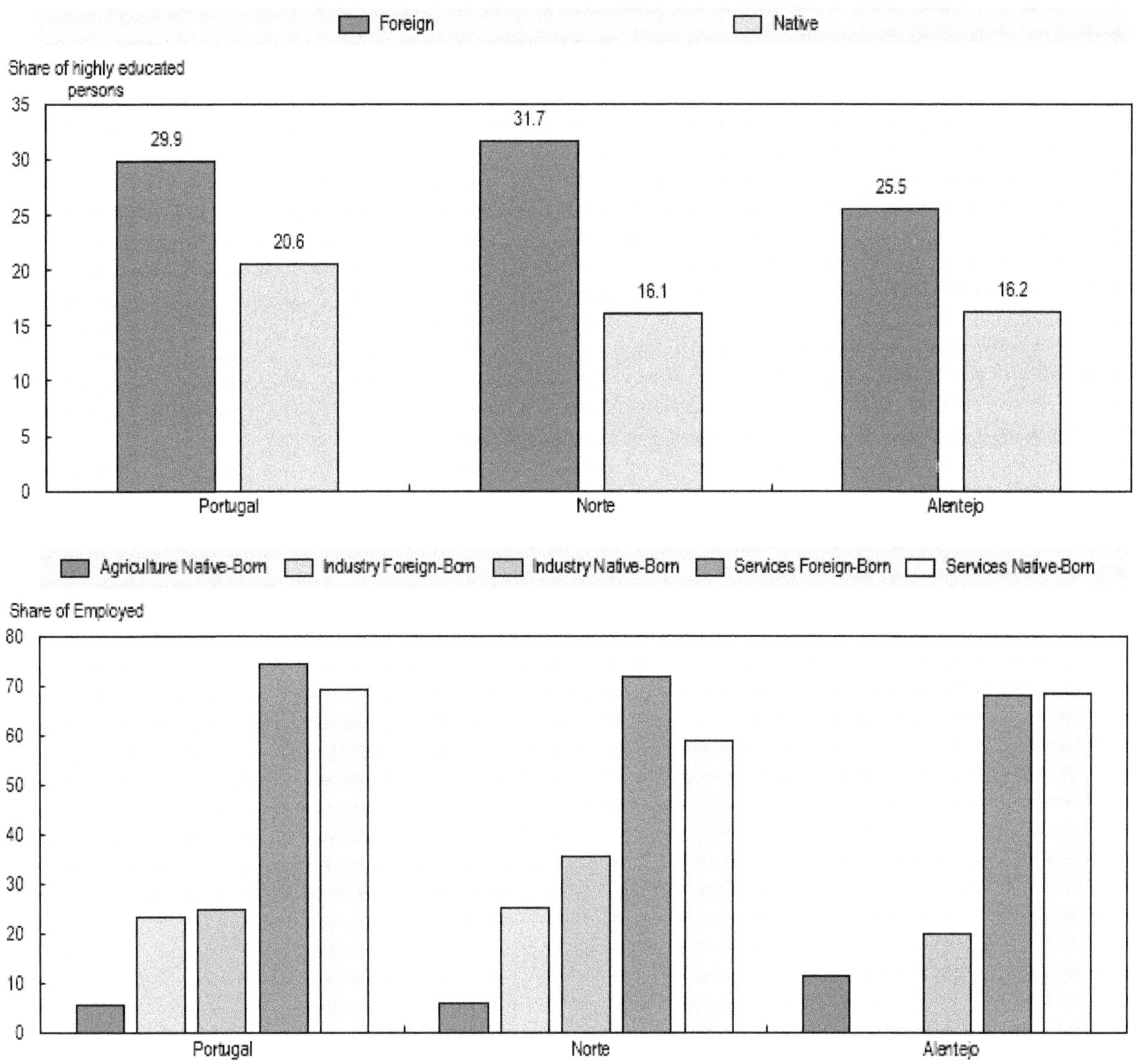

Source: "Regional demography", OECD (2020), OECD Regional Statistics (database), http://dx.doi.org/10.1787/a8f15243-en

Infrastructure and connectivity

The physical and digital connectivity of regions, producers and consumers, is vital to the functioning of regional and global value chains. The development of accessibility infrastructure is crucial for attracting international investment. It is also critical for local SMEs to operate, access markets and strategic resources (OECD, 2019[12]).

Portugal has a peripheral location in Europe and depends on Spanish transport infrastructure to reach the rest of Europe on land. The location is, however, an advantage regarding sea transport in and out of Europe. Portugal ranks high on roads and falls in the middle of pack of OECD countries for railroad infrastructure. (OECD, 2020[13]) The ESPON accessibility index (ESPN, 2021[14]) is calculated as being highest in and around the regions with the busiest airports, i.e. Lisbon, Porto and Faro. The accessibility index in other regions including Alentejo falls into the low category, like other regions in northern Scandinavia and on the eastern and southern edges of Europe.

For Alentejo' regional development, the transport infrastructure has been particularly important. The development of intra-urban and suburban transport networks has helped integrate the rural regions of Alentejo into the local labour market of western Alentejo and Lisboa, thereby creating a greater variety of job opportunities and raising living standards. In addition, the port of Sines is the closest European deep water port to the Panama Canal, placing it in an ideal position for euro-Atlantic logistics. This infrastructure is a key driver for the Sines Complex success.

The digital infrastructure, and connection to the Internet, is another enabler of agglomeration benefits. Whilst in Lisbon almost all buildings have access to fibre optic networks, less than half in Alentejo do (Dijkstra, Poelman and Veneri, 2019[15]). In Norte this is around two-thirds. In Norte, 28% of the population did not use the Internet or did not have a computer in 2019, the highest share in the country and twice more than in Lisbon metropolitan area (OECD, 2020[9]). In addition, digital skills in Portugal are amongst the lowest in Europe, with only 44% of the population having at least a basic level of ICT skills in 2019 (EU average 58%) (EuroStat, 2021[16]).

Access to health and education services and wellbeing

The local availability of quality education and health services, as well as other factors related to lifestyle and wellbeing, could also matter for attracting FDI, a creative class and innovative activities. For Norte and Alentejo, challenges arise from a lack of health service capacity. Alentejo has the lowest number of hospital beds per 1 000 inhabitants in 2018 despite its large elderly population, and half the number of physicians of Norte (2.8 per 1 000 inhabitants in 2019 as compared to 5 in Norte). In Norte a key wellbeing challenge is also the cost of housing. The percentage of household disposable income spent on housing costs is 16.2% in 2018 compared to 15.7% in Alentejo (2017 data).

6.3. FDI-SME linkages and spillovers in Norte and Alentejo

FDI spillovers are possible if significant FDI flow into the region/country, if there is different capacity levels between foreign and domestic firms, i.e. productivity premia in foreign firms, and if the type of investments allow embed FDI in local economy (OECD, 2022[17]).

Potential for FDI spillovers

Portugal is a large receiver of FDI in comparison to other EU countries (see also Chapter 2). FDI inflows are however mainly concentrated in the Lisboa Metropolitan Area and Norte, limiting spillover potential in other regions (Figure 6.5).

Figure 6.5. FDI by region, type of investment and sectoral groups

As a percentage of total investments in the region, aggregates over 2003-20

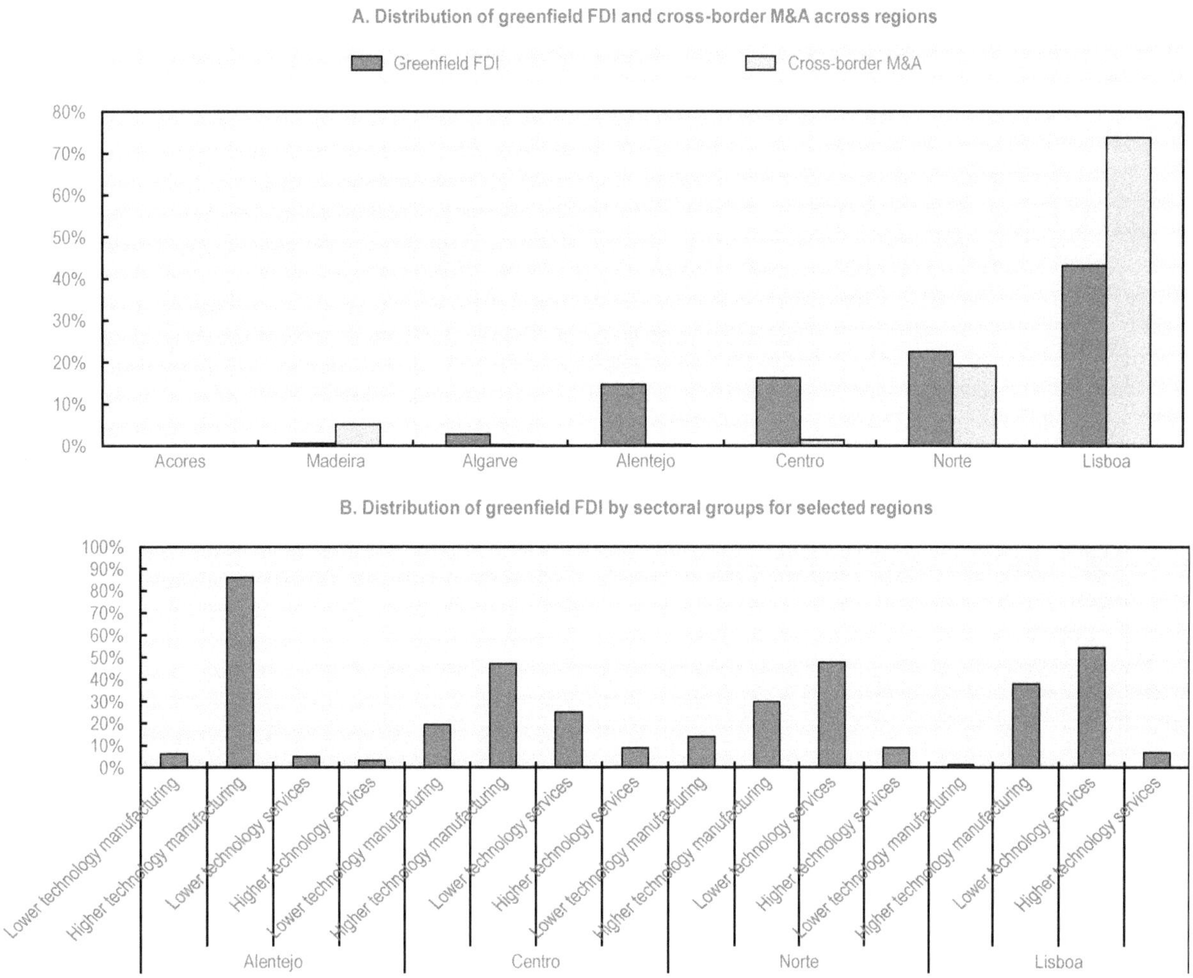

Note: Percentages are based on total capital investment (greenfield FDI) and total M&A deal values over 2003-20. Note that investments into energy and other infrastructure sectors are not included in this analysis.
Source: OECD (2020), OECD Regional Statistics (database), http://dx.doi.org/10.1787/region-data-en, OECD based on Financial Times fDi Markets database and Refinitiv.

Based on the Financial Times fDi Markets database, since 2003, almost 50% of all greenfield FDI and 75% of all foreign acquisitions of domestic firm assets have gone to Lisboa (Figure 6.5, Panel A). Norte received about 20% of greenfield FDI, while Alentejo and Centro received 15% each. Besides Lisboa, only Norte has benefited from some cross-border mergers and acquisitions (M&As) since 2003. Other regions (Acores, Madeira, Algarve) have received only marginal amounts of FDI. It could also be noted that the Lisboa Metropolitan Area is home to many (foreign) companies that have their head office in the capital, even if they operate in other regions as well.

The distribution of greenfield investment by economic activities illustrates that not all regions attract productivity-enhancing FDI (Figure 6.5, Panel B). Most greenfield investments in Alentejo, and to a lesser extent Centro, are made in high-tech manufacturing, while most investments in Lisbon and Norte are made in low-tech services (including mostly logistics, finance and insurance).

The degree of FDI embeddedness also differs across regions, as measured by the percentage of jobs created from foreign investment by sector (Figure 6.6). In Norte, the pattern of investment and related job creation are similar as for the rest of Portugal. Most FDI-driven job creation takes place in post-production services (49%), as defined in this report as including marketing, sales and logistics. High-tech manufacturing (19%) and construction (14%) also attract substantial shares of international investments. The profile of Alentejo differs slightly: more jobs are created as a result of MNE strategies in high-tech manufacturing (36%), infrastructure (18%) and low- and medium-tech manufacturing (16%).

Figure 6.6. Percentage of jobs created from FDI inflows, by sector

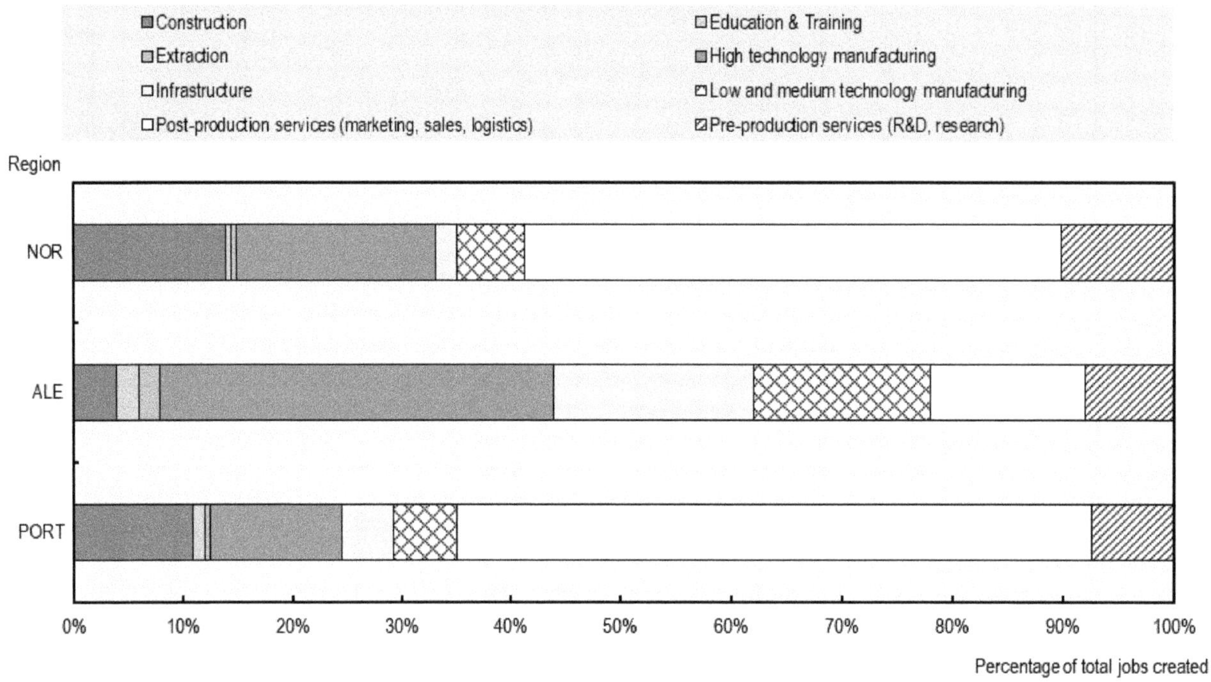

Note: Estimates provided by firms during the investment announcement. See chapters 1 and 2 for definition on pre-production and post-production services.
Source: OECD based on Financial Times fDi Markets database and Refinitiv.

The integration of Norte and Alentejo in FDI flows could also be placed into an European perspective. While the two regions do not seem to compete for the same type of FDI, they do compete with other regions in Europe presenting similar industry structures or specialisation profiles. For example Arnsberg in Germany has a similar business population to Norte and similar dominant industries. So too does the region of Greater Poland. Between 2003 and 2006, Arnsberg saw at most 6 investment projects per thousand inhabitants, at the same time Norte saw up to triple this, whilst Greater Poland saw over 10 times Arnsburg. The same methodology (Castellani and Pieri, 2010[18]) finds Malta has a similar industrial dominance and population size to Alentejo but Malta recorded up to 7 times more projects.

The country where FDI originate also matters for seizing the potential of productivity spillovers (OECD, 2022[17]). Figure 6.7 considers the distribution of FDI into the regions of Norte and Alentejo by country of origin. Spain and France are the two main investors for both regions. Germany, the UK and the US also play a major role in the case of Norte, these top 5 investing countries making up around 70% of total inward investments in the region. On the other hand, Korea, Switzerland and Japan are the next three main investors in Alentejo, making up almost a third of all FDI into the region.

Figure 6.7. Source of FDI to Alentejo, Norte and Portugal, by country of origin

As a percentage of total inward FDI to the region/country up to 2018

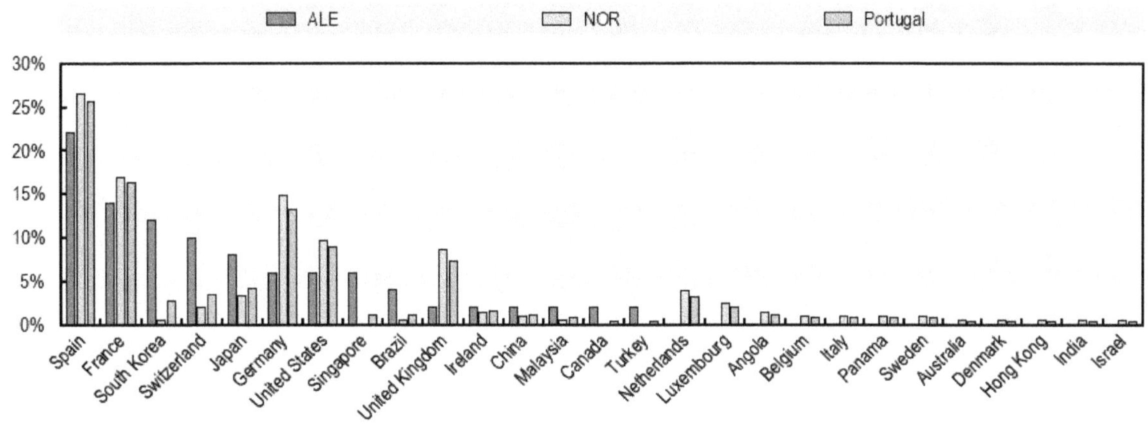

Note: Based on company announcements.
Source: OECD based on Financial Times fDi Markets database and Refinitiv.

Productivity spillovers from international investments are more likely to occur if foreign firms perform better than domestic firms (OECD, 2022[17]). Overall in Portugal, the productivity premium of foreign firms is higher than in other EU peer countries (Figure 6.8). This is a relatively constant feature across regions. However, productivity gaps tend to be lower in metropolitan regions, for instance in Portugal, this gap is the lowest in the Lisbon Metropolitan Area. Similar results exist in Greece, Latvia, Lithuania and the Slovak Republic, where gaps are lower in more developed agglomerations, often close to the capital. Norte and Alentejo that have managed to attract some FDI report the highest differences in productivity between foreign and domestic firms.

Figure 6.8. Performance differences between foreign and domestic firms across regions, selected EU countries, 2019

Are foreign firms more productive than their domestic peers? (yes if value > 0; no if value < 0)

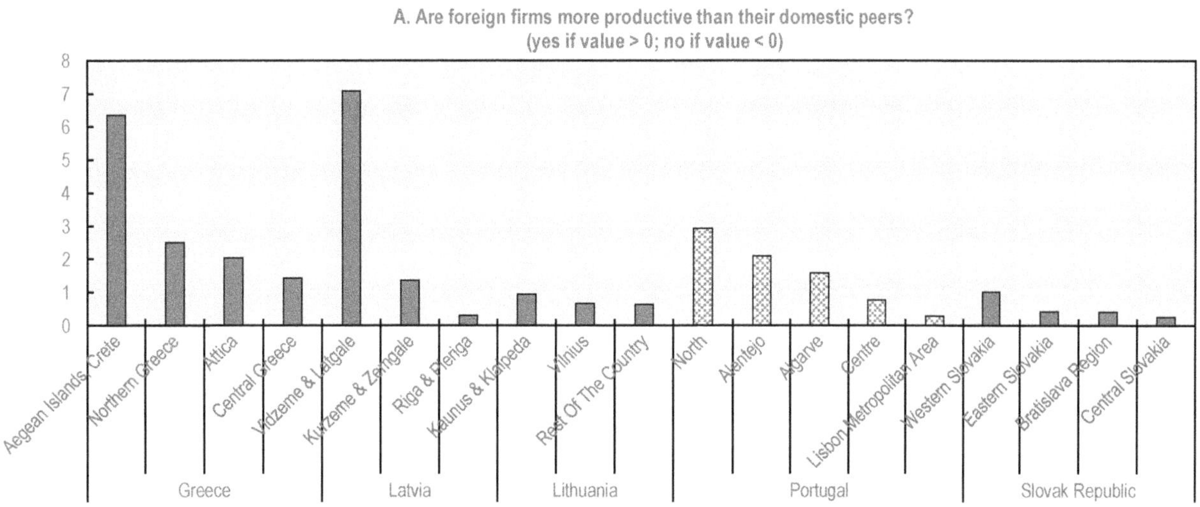

Note: See methodology in OECD (2019[19]).
Source: OECD FDI Qualities Indicators based on World Bank Enterprise Surveys.

SME absorptive capacity

SMEs make a very large part of the business fabric in Portugal - in 2018, 99.9% of businesses in the country counted less than 250 employees (OECD, 2021[20]). This broader point holds across regions. However at greater levels of disaggregation, some variations can be seen: Alentejo as a whole has almost 5 times fewer businesses and SMEs than Norte (around 86 000 compared to around 430 000 in Norte in 2018) (INE. Instituto Nacional de Estadística, 2018[21]). Alentejo has also fewer sole proprietors than other regions of Portugal (Management Association, 2020[22]). In Norte, 12.6% of the microenterprises are in the Greater Porto area, contrasting with other areas in the region, such as the Douro, with only counts 1.7% of the total number of micro enterprises in the region. This testifies to the heterogeneity of the business fabric even within regions (Marques and Couto, 2017[23]).

The large representation of micro and small firms represents a barrier to scaling up local innovation performance, and in turn SME absorptive capacities. Much of Portugal's innovation capacity is concentrated in the metropolitan area of Lisbon. 46.6% of regional employment is in knowledge-intensive services (KIS), as compared to 36% in the country overall (2019) (Table 6.3). The region spends 1.63% of its GDP on R&D (2018), which compares still low vis-à-vis OECD and EU27 averages (2.4% and 2.1% respectively (OECD, 2021[24])). 84% of regional patent applications are filed in cooperation, of which almost 60% with inventors located in foreign regions. If Norte has fewer employees in KIS (which can be explained by its industrial orientation), the region is very active in R&D (1.53% of GDP), second performing region after the capital, and as well integrated in international patent cooperation networks. In fact, Norte experienced a fast rise in patenting activities over recent years (Figure 6.9). Alentejo shows different capacity, with a larger KIS sector but half less R&D expenditure and weaker connections in global knowledge networks. Both regions have however experienced an increase in innovation performance between 2011 and 2017, whilst the remaining five, most significantly in the Algarve, decreased (EC, 2021[25])

Table 6.3. Intensity of innovation activities by region in Portugal

Employment in knowledge-intensive services (KIS), as a percentage of total employment, 2019, intensity of R&D expenditure, as a share of GDP, 2018 and share of co-patenting in total PCT patent applications and co-patenting with foreign regions in total PCT co-patent applications, 2015.

	Employment in knowledge-intensive services	R&D expenditure	PCT co-patent applications	PCT co-patent applications with foreign regions
	As % of total employment	As a share of GDP	As % of total patent applications	As % of co-patent applications
	2019	2018	2015	2015
Metropolitan area of Lisbon	46.6	1.63	83.8	59.7
Autonomous Region of the Azores	39.0	0.32	33.3	100.0
Autonomous Region of Madeira	36.5	0.39		
Central Portugal	34.8	1.31	82.6	61.4
Alentejo	34.6	0.67	57.1	37.5
Algarve	33.1	0.34	45.5	80.0
North (PT)	30.9	1.53	80.9	44.3
Portugal	**36.7**	**1.36**		

Source: OECD (2021), Regional innovation database, http://stats.oecd.org/Index.aspx?DataSetCode=REGION_INNOVATION.

Figure 6.9. Patent applications in Norte and Alentejo, 2001-015

Total number between 2001 and 2015 and share of co-patenting and foreign co-patenting, 2015

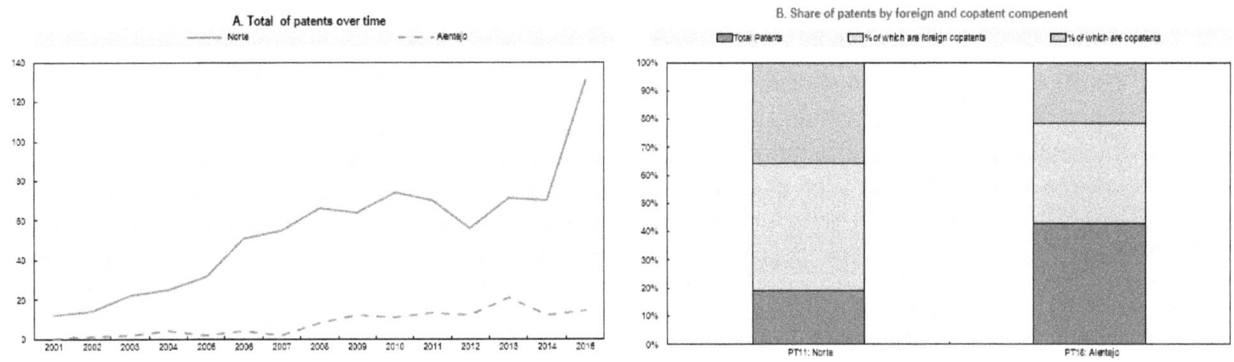

Source: "Patents", OECD (2020), OECD Regional Statistics (database), http://dx.doi.org/10.1787/region-data-en

6.4. Regional and local policy initiatives for FDI-SME linkages and spillovers

Using the broad policy areas discussed in chapters 4 and 5, this section focuses on improving regional specific actions to make the most of FDI at local level (see Box 6.2 for an overview of governance arrangements in Norte and Alentejo).

Attracting productivity-enhancing FDI

Portugal Global, the Trade and Investment Agency (*Agência para o Investimento e Comércio Externo de Portugal, AICEP*) and the SME Competitiveness and Innovation Agency (*Agência para a Competitividade e Inovação, IAPMEI*) have different subnational footprint (see Chapter 4). The largest AICEP regional footprints are in Centro and Norte, with limited presence in Alentejo and other regions. The absence of an official branch of AICEP in Alentejo may provide challenges for FDI attraction and embeddedness.

Invest Porto and Invest Braga are the two main public agencies for investment promotion and attraction in the Norte region. They work with representatives from AICEP but are not directly a part of them. Invest Porto was established in 2015 by the Porto City Council as an operational division of the city's Economy Department. The agency's mission is to contribute to a favourable and competitive business environment in the city of Porto and support investment, innovation and local development. Similarly, Invest Braga was created in 2014, to act as the economic wing of the Braga municipality, with the mission of promoting the economic development of Braga and attracting investment and entrepreneurs to the region. Its strengths lie in closer ties with local governments and other public bodies with decentralised powers leading to a stronger capability to address investors' operational concerns.

Other European economies have mixed IPA models. For example Italy has some regions that have their own IPAs; in Sweden subnational IPAs cover different types of geographies, some being responsible for large territories such as regions, while some only focus on individual cities - in a similar manner to Portugal; and, in Spain, Germany and Poland all administrative regions have their own IPA. In the Polish case, regional IPAs were established simultaneously in 2011 thanks to the financial support of the European Cohesion Policy.

Policy approaches to the attraction of FDI extend beyond financial incentives. Subnational agencies such as IPAs have an essential role in reducing the information asymmetries firms face when searching for a location and simultaneously use this knowledge of firm preferences to promote their regions. Governments' one-stop-shops and digital platforms are instrumental in promoting locations.

- Invest Braga and Invest Porto highlight the benefits of national measures through the promotion of the government Simplex website (www.simplex.gov.pt), an information repository containing all measures taken to reduce bureaucracy. They also promote the Empresa na Hora initiative (a company in one hour) (https://justica.gov.pt/Servicos/Empresa-na-Hora), which allows companies to incorporate in less than an hour.
- Through the European Social Fund and Alentejo 2020 programme, a dedicated website (https://invest.alentejo.pt/) and staff based in Evora have been set up to focus on promoting international investment in the Alentejo region. Alentejo's website has a strong focus on wider environmental features such as infrastructure and quality of life, essential for effective promotion.
- The national IPA (AICEP) is the major shareholder of AICEP Global Parques, an entity that manages three industrial parks in Portugal and that has developed a Site Selection Service platform for FDI. The regions that host the business parks are responsible to provide to AICEP Global Parques site location options to include in this Platform, in collaboration with a private business Global Parques, who also run several industrial parks. The Platform is a business locations procurement tool for investment projects in Portugal. It provides information for projects regarding industry, logistics and services. It uses multi-criteria analysis, to choose, easily and effectively, a site in Portugal that best fits a business project´s requirement; to get to know about available sites by browsing the map or searching by geographic region; to identify the best solutions that fit the investment project - size; site type; proximity to relevant infrastructures, among others. AICEP provides site selections' support to investors: it presents different site proposals according to project specifications and help setting up direct contacts with local entities.

Having a shared understanding of the wider regional and national investment promotion agenda can ensure regional authorities avoid competition amongst themselves. At the same time national FDI attraction policies and instruments (such as eased administrative and licensing regimes, investment tax incentives) can consider how each region is unique in the way it competes in global investment networks.

Box 6.2. Governance arrangements in Norte and Alentejo

The Portuguese governance system is quite centralised as compared with other European and OECD countries (see chapter 4). General public services spending share for subnational governments is much larger than the OECD average. The OECD World Observatory of Subnational Government Finance and Investment (SNGWOFI, 2021[26]) notes for Portugal some of the lowest levels of subnational government expenditure in the OECD area (Figure 6.10).

Figure 6.10. Subnational government expenditure, 2018

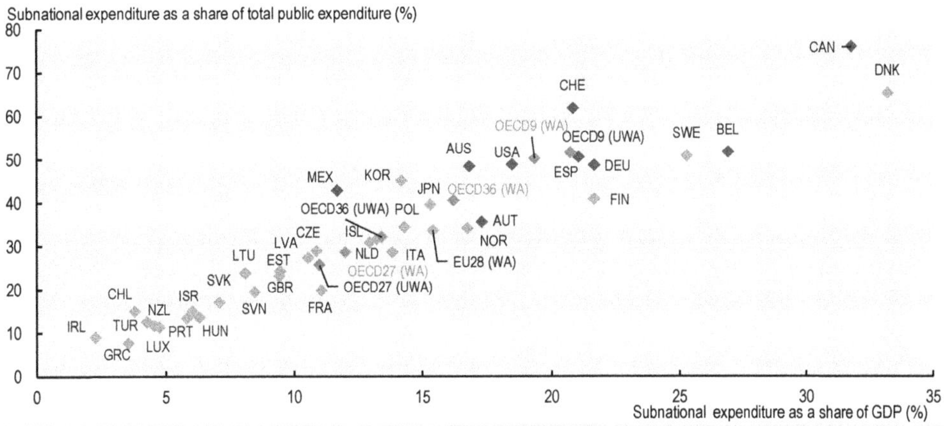

Source: (OECD, 2020[9]), Regions and Cities at a Glance 2020, p. 111, https://doi.org/10.1787/959d5ba0-en.

Portugal has not established a regional government level, unlike many other EU countries. Instead, there are five regional planning and co-ordination entities, the Comissão de Coordenação e Desenvolvimento Regional (CCDR), one for each of the five NUTS 2 regions of mainland Portugal, i.e. one for Norte and Alentejo also. The CCDRs are decentralised branches of the government and carry out tasks in the areas of the environment, land and town planning, and regional development. The CCDRs are responsible for the territorial co-ordination of central government services in each region. One of their main missions is to manage regional operational programmes of the European structural and investment funds.

There are currently 308 municipalities with an average municipal size of 33 524 inhabitants. They have assignments that span several areas such as housing and civil protection, energy and local development, social assistance, urban planning, transport, education and health amongst others. Portugal has attempted to enhance inter-municipal co-operation by establishing 23 Inter-Municipal Councils (IMCs), which correspond to the TL3 regional level, in order to leverage benefits that go beyond the borders of single municipalities. Alentejo holds 5 of these and Norte 8. Portugal also created metropolitan areas for Lisbon and Porto.

However, the role of inter-municipal co-operation remains limited as most powers are in the hands of municipalities and central government. While membership in an IMC is not compulsory, all municipalities are currently members, as municipalities are steered to join by upper-level incentives associated with the management of the EU Structural and Investment Funds. Although, they can take on the functions and tasks assigned by law to the municipalities, IMCs can only provide services that are assigned to them by the municipalities that make up their membership.

Embedding FDI in the local economy

Invest Braga and Invest Porto agencies act beyond attraction and facilitation (e.g. tackling any practical problems such as bureaucratic difficulties) to also consider matchmaking with local firms. The national Portuguese Suppliers Directory identifies Portuguese producers by sector/market/product/service. The extent to which this is proactively advertised and monitored is unclear though. The literature points out greenfield investors will actively seek out means to build links with domestic producers whilst M&As will not as such (Creszenzi, 2018[27]), thus without active matchmaking there are likely to be missed opportunities.

AICEP in its Internationalise 2030 acknowledges the importance of building intelligence though creating a specific axis on business and market intelligence. This information could be used by both regional agencies and businesses for informed decision making on building, embedding and reshaping GVCs. Such information is contained in the Smart Specialisation Strategies however one of the most recent reports of its implementation in Portugal (EC, 2020[28]) identifies that at regional level, the management teams of the strategy need to be substantially reinforced. The new powers allocated to CIMS may help this.

An example of where this has been done relatively successfully is Scotland (OECD, 2014[29]). The Output Monitoring Framework (OMF) was developed by Scottish Enterprise, the national economic development body for Scotland to meet the needs of a federated network of regional bodies known as Local Enterprise Companies. These had to work in close co-operation and partnership with Locate in Scotland (Scotland's one-stop shop for inward investors), Scottish Enterprise, and regional authorities. The OMF developed a common framework of monitoring and evaluation of network activity, including inward investor support, across a regionally federated structure. This aided understanding of all inward investment, domestic business competitiveness and the establishment of new businesses. In addition, information on skills and knowledge, physical business infrastructure and environment and access to opportunity were also collected. The latter forms of information proved essential for successful embedding.

Evidence from Costa Rica shows mapping and matching is not the end. (Crespi, Fernández-Arias and Stein, 2014[30]) found that 80% of SMEs matched with MNEs did not end up successfully integrating into the value chain. Thus, other activities such as reinforcing SME absorptive capacity and local infrastructure and environment are equally important.

Further coordination with IAPMEI or other government agencies can improve FDI embeddedness, further ensuring that attraction is even better targeted to local capability. For example, the Esposende municipality in Braga has created Start Esposende, an investment funding agency and business incubator, which provides a range of services to support local entrepreneurs and investors that aim to establish themselves in the municipality. Working with Invest Braga can ensure conversations are a two way street. Invest Braga can share more information of MNEs' customers and objectives and Start Esposende can share further information on the sorts of businesses coming through its doors – to establish connections immediately e.g. removing potential supply chain bottlenecks from the start.

Improving domestic SME absorptive capacity

There is a vast amount of regional policies aimed at SMEs. Officials in both Alentejo and Norte have a good record of the number of SMEs signed up to programmes, but information on the share of eligible businesses involved and why those eligible do not sign up is difficult to gather. Often SMEs may need assistance to understand the value of the programme, particularly if the investment is resource intensive.

One implicit way both regions do this is by reducing the transaction costs of participation in the programme or removing disincentives. For example, Norte's regional agency policy on intellectual property rights protection encourages firms to see the long-term benefits of their collaboration. Over the last 3 years, this policy has benefitted over 50 firms. Financial incentives are the key method for all regions of Portugal to support local SMEs, including nationally implemented tax breaks or subsidies. There are also policies implemented at the regional level, for example, the CCDR Alentejo provides financial support to encourage innovation. As part of the EU funds' Operational Programme, assistance can be received by those projects that contribute to innovative and qualified activities, to their progression in the value chain or to tradable and international production.

The EUR 200 million Fund, financed by the regional OPs from the mainland, carries out equity and quasi-equity investment operations in SMEs under a co-investment regime with the objective of:

- encouraging the establishment or capitalisation of companies, as a priority, in the start-up phases (seed, start-up, later stage venture) and;
- mobilising specialised national and international venture capital entities that - besides the financial investment - enable companies to acquire knowledge and technical, commercial and financial experience.

However, despite substantial backing – the Fund results from a protocol between AD&C, IP and Banco de Fomento and a relatively healthy EUR 6 million annual budget – the fund has so far only aided a limited number of firms. The low success rate could be rectified through an increased awareness of co-investment and risk-sharing policy by the agencies. As mentioned in the section above and via the example of Costa Rica, mapping is key to improve targeting.

Most recently, public funding has been related to COVID-19 recovery. The OCDE-CoR survey (OECD, 2020[31]) points out to substantial funding provided at the regional level but with the limited ability of regional governments to effectively help. Comunidade Intermunicipal do Alto Minho in Norte for example notes that the notices for SMEs to apply for support had to be longer because firms struggled and thus took more time to gather all relevant information and submit applications.

In addition, considering all funds together will allow for a greater understanding of the possible debt burdens on SMEs or the benefits they face e.g., Annual Investment Allowance, R&D tax credits, COVID support schemes, and wider business taxes.

Responses to the EC/OECD Survey on Policies enabling FDI spillovers to domestic SMEs suggest that while regional authorities in Norte and Alentejo have been successful in improving SME absorptive capacity, greater investment in management capacity would allow better monitoring of project implementation and eventual break even rates, with a view to better understanding the risks associated with the projects implemented. Regional governments can help simplify procedures directly and build links with civil society organisations and other firms, which typically includes associations, cooperatives, foundations and social enterprises, if they have the capacity to do so.

Enabling strategic partnerships and knowledge exchange

Many initiatives in Norte and Alentejo do not directly target SMEs and FDI firms simultaneously. A successful example of potential methods of working can be derived from Ireland. The Irish National Linkages Programme had two key components. One working to account for firm heterogeneity and the other SME upgrading. Through targeting both MNEs and local firms the programme both found links and helped build capacity. This targeting process also looked at SMEs and their ability to improve or upgrade their capabilities (Crespi et al., 2014). The successful programme has now evolved into a wider initiative working at incorporating Irish companies into GVCs.

In Portugal, many programmes from the national level run informally, making regional monitoring and evaluation more challenging. For example, ANI (the national innovation agency) hosts a range of policies including Co-development R&D Centre for SMEs and larger firms to form informal relationships. The success of these relationships can only be seen for those who apply for formal grants for participating in European R&D programmes. Further programmes are implemented by CIMs and CCDRs, as discussed in chapter 5.

Chapter 5 notes that knowledge transfer infrastructures, such as Technological Interface Centers and Collaborative Laboratories, are less widespread in the region of Alentejo. The incorporation of cutting-edge thinking, University start-ups and accelerators should see two-way benefits, at MNE and regional level. At the same time, the partnerships *between universities* can work as a further channel for information sharing, and partnerships are more likely to occur if MNEs are directly integrated into these programmes.

A successful example can be seen as part of the EU innovation Hub network. The EIT Digital Innovation Hub in Italy, headquartered at the Povo Scientific and Technological Centre in Trento, focuses on leveraging digital technologies to help improve quality of life. Italy can be taken as an example of successful innovation hub governance. Located at the core of the Trentino Region, an area rich in communications infrastructures and bristling with innovative companies, the centre unites the leading digital players in Italy. Its core partners are Engineering, Telecom Italia and TrentoRISE, while affiliated partners have activities all over Italy (CNR-National Research Council) and have labs, connected to the Innovation Hub, in Lombardy (Politecnico of Milan), Piedmont (Politecnico of Turin), Emilia Romagna (Alma Mater Studiorum – Università di Bologna) and Tuscany (Scuola Superiore Sant'Anna). Affiliated industrial partners include CFR (FIAT Research Centre), Cooperazione Trentina, PosteItaliane, Reply and ST Microelectronics. (European Institute of Innovation and Technology, 2021[32])

Promoting clustering

Portugal has about 20 clusters of competitiveness that are recognised by IAPMEI since 2017 (Table 6.4).

The Sines complex in Alentejo is one of the leaders of green energy production in the country. Various sectors including manufacturing, petrochemicals and energy work in tandem to boost the region's economy. Its new technology park (Sines TECH – Innovation & Data Center Hub) provides a space for information exchange with logistical constraints of conference centres, warehouses and office blocks all covered in the complex. There are spaces for special courses to upgrade skills on technology, industry and welding. However Sines is relatively detached from the rest of Alentejo and therefore its linkages with firms outside of the complex but within Alentejo are limited. Even its brochures relate to linking investors with "land for tourism and real estate across the municipalities". Therefore the dual objective of economic growth and regional development may struggle to be achieved if connectivity across the region is limited.

Portugal has been particularly active in developing cluster policies through active engagement: 14% of national policies identified in the EC/OECD mapping on policies strengthening FDI-SME spillovers aim to develop clusters, including the IAPMEI coordinating the recognition and establishment of 18 industrial clusters (EU/OECD, 2021). At the same time, the subnational regions continue to implement their own cluster policies. In Norte the Norte Regional Operational Programme 2014-20 include a number of initiatives in favour of clusters, such as the Sistemas de Incentivos à Internacionalização by CCDR Norte. These initiatives focus on Smart Specialisation industries, as the choice of a large number of domains does not favour the concentration of resources in projects and activities that would generate spillovers (European Commission Smart Specialisation, 2019[33]). At the same time a top-down imposed formation of a cluster is less likely to succeed in the long term.

The recent signing of sectoral pacts[1] can help coordinate action between private and public sectors, but the method proposed for monitoring and evaluating cluster policies at the regional level is unclear.

Table 6.4. Clusters in Portugal, IAPMEI labelled, 2019

	Employment	Turnover (EUR million)	Exports (EUR million)	GVA (EUR million)	Strategic objectives		
					Internation-alisation	Cooperation and partnerships	Supporting business and entrepreneurs' capacity
Aeronautics, Space and Defense Cluster	21 000	4 717	4 049	1 119	X	X	X
AgroFood Cluster	24 400	5 313	1 425	962	X		X
Architecture, Engineering and Construction Cluster	11 100	1 915	587	490	X	X	
Automotive Cluster	14 900	5 557	4 231	688	X		X
Engineering & Tooling Cluster	8 700	997	552	331	X	X	X
Footwear and Fashion Cluster	24 000	1 770	1 253	491		X	
Habitat Cluster	11 500	2 852	1 314	639		X	X
Health Cluster	23 600	3 776	493	1 284	X		
Mineral Resources Cluster	1 900	287	222	101	X	X	X
Ocean Cluster	7 800	1 074	312	406	X		
Petrochemicals, Chemicals and Refining Cluster	8 800	12 095	4 366	995	X		X
Production Technologies Cluster	39 500	2 242	1 166	822	X		X
Railway Cluster	8 500	994	325	330	X	X	
Smart Cities Cluster	n.a	n.a	n.a	n.a	X	X	X
Textiles Cluster: Technology and Fashion	8 200	737	543	215	X	X	
ICT Cluster	14 400	5 280	1 249	1 417	X	X	X
Tourism Cluster	n.a	n.a	n.a	n.a		X	
Vine and Wine Cluster	5 100	1 455	641	328		X	
Ocean Cluster	7 800	1 074	312	406	X		X

Note: Data on employment, turnover, exports and GVA not available for the Smart Cities Cluster, the Tourism Cluster.
Source: IAPMEI (2021[34]).

For Norte and Alentejo, the effectiveness of cluster strategies depends on their ability to make clusters *evolve* with global value chains. Portugal has in place a system to periodically evaluate the success of its strategy which can be beneficial for all levels of government to learn from. The Portugal 2020 Global Evaluation Plan (PGA PT2020) is a guiding document of the Portugal 2020 Evaluation. It enables the design and implementation of policies and programmes to benefit from quality assessments, supported by evidence on the effectiveness, efficiency and impact of interventions. It means there is room for policies to evolve as the environment changes around them. The most recent evaluation is from January 2021 which can provide a basis for future strategies.

Consolidating agglomeration benefits

Transport infrastructure

Good transport links to Central Europe are a key part of Portugal's historical success. Projects with the European commission to extend rail links across Europe have included substantial participation from Portuguese regions. However, in Alentejo, the within-region transport system is more limited. The Alentejo Platform was created in 2018 by leaders of business organisations, public and private entities and citizens movements and "civically committed" citizens, to require the Government to carry out projects in the areas of accessibility and road and rail transport which they consider fundamental for the sustainable development of the region. As such, the government commissioned Infrastructures de Portugal to conduct studies on ways to improve the regional connectivity.

Labour markets

Norte's mission 2020 has the ambition to increase the number of workers and employers that are able to adopt new techniques, technologies and organisational methods to improve their employability. Specifically, in partnership with businesses, including MNEs, they aim to increase the hiring of highly skilled human resources, thereby contributing to increase entrepreneurial skills in R&D&I and intensify interactions between companies and regional entities. Given the population density of Norte, this may be easier to achieve should the skills gap be small enough (in a similar concept to SME absorptive capacity).

There are several universities in Norte which help increase the capability of the local labour market. Between 2008-2018 one of the highest increases in student attainment across OECD countries was noted. However as the working age population remained below average, Norte's 2018 smart specialisation report (Interreg Europe, 2018[35]) points to policies investing in education, training and vocational training for skills and lifelong learning. Across Portugal, the OECD finds within the education sector, Portugal faces the challenge of ensuring that only effective programmes or initiatives are scaled up or systematised. In addition, to improve implementation, the OECD advises that different parties should be involved in design processes and receive practical support. (OECD, 2019[36])

These programmes aim to ensure the skills developed match the current and future demands of the region. Thus to counteract high unemployment rates, it is imperative to improve the matching between workers and firms.

Such infrastructure can improve local skills, but in the short term it may be difficult to attract the right people to the region. Alentejo's foreign born population is just 4% (Portugal average 6.8%, OECD average 10%). The population within Alentejo over the last 50 years has been seen to favour most coastal regions of the territory than the interiors (OECD forthcoming, 2022). National government programmes such as specialised visas discussed in chapter 3, can help attract foreign labour. In this case attraction and preservation would need to ensure salaries are globally comparable, unless the non-financial benefits can compensate for this (access to world class businesses, knowledge, technologies). However, the distance from urban areas with a greater variety of skills can pose a challenge to attract local labour e.g. from Lisbon for Alentejo and from Porto to inner parts of Norte.

Regional skills can be strengthened by improving collaboration between public authorities, local businesses, and not-for-profit organisations to ensure local education and training match the current and future needs of rural firms and harness digital technologies to support lifelong learning for youth and experienced workers. In theory the role of remote working may prove a challenge, particularly for value chain functions that can be conducted in such a way. For the majority of occupations in Alentejo and Norte, it is likely there is still a large need for in person employment.

Quality of Life

Invest Alentejo websites host a dedicated section relating to the lifestyle benefits for investors – e.g., tourism, affordable housing. Improving healthcare services and education would likely lead to more settlements for investors and their families. Invest in Sines brochures includes sections on tourism and quality of life. Both of which point to the acknowledgement of the importance of portraying and creating a good quality of life for building intrinsic human links to the region, thereby increasing embeddedness. This includes access to essential services such as health and education.

Improving FDI-SME policy co-ordination at regional level

The national strategic references for regional planning are the Portugal 2030 Strategy and the National Spatial Planning Policy Programme (PNPOT), although the responsibility is spread across ministries. The Ministry of Planning looks after strategy of economic and social development, namely convergence and cohesion policy; the Ministry of Territorial Cohesion looks after regional development and inner areas; the Ministry of Environment and Climate Action looks after spatial planning and forestry; and then there are other sectoral ministries responsible for the provision of public and collective services and other territorial interventions.

At a subnationalal level, as well as the CCDR, a number of institutions represent each of the key regions on the mainland. The regional directorates implement agricultural policy, including those addressing rural development measures. They provide analysis, approval, monitoring, and validation of projects supported by public funds in their respective regions. Yet their links with integration with local FDI which would accelerate development and exportability is unclear. Taking the example of one programme, the Mainland Rural Development Programme (PDR 2020) supported by European funds (EAFRD) is operational in Alentejo. It supports the tradable goods sector and farmers directly involved in adding value through agro-forestry activities through a wide range of policies including building conditions for economic and social dynamism. Explicit co-ordination with local foreign investors is not evident.

Box 6.3. The alternative TL3 typology

This OECD methodology classifies TL3 regions into metropolitan and non-metropolitan according to the following criteria:

- ***Metropolitan TL3 region,*** if more than 50% of its population live in a functional urban area (FUA) of at least 250 000 inhabitants. Metropolitan regions are further classified into:
  - **Large metropolitan TL3 regions**, if more than 50% of its population lives in an FUA of at least 1.5 million inhabitants.
  - **Metropolitan TL3 regions**, if the TL3 region is not a large metropolitan region and 50% of its population lives in an FUA of at least 250 000 inhabitants.
  - ***Non-metropolitan TL3 region***, if less than 50% of its population live in an FUA. These regions re further classified according to their level of access to FUAs of different sizes into regions:
    - **With access to (near) a metropolitan TL3 region**, if more than 50% of its population lives within a 60-minute drive from a metropolitan area (an FUA with more than 250 000 people); or if the TL3 region contains more than 80% of the area of an FUA of at least 250 000 inhabitants.
    - **With access to (near) a small/medium city TL3 region**, if the TL3 region does not have access to a metropolitan area and 50% of its population has access to a small or medium city (an FUA of more than 50 000 and less than 250 000 inhabitants) within a 60-minute drive; or if the TL3 region contains more than 80% of the area of a small or medium city.
    - **Remote TL3 region**, if the TL3 region is not classified as NMR-M or NMR-S, i.e., if 50% of its population does not have access to any FUA within a 60-minute drive.

Source: (Fadic et al., 2019[11]),"Classifying small (TL3) regions based on metropolitan population, low density and remoteness" https://dx.doi.org/10.1787/b902cc00-en.

References

Castellani, D. and F. Pieri (2010), *The Effect of Foreign Investments on European.* [18]

CENSOS (2021), *Instituto Nacional de Estatística.* [8]

Crespi, G., E. Fernández-Arias and E. Stein (2014), "A World of Possibilities: Internationalization for Productive Development", in *Rethinking Productive Development*, Palgrave Macmillan US, New York, http://dx.doi.org/10.1057/9781137393999_8. [30]

Creszenzi, R. (2018), *MOVE ON UP! Building, Embedding and Reshaping Global Value Chains Through Investment Flows: Insights for Regional Innovation Policies.* [27]

Dijkstra, L., H. Poelman and P. Veneri (2019), "The EU-OECD definition of a functional urban area", *OECD Regional Development Working Papers*, No. 2019/11, OECD Publishing, Paris, https://dx.doi.org/10.1787/d58cb34d-en. [15]

EC (2021), *Higher Education for S3 in Portugal.* [25]

EC (2020), *Implementation of Smart Specialisation Strategies in Portugal: An assessment.* [28]

ESPN (2021), *Territorial patterns and relations in Portugal.* [14]

European Commission Smart Specialisation (2019), *Smart Specialisation Platform*, https://s3platform.jrc.ec.europa.eu/documents/20182/449628/Apresenta%C3%A7%C3%A3o+S3+in+Portugal+-+ENG.pdf/954d2ed3-2e13-40db-b62c-82a1dbe12715 (accessed on 3 June 2021). [33]

European Institute of Innovation and Technology (2021), *EIT Innovation Hubs*, https://eit.europa.eu/our-communities/eit-innovation-communities/innovation-hubs. [32]

EuroStat (2021), *Employment by sex, age, economic activity and NUTS 2 regions*, https://appsso.eurostat.ec.europa.eu/nui/show.do?dataset=lfst_r_lfe2en2&lang=en. [16]

EuroStats (2021), *Population on 1 January by age group, sex and NUTS 3 region*, https://ec.europa.eu/eurostat/databrowser/view/DEMO_R_PJANGRP3__custom_859397/default/table?lang=en. [10]

Fadic, M. et al. (2019), "Classifying small (TL3) regions based on metropolitan population, low density and remoteness", *OECD Regional Development Working Papers*, No. 2019/06, OECD Publishing, Paris, https://dx.doi.org/10.1787/b902cc00-en. [1]

Foray, D., P. David and B. Hall (2009), *"Smart Specialisation – The Concept"*, https://ec.europa.eu/invest-inresearch/pdf/download_en/kfg_policy_brief_no9.pdf?11111. [5]

IAPMEI (2021), *Clusters de competitividade reconhecidos pelo IAPMEI*, https://www.iapmei.pt/Paginas/Clusters-de-competitividade-reconhecidos-pelo-IAPM.aspx. [34]

INE. Instituto Nacional de Estadística (2018), *INE. Instituto Nacional de Estadística*, https://www.ine.es/ (accessed on 10 October 2021). [21]

Interreg Europe (2018), *Norte Region Smart Specialisation Strategy (NORTE RIS3).* [35]

Management Association, I. (ed.) (2020), *Start-Ups and SMEs*, IGI Global, http://dx.doi.org/10.4018/978-1-7998-1760-4. [22]

Marques, A. and A. Couto (2017), "SMEs and Family SMEs: Specificities from the Portuguese Socio-Business Context", *European Journal of Economics and Business Studies*, Vol. 3/2, pp. 190-199, https://journals.euser.org/index.php/ejes/article/view/2467. [23]

McCann, P. and R. Ortega-Argilés (2013), *"Smart Specialisation, Regional Growth and Applications to EU Cohesion Policy"*, Regional Studies, available at, http://ipts.jrc.ec.europa.eu/docs/s3_mccann_ortega.pdf. [6]

OECD (2022), *FDI-SME linkages, productivity and innovation spillovers*, OECD Publishing, Paris. [17]

OECD (2021), *Figure 6.88. COVID-19 impact on business dynamics and policy responses in Portugal*, http://dx.doi.org/10.1787/888934251979. [20]

OECD (2021), *Main Science and Technology Indicators, September 2021 edition*, https://www.oecd.org/sti/msti.htm (accessed 28 October 2021). [24]

OECD (2020), *OECD Regions and Cities at a Glance 2020*, OECD Publishing, Paris, https://dx.doi.org/10.1787/959d5ba0-en. [9]

OECD (2020), *Rural Well-being: Geography of Opportunities, OECD Rural Studies*, OECD Publishing, Paris, https://doi.org/10.1787/d25cef80-en. [7]

OECD (2020), "The impact of the COVID-19 crisis on regional and local governments: Main findings from the joint CoR-OECD survey", *OECD Regional Development Papers*, No. 05, OECD Publishing, Paris, https://dx.doi.org/10.1787/fb952497-en. [31]

OECD (2020), *Transport infrastructure trends and regional development*, https://doi.org/10.1787/b261814f-en. [13]

OECD (2019), *Education Policy Outlook 2019: Working Together to Help Students Achieve their Potential*, OECD Publishing, Paris, https://dx.doi.org/10.1787/2b8ad56e-en. [36]

OECD (2019), *FDI Qualities Indicators: Measuring the sustainable development impacts of investment*, https://www.oecd.org/fr/investissement/fdi-qualities-indicators.htm. [19]

OECD (2019), *OECD SME and Entrepreneurship Outlook 2019*, OECD Publishing, Paris, https://doi.org/10.1787/d2b72934-en. [12]

OECD (2014), *Monitoring and Evaluation of Foreign Direct Investment in Kazakhstan*, https://www.oecd.org/cfe/leed/oa20-Monitoring-Kazakhstan.pdf. [29]

OECD (2014), *OECD Science, Technology and Industry Outlook 2014*, OECD Publishing, Paris, https://doi.org/10.1787/sti_outlook-2014-en. [3]

OECD (2013), *Innovation-driven Growth in Regions: The Role of Smart Specialisation*, OECD, https://www.oecd.org/sti/inno/smart-specialisation.pdf (accessed 28 October 2021). [4]

PORDATA (2021), *Education data*, https://www.pordata.pt/Tema/Portugal/Educa%c3%a7%c3%a3o-17 (accessed on 1 June 2021). [2]

PORDATA (2019), *Non Financial Enterprises by size*, https://www.pordata.pt/en/Municipalities/Non+financial+enterprises+total+and+by+size-916-6374 (accessed on 1 June 2021). [37]

Skills Panorama (2016), *Portugal: Mismatch priority occupations*, https://skillspanorama.cedefop.europa.eu/en/analytical_highlights/portugal-mismatch-priority-occupations. [11]

SNGWOFI (2021), *SNG-WOFI Database*, https://www.sng-wofi.org/data/. [26]

Note

[1] In 2019 the AEC Cluster – Architecture, Engineering and Construction, managed by the Portuguese Technological Platform for Construction (PTPC), signed a Sectoral Pact for Competitiveness and Internationalisation with the Ministry of the Economy.

www.ingramcontent.com/pod-product-compliance
Ingram Content Group UK Ltd.
Pitfield, Milton Keynes, MK11 3LW, UK
UKHW051504290926
15471UKWH00008B/1416